The Simpol Solution |

'It's ambitious and provocative. Can it work? Certainly worth a serious try.'

Noam Chomsky

'National competitiveness has become one of the central myths by which we are governed. It is, in essence, a wholly corrosive process that undermines the state's capacity to raise taxes at the same time as it tells most of us that our labour should be valued less highly. Bunzl and Duffell perform the important public function of debunking this myth, but they also go much further than that. They provide an eye-catching blueprint for thinking a radically different world into being. Challenging conditions require expansive thinking, and this book delivers suitable ambition many times over in its efforts to move us beyond the neoliberal dystopia engendered by national competitiveness discourse. It deserves to be widely read and its central aims to be widely debated.'

Matthew Watson

Professor of Political Economy, University of Warwick

UK Economic and Social Research Council Professorial Fellow

'I nodded until I got a crick in my neck. I haven't read a book for years that I agreed with so deeply and so consistently – nor felt so keenly that these are messages the world needs to hear. The clarity, simplicity and profound importance of this book are beyond question. Please read it, and please encourage others to do the same.'

Professor Simon Anholt

Founder, the Good Country, the Good Country Index and the Global Vote

'The Simpol Solution is an encouraging first step, truly workable and pragmatic, toward a world governance platform. A fully functional world governance is likely still a considerable way off, but the Simpol Solution consists of actions that can – and in many cases already have – been taken that create beginning networks of internationally indexed and unified governing agreements. It's something that true cosmopolitans, frustrated over the inevitably slow-motion of putting a fully functioning world government into place, can get behind right now and start to see at least some of their dreams and visions actualized. This is the best thing we have, at this time, for anything resembling a genuine and functional world governing system.'

Ken Wilber Consciousness theorist

Author of *The Integral Vision*

'Simpol represents a very powerful new idea for solving global problems. Yet it demands a mind-shift which the book's innovative psychological approach permits readers to make. Having made that shift, I hope NGOs around the world will participate in Simpol, that philanthropists will come forward to fund an information campaign and, above all, that we citizens start to use our votes in the way Simpol suggests. If we do, we'll find ourselves becoming part of the global political solution.'

Scilla Elworthy
Peace builder and founder of Oxford Research Group
Author of *Pioneering the Possible: Awakened Leadership for a World That Works*

'*The Simpol Solution* combines a razor-sharp description of today's competitiveness conundrum – vital yet now locking us into self-destructive patterns – with an equally pithy practical solution. I'd love to see Bunzl put his plan in motion.'

Dr Sally Goerner
Author of *After the Clockwork Universe*
Science Advisor, the Capital Institute

'*The Simpol Solution* takes a welcome fresh look at political/economic reality and clearly explains the psychology behind why we need new eyes to see how we might force politicians to change the world on our behalf.'

Joris Luyendijk
Author, journalist and talk-show host

'We urgently need to complement the competition of our global market with self-regulating governance and cooperation on the same scale, so the authors argue, laying their brilliant Simpol as the blueprint to get us there. All we have to do is get involved and actively spread its DNA!'

Elisabet Sahtouris, Ph.D.
Evolution biologist and futurist
MBA Professor, Chaminade University, Honolulu
Author of *Gaia's Dance: The Story of Earth and Us*

'Bunzl and Duffell offer an ambitious and thought-provoking account of how destructive competition between nation states might be transformed into globally beneficial cooperation. Their aim is "simultaneous policy", where multiple issues would be negotiated among all states, offering each important benefits and making possible fully global implementation. They outline an ingenious method, already trialled in the United Kingdom, of pressuring national politicians to pledge advance support for pursuing such global solutions. They draw on an impressive range of sources and disciplines – from political science and psychology to economics and evolutionary biology – while writing in a highly accessible style and offering a number of engaging anecdotes to reinforce their claims. This book will make an important contribution to the dialogue on global governance alternatives and the harms that seem inevitably to arise within a system of competitive sovereign states.'

Professor Luis Cabrera
Convenor, World Government Research Network
Griffith University, Brisbane

'A courageous and urgently needed book. It points to the crux of the issue: "We can't solve the problems of the world with the same thinking that produced them." Einstein said this, and Bunzl and Duffell point the way to acting on it. This book needs to be read by just about everyone!'

Ervin Laszlo
Author, philosopher and evolutionary systems theorist
Founder, Club of Budapest

'With the major challenges facing humanity being global in nature, new frameworks, philosophies and approaches are essential for societies to survive as we know them. The Simpol approach provides a starting point on the long path to a global governance system that creates an inclusive sustainable future'

Steve Killilea
Founder, the Global Peace Index and the Institute for Economics and Peace

'I have been following the work of John Bunzl for some time, and this inspirational new book, bolstered by a psychological dimension provided by Nick Duffell, is the most comprehensive case for the power of this new global way of thinking and resolving our collective systemic challenges – worldwide cooperation in terms of simultaneous policy is an evolutionary imperative if we are to thrive rather than just survive and drift towards the breakdown of civilisation, the early stages of which we are already witnessing. Essential reading for all global citizens.'

David Lorimer
Programme Director, the Scientific and Medical Network

'Imaginative, learned and full of passion, this book provides an elegant introduction to the damage created by the competitive imperatives of contemporary globalized capitalism. It shows the real possibilities of a worldcentric paradigm shift, transcending from a competitive to a cooperative evolution and mode of consciousness. A real pleasure to read and a potential political pathbreaker.'

Ugo Mattei
Co-author of *Plunder: When the Rule of Law Is Illegal* and *The Ecology of Law: Toward a Legal System in Tune with Nature and Community*

'The time has never been more ripe for global solutions to what are global problems such as climate change, economic inequality and unending violence. The great strength of the approach Bunzl and Duffell are developing is that it makes use of the energies tied up in today's global competitiveness but flips them in the direction of global cooperation. Here is a radical and challenging approach to conventional political orthodoxies. Its great psychological strength is that it works at many levels, from government to the individual citizen.'

Andrew Samuels
Author of *A New Therapy for Politics?*
Professor of Analytical Psychology, University of Essex

'Houston, we have a problem! Capital has become transnational and has instituted a regime of global competition which is extracting value from communities and nature without reinvesting it in sustainable infrastructures and livelihoods. But the nation state and its citizens have lost the power at the national level. So what can we do? While many suggest a return to the urban level, this book suggests an equally important strategy: the trans-nationalization of change. What needs to be done what needs to be done by citizens and movements straight at the transnational level, through simultaneous policy campaigns. The challenge of building and getting to this new capacity is laid out in this important book, which is a guidebook to the necessary politics of our times in which the local is always linked to the global.'

Michel Bauwens
Founder, the Peer-to-Peer (P2P) Foundation

'To address the multiple problems of our planet and to capitalize on the enormous scientific and technological opportunities we have, we first need imaginative and far-reaching proposals. John Bunzl and Nick Duffell offer a highly innovative view. Even if provocative, it will certainly help us to look at contemporary impasses with new eyes.'

Daniele Archibugi
Italian National Research Council and the University of London

'Do you want to help make a better world but feel powerless to do so? This extraordinary book lights the way forward.'

John Stewart
Author of *Evolution's Arrow: The Direction of Evolution and the Future of Humanity*

'*The Simpol Solution* targets the trap at the heart of the neoliberal race to the bottom – the imperative to compete. Only through simultaneous policy change across nations could we hope to escape the iron grip of a competition regime that prevents governments from embracing the true public interest. Simpol's ingenious technique for such worldwide action is under way – and everyone needs to know about it.'

Dr Kerryn Higgs
Historian and author of *Collision Course: Endless Growth on a Finite Planet*

'I've been tracking Simpol for years now as it struck me from the very beginning as one of the only workable solutions out there to the global challenges we are facing. With this book the authors lay out the case in a clear and compelling way, giving us no excuse to ignore the implications.'

Peter Merry
Chief Innovation Officer, Ubiquity University

John Bunzl is a director of an international textile company, a writer and international campaigner with a simple and powerful vision for more effective global cooperation. For over a decade he has worked with policy-makers and politicians, academics and non-governmental organizations, activists and citizens around the world to promote and inspire more effective cooperation. From the behavioural and evolutionary science behind why we cooperate to the political implications of a world without adequate binding international agreements, John is interested in finding cooperative solutions to our most challenging problems.

In 2000 John founded the International Simultaneous Policy Organization (ISPO) and launched the Simultaneous Policy (Simpol) campaign. John is a regular contributor to the *Huffington Post* and has spoken at various TEDx events. He has also presented to the World Social Forum, the World Trade Organization, the Schumacher Society and at various universities including the London School of Economics.

Nick Duffell is a psychotherapist, trainer and psychohistorian with wide experience as a facilitator in leadership development. He writes and broadcasts on psychological issues and has published several books. His *The Making of Them* (2000) received wide critical acclaim, and his 2004 book *Wounded Leaders*, which provides a challenging psychological analysis of the British political scene, is still making waves. Nick and his wife Helena founded the Centre for Gender Psychology in 1996 and co-authored the popular book *Sex, Love and the Dangers of Intimacy*.

THE
SIMPOL
SOLUTION

Solving Global Problems Could
Be Easier Than We Think

John Bunzl and Nick Duffell

PETER OWEN
London and Chicago

Peter Owen Publishers
81 Ridge Road, London N8 9NP

First published by Peter Owen 2017

Paperback ISBN 978-0-7206-1931-7
Epub ISBN 978-0-7206-1932-4
Mobipocket ISBN 978-0-7206-1933-1
PDF ISBN 978-0-7206-1934-8

A catalogue record for this book is available from the British Library

Designed by Danica Rosso
Printed and bound by CPI Group (UK) Ltd, Croydon, CR0 4YY

Acknowledgements

Excerpts from *Janus: A Summing Up* by Arthur Koestler, copyright © 1978 by Arthur Koestler, used by kind permission of Random House, an imprint and division of Penguin Random House LLC, all rights reserved. Quotations from Michael E. Porter excerpted from pp. 16 and 45 of *On Competition* by Michael E. Porter, Harvard Business Press Books, Cambridge, Massachusetts, 2008. Quotations from the *Financial Times* newspaper are used under licence from the Financial Times, all rights reserved. Excerpts from Robert Wright, *Nonzero: History, Evolution and Human Cooperation*, Abacus Random House, New York, 2001, used by kind permission of Penguin Random House. Extracts from George Soros, *The Crisis of Global Capitalism: Open Society Endangered*, 1998, used by kind permission of Little, Brown and Co. and Perseus Books Group. Excerpts from William Davies, *The Limits of Neoliberalism: Authority, Sovereignty and the Logic of Competition*, London, 2014, reprinted by kind permission of Sage Publications. Excerpts from Pauline Vaillancourt Rosenau, *The Competition Paradigm*, Lanham, Maryland, 2003, included by kind permission of Rowman and Littlefield. Transcript from Channel 4 News bulletin by kind permission of ITN Source. Excerpts from David Sloan Wilson, *Does Altruism Exist? Culture, Genes, and the Welfare of Others*, New Haven, Connecticut, 2015, used by kind permission of Yale University Press. Transcript of a TED Talk by George Papandreou, 2013, reproduced by kind permission of TEDGlobal. Quotations from the *Guardian* newspaper and website courtesy of Guardian News and Media Ltd. The quotation from *The Times* is courtesy of News Syndication. Excerpts from Don Edward Beck and Christopher C. Cowan, *Spiral Dynamics: Mastering Values, Leadership, and Change*, Oxford: Blackwell Publishing, 1996, used by kind permission of Wiley. Quotations from William Stafford used by kind permission of the Permissions Company, Inc., reprinted with permission of the publisher. Excerpt from *When Corporations Rule the World*, copyright © 1995 by David Korten, Berrett-Koehler Publishers, Inc., www.bkconnection.com, used by permission of the publisher. Thanks to the National Institute for the Clinical Application of Behavioral Medicine for permission to quote from Ruth Buczynski's interview with Daniel Siegel, 'How Brain Science Can Lead to More Targeted Interventions for Patients Healing from Trauma'.

Extract from page 2 of the Introduction and page 5 from Chapter 1, 'Freedom's Just Another Word', from *A Brief History of Neoliberalism*, David Harvey (2005), by kind permission of Oxford University Press, Oxford. Extract from *The Enigma of Capital*, David Harvey, by kind permission of Profile Books, London.

Thanks go to all those who helped by reading and critiquing the manuscript for this book, especially to Alexander Lyons, Jacq Burns and Rob Bruce, to Andrew Wallace for his special help and to all the many Simpol supporters who already help to put the ideas into practice and to the team at Peter Owen Publishers for their extraordinary professionalism.

John would like to express particular gratitude to Ken Wilber for his invaluable help in refining parts of the book, to Jenni Camplin, who introduced him to Nick, and to Anne and his children, Alexandra, Tom and Jake for their unstinting love, help and support.

Nick wants especially to appreciate Helena Løvendal for her loving enthusiasm and helpful contributions and to thank Hilde Bland, Nick Dawson, Anne-Marie Diepeveen and Andrew Mullis for their belief and righteous anger, as well as Peter MacFayden, Jo McCrum and Kristen Harrison for their support.

Contents

Introduction

The future?

Imagine the scene, about a hundred years from now: a small girl, sheltering with her family against the ravages of the climate and the constant danger of violent marauding bands, looks at her grandfather and says accusingly, 'Grandpa, why didn't you *do* anything?'

It is a terrifying vision of the future. A 2009 British movie directed by Franny Armstrong called *The Age of Stupid* featured a similar idea, with an old man looking back in regret on a world gone wrong.

Although we can never predict the future it is realistic to be very concerned. We don't need to tell you that the problems besetting our world in the second decade of the twenty-first century are huge: climate change, freak weather, polluted seas, increasing wealth inequality. We are assaulted by out-of-hand religious fanaticism, mass migration, corporate powers overshadowing national governments, interminable local wars, failed states, a fragmenting European Union, population growth out of control; the politics of fear, blame and denial are spreading as fast as political apathy among the young. And the new dilemmas of the future – such as data banks, genetic engineering and robotics – threaten to arrive on top of the unsolved crises of today.

Need we say more? We all know these problems affect all of us on the planet, but we seem incapable of solving them, and time is running out. Do we really want some future grandfather to be accountable for our inaction? Why can't we just sort it out?

Is it just because the issues are too big? Or is it that political leaders cannot find the will to deal with them? Is it that greedy financial interests are bent on total destruction in the service of profits? Are we too selfish, too ostrich-like or, worse, too lemming-like?

Or are we just not thinking about them in the way we need to?

A global impasse needs a global solution

In answer to these pressing questions this book makes four main claims.

First, that there is just one single barrier that prevents us from solving all of these problems: the pursuit of international competitiveness. We show how every government's need to keep its economy attractive to corporations and investors – its need to stay internationally competitive

– makes it impossible for any nation to make the first move. Whether it's climate change, fair corporate taxation, poverty reduction, migration or almost any other global issue, we will show that it's the fear of competitive disadvantage that stands in the way.

Competitiveness isn't only a way to attract investment and jobs: it has a rarely recognized destructive side that operates as a vicious circle preventing action on global and many national problems. The relentless drive for competitiveness – the very pursuit we are told will assure our prosperity – turns out to be slowly killing us. We call this vicious circle 'Destructive Global Competition' or DGC for short, and the solution, we argue, lies in a new form of global cooperation.

Our second claim is that there is a way to break the vicious circle and to achieve global cooperation. We outline a global campaign that offers a means of overcoming the first-mover competitive-disadvantage problem, called the Simultaneous Policy. Simpol is founded on three principles:

1. *Simultaneous implementation*
   If all or nearly all nations can be brought to implement appropriate policies simultaneously, no nation, corporation or citizen would suffer a competitive disadvantage. All nations win, and the vicious circle of DGC is broken.

2. *A multi-issue framework*
   Addressing global problems one at a time, as the world is now, is unlikely to be successful – in fact, it's designed to fail. This is because dealing with any single issue means there will always be some nations that win and others that lose, and the losers have no incentive to cooperate. Simpol offers a framework for negotiating two or more issues together so that nations that might lose on one issue can gain on another. Not only will this vastly improve the chances of reaching substantive agreements it can make action in every nation's immediate interest. It can make nations want to act now.

3. *A new way to use our votes*
   Today there is little incentive for politicians to reach or uphold international agreements. If they fail they can always claim 'the national interest' as a legitimate excuse. A powerful carrot-and-stick inducement is required to encourage politicians towards productive outcomes.

Simpol provides this by inviting us to use our votes in an entirely new way, driving national governments towards the target. As we'll show, it's like having two votes rolled into one: the vote you already have that works nationally and a new one that works globally. We'll prove to you that you already possess both, and that they both work. Just when many of us sense that voting has lost its potency, Simpol transforms our votes into the most powerful weapon for global solutions.

The third claim we make is that global cooperation, as outlined above, cannot come about until there has been an *inner revolution* in the way we *think about* and *see* the world. At the heart of this book is a re-evaluation of our habitual ways of thinking, because unless we find a way to change how we see the world and think about its problems we will not be capable of effective action on a global scale. We will not even understand why there is no useful option but cooperation.

In a statement widely attributed to Albert Einstein, perhaps the greatest genius of modern times, this inner revolution was predicted when he sagely advised that we will not solve our problems with the same thinking that created them. Unless our world finds a way to think differently, the image of the little girl and her grandfather risks becoming all too real.

Changing the way we think is always a mighty challenge and you may be wondering whether it can really make much difference. 'How can a handful of people who read a book like this possibly change the world?' you may be asking.

Our answer is also our fourth claim, that it doesn't take masses of people to change the world – in fact, it never has. We will show how many key transitions in human history were catalysed by small numbers, and we'll show how Simpol fits this pattern, too. That's why you matter.

Our four claims leave us with three steps:

- Step 1 is to recognize exactly how stuck we are and what keeps us stuck;

- Step 2 is to understand the nature and value of the cooperation imperative; and

- Step 3 is to evolve a new way of thinking and seeing that enables us to take swift, appropriate and effective cooperative global action.

We invite you to come on a journey with us to explore the implications of our claims and to join us in taking these steps. To give you a closer idea of where we're headed, here's the itinerary we propose.

Understanding DGC and the cooperation imperative

Global problems have diverse causes, but in Chapter 1 we explain how the vicious circle of Destructive Global Competition – DGC – is the single road-block to solving just about all of them. Individuals, political parties, governments – even corporations – are all subject to the tyranny of DGC, and yet almost no one seems to be aware of it. This blindness, we explain, is because society as a whole only sees competition's constructive side, while we expose its hidden destructive side.

DGC achieves this dominance because capital moves freely and globally, flowing to wherever the best returns are found. Since capital and investment are the cornerstones of healthy economies, governments must compete to attract them. That's why politicians harp on about keeping their economies internationally competitive. If the policies needed to solve global problems made firms and nations more competitive, there'd be no problem. But such policies are not attractive to global markets; tighter regulations and higher corporate taxes increase costs and make firms and nations *less* competitive.

So governments are stuck. No nation wants to move first. The UK's former Chancellor of the Exchequer, George Osborne, made no bones about it, emphasizing that the planet wouldn't be saved by putting his country out of business.[1]

With governments hesitant to regulate, we show how competition between corporations also turns destructive and there is no way out: the vicious circle affects everyone. Worse, it even subverts democracy itself. Whichever party may be in power, all are confined to a very narrow competitiveness agenda that is incompatible with social justice or environmental sustainability. Paralysed by DGC, we are left with what this book calls 'pseudo-democracy'. No wonder political parties are in turmoil while voters see little difference between them and turn to apathy, cynicism or the politics of fear.

We're not suggesting that governments can't take any action at all on global problems, only that the issue is one of perspective. Imagine a vintage car moving steadily along a highway. For its age it may be moving along quite nicely, but as we focus on it we fail to notice a sports car tearing down the fast lane. The vintage car represents the present rate of progress that governments are making and the sports car the rate at which global problems are worsening. With an eye on both vehicles it's perfectly clear who's going to win.

We are left facing a simple imperative: find a way to cooperate globally to escape DGC's vicious circle or face unparalleled chaos and potential ruin.

'Another fine mess . . .'

Having acknowledged the centrality of DGC, our predicament may initially seem hopeless. And yet, at least our task is now straightforward: all prescriptions about what needs to be done – reducing emissions, equalizing wealth or reregulating financial markets and so on – become secondary. Instead, the primary issue is how to overcome DGC. The vital questions are not what but how: how did we get here, and how do we overcome DGC?

Chapter 2 explains how we arrived at this perilous state. DGC turns out to be less a result of some evil conspiracy than that the world's *context* has irrevocably changed. This context is no longer national nor even European, Asian, African or American; it is irreversibly global. However, our world is yet to fully understand the implications.

It's as if we are just not seeing far enough yet. Everyone knows you have to go up a hill to get the best view, but we are still looking and thinking about our problems from a flat plain. What we clearly see from the top of the hill is that we have entered what we call 'a new context for governance', and we need to reorganize ourselves in line with it.

Understanding this new context is crucial, and yet changing contexts are part of an old story. New contexts such as the kind we are experiencing under globalization are inevitable and belong to the unfolding story of human evolution. The crises they create are always resolved by increasing levels of complexity, cooperation and governance. Our predicament, we now see, is not so much a calamity as it is humanity's need to grow up. We must now learn to cooperate and consciously self-regulate ourselves, just as an adolescent cannot leave home with genuine autonomy before having developed these skills.

'. . . and it's all YOUR fault!'

But here's the rub. Like anyone who has to grow up, we are busy resisting. Not only does changing our thinking present a challenge, it means we must take responsibility. But instead we stay stuck in the blame game: blaming politicians, blaming corporations, blaming immigrants or blaming 'the system' for the state we are in. How such immature thinking keeps us stuck is the topic we turn to in Chapters 3 and 4.

Thinking is crucial, yet most books on globalization concentrate on what we call its *outer* characteristics – trade, technology, communications, the environment, financial markets and so on. This book takes an entirely fresh approach by focusing on globalization's *inner* aspects – the way we *think* and *feel* about it as individuals and as cultures and how it impedes our ability to solve global problems.

This may at first sound simplistic, but the way we think is an integral and very emotive part of our identity and changing it can be far more difficult than we imagine. It involves confronting the terror we feel at abandoning our entire worldview. This is all the more difficult when we can't yet see a solution. 'How', you might ask 'can I be expected to jump off one boat before you've shown me a better one to jump on to?'

The problem is that adopting new thinking means first loosening and letting go of our existing way, and this involves a terrifying transition. Rather like the mythological bird the phoenix that first had to die and turn to ashes before being reborn, new life can only arise when something has been let go. We have to go through a grieving process for what we are losing, similar to the one we might experience if someone close to us dies. It can be thought of as a difficult journey – painful but necessary.

On the road again

Taking this journey means we have to choose an emotional road, because fully embracing any new context means contending with many difficult feelings. Our familiar, polarized thinking will not last the distance. The road will be particularly uncomfortable for some: as much for those who imagine yet more competition to be the answer as for those environmentalists and campaigners who see themselves as already equipped with the answers.

On this road we encounter the psychological obstacles to adopting new thinking as recognizable staging posts along the road: *denial, anger, bargaining, depression* and, finally, *acceptance*. First, in Chapter 3, we consider the role of denial: how we hide the reality of DGC from ourselves, how society normalizes it and how we compartmentalize and compensate for it. In Chapter 4 we turn to anger: how we vent our frustration in polarized politics, protest and apathy. Then we look at how we impotently try to bargain with the DGC monster before acknowledging, finally, that present approaches to solving global problems cannot work, that we are depressed, grieving and fearful for the future.

Our difficult journey ends in acceptance. Not an acceptance of hopelessness but an acceptance that our familiar nationcentric way of thinking no longer serves us and we can let it go. Acceptance, then, is not a capitulation but a new liberation: we learn to see ourselves and the world with fresh worldcentric eyes. Accepting the reality of DGC and relinquishing the blame game, we are now more ready to consider innovative solutions.

A new thinking platform

Before we can embark on practical action we need to understand the different ways in which people and cultures think and how new thinking develops or gets blocked. In Chapter 6 we do this by introducing a comprehensive model of thinking platforms developed by social scientists over the last decade. This model – applied here for the first time to the problems of globalization – categorizes a range of different levels of thinking. It explains why people see the world in different ways and how those different perspectives interact. This understanding helps us to see better why there is so much conflict in the world and where our thinking needs to go next.

It also shows how human thinking is subject to the same natural evolutionary processes as the rest of life – differing and evolving levels of thinking are part of our universal inheritance. Drawing on such diverse disciplines as evolutionary biology and psychohistory we reveal why outdated worldviews always hold sway until a sufficient head of steam is built up to push people into accepting a new emerging perspective, and we show that these transitions are often catalysed by a relatively small number of people.

Seeing the world in this way is like a breath of fresh air; it is an integral part of the new worldcentric level of thinking that our model introduces. Our hope is that, by this point, you'll be starting to see the world in this way, too, because it is this level that permitted us to identify the global phenomena of DGC and pseudo-democracy. It is this level that opens the door not only to understanding global problems but also to new ways of resolving them.

'Five minutes' to change the world

Born in 1879, Einstein did not have the benefit of depth psychology or psychohistory, which are as radical tools to study human thinking and the organization of societies as quantum theory was to the study of physics. However, the wise man knew a thing or two. He was once asked how he would spend his time if he were given one hour to solve a difficult problem. His answer was that he'd spend fifty-five minutes defining the problem and five minutes solving it.

In our book's final 'five minutes' we first discuss the criteria that a new worldcentric form of politics would have to meet (Chapter 7). We explain why existing global institutions such as the United Nations don't fit the bill. Then, in Chapter 8, we introduce the Simultaneous Policy campaign, demonstrating that it meets the necessary criteria.

Already in early operation, Simpol is achieving encouraging results: considering the low number of people involved so far, the high level of support it has gained from politicians is remarkable. This, as we'll show, is no accident but the result of the powerful carrot-and-stick voting incentive that Simpol advocates and which its supporters are already adopting. Rather like the hundredth monkey principle – in which a new idea rapidly spreads widely once a critical number of people start to espouse it – they're demonstrating our fourth claim: *you don't need many people to change the world.*

Is Simpol *the* solution to global problems? That will be for you and others to decide. Our purpose is not to prescribe but to provide a pragmatic example of the kind of initiative that worldcentric thinking leads us towards.

We end by evoking scientific disciplines, such as evolutionary biology and neuroscience, to show how Simpol closely mimics the way that evolution itself resolves its own naturally occurring crises. Our current predicament, we discover, is part of a deeper evolutionary process of which we, too, are part. The challenge we face, it turns out, is not an arbitrary impending catastrophe but evolution's way of calling humanity to embrace its maturity. Beyond the need to survive, our challenge is an opportunity to fulfil our evolutionary destiny: our chance, in the deepest sense possible, to come home to who we really are.

Our hope is that you'll finish this book feeling liberated from impotence and political apathy, eager to re-engage from a more inclusive perspective, equipped with more powerful political tools. The campaign we outline recognizes that leaders are still needed but embodies the reality that real change comes about when a critical number of us alter our way of thinking and find new ways to act together that reflect it. And, as we all know in our hearts, when enough of us get really focused on an issue nothing can stop us.

1. The Staggering Power of Competition

The neoliberal miracle

Michael E. Porter is a trim baby boomer who oozes brains, confidence and fitness. A senior professor at the Harvard Business School and founder director of the Institute for Strategy and Competitiveness, Porter is the doyen of living management gurus, but he could have been a professional golfer. Right from the start he excelled as an all-rounder, first in his class while starring at team sports then majoring with honours in aerospace and mechanical engineering at Princeton before gaining an MBA with high distinction and a Ph.D. in business economics from Harvard. Porter is the founder of the modern business-strategy field and one of the world's most influential thinkers on management and especially on the topic we address in this chapter: the concept of international competitiveness. In 2012 Geoff Colvin, senior editor-at-large at *Fortune* magazine, suggested that Porter had influenced more executives and more nations than any other business professor on earth.[1]

If there's one idea that's central to the Porter doctrine on competitive strategy and the development of nations, states and regions, set out over nineteen books and 125 articles, it's that competition is beneficial. Said to be frustratingly unquotable, in his book *On Competition* Porter makes himself uncharacteristically clear:

> If this collection [of essays] could convey only one message, I would want it to be a sense of the staggering power of competition to make things better – both for companies and for society.[2]

Porter is far from alone in holding this view. In fact, the notion that competition is necessarily beneficial is the central tenet of the economic doctrine known as 'neoliberalism' that since the 1980s has come to dominate economic thought the world over. Neoliberalism, as Professor David Harvey of the City University of New York explains, is:

> A theory of political economic practices that presupposes that human well-being can best be advanced by liberating individual

entrepreneurial freedoms and skills within an institutional framework
characterized by strong private property rights, free markets, and free
trade.[3]

Neoliberalism proposes that markets rather than governments are the
best way to secure prosperity and well-being. Now the purpose of a market
is to match supply to demand. Operationally, it tends to produce winners
and losers, whereby resources are automatically allocated in the most
economically efficient manner. So, essentially, a market *is* a competition,
and a free market indicates not only entrepreneurial freedom but also
includes the belief that markets and trade should remain as free as possible
from government intervention. According to neoliberal orthodoxy, all
governments need to do is to keep competition going and prosperity and
well-being will result.

Founded on this assumption that competition is eternally beneficial,
neoliberalism has by now thoroughly pervaded governments, universities,
economists, think-tanks, the media and public opinion. But what
underlies the unquestioned dominance of such a notion? Professor
of management and policy science at the University of Texas, Pauline
Vaillencourt Rosenau, suggests:

> There seems to be something almost religious or magical about
> competition, especially in the marketplace, that is so evident that it
> does not need to be subjected to inquiry . . . More competition is
> assumed to be better than less, no matter what the circumstances or
> the type of competition involved.[4]

Competition, it seems, comes very naturally to us, for it appeals, as
Harvey suggests, to our innate sense of personal autonomy:

> The founding figures of neoliberal thought took political ideals of
> human dignity and individual freedom as fundamental, as 'the central
> values of civilisation'. In so doing they chose wisely, for these are
> indeed compelling and seductive ideals . . . Concepts of dignity and
> individual freedom are powerful and appealing in their own right.[5]

Our acceptance of these ideas is neither irrational nor surprising
since freedom and competition are natural and indispensable parts of life.

Competition not only appeals to these deep values but genuinely has a beneficial side, spurring innovation and excellence while also making sure of lower prices for consumers.

In the context of recent economic history, it is easy to see why neoliberal ideas so comprehensively captured the imagination of politicians and economists eager for economic growth to recover during the economic stagnation that pervaded the 1970s and why their infatuation with them – and our complicity – continues unabated. Today the neoliberal cult extends to all corners of life – to all levels of politics, economics and culture. In the banking industry, betting on winners and losers has taken economic-market risk to new levels in the practice of financialization. Not only do individuals and firms need to be competitive, so do cities, regions and whole nations. The need for all and any entity to stay competitive constitutes the philosophical platform that underpins virtually all decision-making.

The worship of competitiveness is promulgated by many influential organizations. Take the World Economic Forum (WEF), which holds its annual meetings in the exclusive Swiss ski resort of Davos, attended by heads of government, business leaders and economics gurus. The WEF's strapline proclaims it is 'Committed to improving the state of the world', and its flagship publication is the *Global Competitiveness Report*, the purpose of which, according to its preamble, is to assess 'the competitiveness landscape of 144 economies, providing insight into the drivers of their productivity and prosperity'.[6]

At the core of this mission statement 'competitiveness' and 'prosperity' are seamlessly linked, revealing the – now familiar – assumption that competition is invariably only beneficial. Each year, when the WEF releases its annual report, frenzy breaks out as the media, economists, politicians, think-tanks and business schools comment on each nation's ranking and whether a nation has risen or slipped lower.

The culture of international competitiveness, along with the uncertainty and anxiety it induces, reaches every industry in every corner of the globe. Witness this report on the Caribbean tourist industry:

> irrespective of how it is conceptualised, international competitiveness would continue to remain a dynamic issue. Hence, in as much as our tourism industries may very well appear to be highly competitive at the moment, that situation can quickly reverse itself, rendering many of our destinations uncompetitive in the process.[7]

Inherent in this culture, in the need to stay ahead, in the fear of a situation that 'can quickly reverse itself', we cannot fail to notice a level of menace, as senior lecturer in politics at London's Goldsmith's University Will Davies explains:

> What I have characterized as the 'violent threat' of neoliberalism has come to the fore, whereby authority in economic decision-making is increasingly predicated upon the claim that 'we' must beat 'them'.[8]

Whether you are competitive or uncompetitive, ranked high or low, the message that competition's 'violent threat' communicates remains the same: do whatever is necessary to maintain or enhance your competitive position. Fail to stay competitive and you will lose out in 'the global race'.[9]

And the threat works. Competition and competitiveness have become as unquestionable in the modern world as God, His angels and the Devil were in the medieval. Fear of damnation in the future is ubiquitous. Today government leaders universally see it as their duty to pursue their nation's international competiveness as unrelentingly as the defence of the realm and far more enthusiastically than regulating business or collecting taxes.

But if competition is really so beneficial, why do global problems seem to be getting worse rather than better? If the markets in which we're all embedded are competitions, and if competition only produces benefits, as neoliberal ideology insists, you'd have thought that its 'staggering power to make things better' would, by now, have caused many of our problems to disappear.

Clearly, something doesn't quite stack up.

There's nothing we can do

In fact, the noticeable thing about our age is the strange combination of the knowledge and clarity we have about global problems, and our inability – or unwillingness – to tackle them effectively. Instead, governments appear increasingly impotent, both economically and politically, while we, the public, alternate between anger and apathy about our leaders' ability to do anything but help the wealthy prosper and, in particular, about our own ability to make a difference.

If the pursuit of competitiveness has the power to generate an increase in prosperity, health and well-being, as is claimed, then it comes at a staggering price: a sense of widespread public powerlessness and anger. This sense of impotence comes at a time when information has never before been so widely available: broadcast news and the internet reaches every corner of the planet, while at the same time only fear and nationalism appear to prompt people to use their hard-won right to vote in any sizeable numbers. And the sense of powerlessness is spreading to all areas of concern. Paul Mason, who has served as senior economic correspondent on the BBC's flagship television news programme *Newsnight* and subsequently *Channel 4 News* in the UK, suggests that the fundamental economic problems have not been solved but merely palliated and that this is destroying the public's confidence in 'agency' – the human ability to avoid danger, mitigate risk and regain control over fluid situations. One sees it clearest of all, Mason suggests, in people's attitudes to war and disaster, recalling how the editor of the BBC Radio 4's *Today* programme admitted that he was having trouble retaining listeners in the face of relentless bad news: Syria, Isis, Libya, Gaza. It was not the scale of the horror that turned the public off, it was their own powerlessness in the face of it.[10]

Such feelings are not to be ignored, nor are they irrational, as Mason points out:

it is logical to feel powerless if you witness the best educated and briefed people of your generation flounder – as politicians and diplomats have – in the face of a collapse of global order.[11]

Mason is not alone in this view. Joris Luyendijk is a Dutch news correspondent and talk-show host educated in Amsterdam, Kansas and Cairo. He was a news correspondent in the Middle East for a number of years, based in Egypt, Lebanon and Israel, reported on the Second Gulf War in Iraq and has written extensively on Western ineffectiveness in these regions.[12]

Since 2011 Luyendijk has been based in London at the *Guardian* newspaper, in which his banking blog offers an anthropological perspective on the financial world. His latest book is a result of some 300 interviews with bankers and other people in the London financial industry with the aim of understanding how the 2008 financial crisis could have happened. What sparked his curiosity is the phenomenon that the public seem very interested in topics in which they have a personal stake, such as whenever it looks like somebody wants to steal their entire life savings, but soon lose attention when an issue such as financial reform comes up.[13]

Interestingly, Luyendijk has become much in demand as a speaker on economics, and, ironically, a recent lecture engagement in Amsterdam that expounded the increasing powerlessness of ordinary people in the face of vast economic and political forces was an instant sell-out.[14] Despite our widespread apathy, when this powerlessness is named we instantly recognize it.

The picture that emerges is that over the last thirty years, since our world has become increasingly globalized, economically deregulated, driven by market forces and financialized, based on a central philosophy that holds competition to be an unremitting good, there has been a profound change. People feel increasingly uninvolved as if they no longer have any agency, while global problems continue to pile up. Could it be that the concept of competiveness being only beneficial may itself be faulty?

Our own doubts about competition led us back to first principles: we decided we needed to go back to school.

Fair play

It is a chilly day in south-east London and not one for hanging around a bleak expanse of playing fields shrouded in grey skies. But we, the authors, are on a mission. We have managed to get permission to visit an inner-city comprehensive school on sports afternoon and to speak to some of the kids about their attitudes to competition, on condition that we don't name anyone or the school.

School is apparently where Professor Porter, who played American football, baseball and basketball growing up and later, at Princeton, was on the NCAA championship golf squad, says he first got thinking about competition.[15]

So what can we learn from a brief return to the school sports field?

First we try to find out what part sport plays in the school curriculum. How much sport is there at school these days, we ask the teacher. In a state school, much less than there was thirty years ago, she replies, and only a quarter of what is offered by private schools costing parents an average of £30,000 a year. The Youth Sport Trust, the UK charitable organization that monitors and coordinates school sport, published figures in early 2015 that showed the average amount of physical education in state schools had dropped well below the recommended two hours minimum per week. Despite Britain's investment in the London Olympic Park, the chairperson, Baroness Sue Campbell, said it painted a 'bleak and worrying' picture.[16]

But the picture we witness on the sports ground is far from bleak, despite the weather. Three groups of youngsters aged from eleven to thirteen are busily rushing around chasing footballs and yelling at the tops of their voices 'Man on!' and 'To me!' to the background noise of thudding balls and the shriek of whistles. They seem to be loving it.

The following day we show up at the school itself and notice how many of the children choose to use their break-time to organize their own brief games of football, which we are allowed to observe. When the bell for lessons sounds, we use our special permission to ask the children some questions. What were they actually doing out there? Did their impromptu football games simply involve competition, or were there other elements involved?

'OK, we want to know what you were doing out there. Was your game about cooperation or competition?' we ask.

'Competition!' they shout back gleefully.

Clearly, competition comes as naturally to them as to anyone else, but when we point out our take on their activity, they are surprised to learn how much they also cooperated. We remind them that before even starting to play their games they were cooperating in picking teams, deciding where the goals should be, when the ball would be deemed out and so on. They hadn't realized how much cooperation was involved in setting up a break-time kick-about.

'What would happen if you hadn't cooperated to set these rules?' we enquire. 'What if there were no rules at all?'

Some kids respond that it would have become a riot or free-for-all; others that the bigger kids would have the ball all the time – no fun at all, not even a competition any more.

So, what lessons did we learn?

Apart from confirming our own view that competition comes naturally to most of us, the paradox we came away with is that to be healthy and productive competition needs to be complemented by what appears to be its opposite. Competition needs cooperation and governance – rules and regulations. Without cooperation and governance to police competition it turns into a destructive free-for-all.

Competition, it seems to us, comes in two varieties: it can be either *constructive* or *destructive*, depending on whether adequate cooperation – adequate agreement on the rules – are present or not and whether they are properly enforced. This is a distinction also made by Vaillancourt Rosenau in her extensive study of competition, *The Competition Paradigm*:

When competition is constructive, it involves competing at efficiency in *controlled circumstances*. Destructive, excessive, or *unfettered* competition seems to be associated with serious, negative, though sometimes unintentional side-effects [authors' italics].[17]

We will investigate some of the side-effects of global economic competition shortly, but for now we need only note how strange it is that this all-important distinction between constructive and destructive competition seems to be ignored by neoliberal thinkers – even by such luminaries as Professor Porter as he played on the fields of Princeton and theorized in the seminar rooms of Harvard – in favour of its beneficial aspects.

In acknowledging only one side of competition – the constructive aspect – economic experts are actually making life harder for themselves, like driving with one arm in a sling. Under such conditions, whenever an economy falters or whenever a so-called market failure is identified, mainstream economists predictably prescribe yet more competition as the solution. If markets fail, they tell us, it's because they are not deregulated enough, as Vaillancourt Rosenau observes:

More competition is assumed to be better than less, no matter what the circumstances or the type of competition involved. Qualifiers are forgotten, counterevidence is neglected, and the existence of a spiral of destructive competition is ignored.[18]

The existence of such a destructive spiral changes everything, as we will demonstrate shortly, but we will also show that the ability to tackle problems on a global scale depends on competition and cooperation operating symmetrically – in other words, over similar ranges and on the same scale. As any school kid knows, it's no good governing just one part of the football field or basketball court and letting the other be a free-for-all.

The shadow side of competition

Our current myth of competition seems therefore to need some serious revision: it's not entirely faulty just fundamentally incomplete. It is not that competition brings no benefits nor that it's not an essential and vital component in any healthy and vibrant economy – economists, neoliberal or otherwise, are not wrong about the staggering and often beneficial power of competition – it is just that they're only seeing *half* the picture.

And this omission is a seriously crippling problem, because if what we in this book call competition's destructive or 'shadow side' is allowed to gain a foothold, it starts to take over exponentially, as Vaillancourt Rosenau points out:

Destructive competition drives out constructive competition . . . Groups, individuals, and countries practice destructive competition when they win by cheating on the rules or when they cheat more than their competitors.[19]

The problem is that if one player finds a way to undermine or circumvent the rules and gets away with it then the others have no choice but to follow. If they don't they'll lose out. If there is no entity of governance to restore adequate rules and to enforce them, a vicious circle is set in train. This is where the staggering power of competition's shadow side kicks in. What was initially a constructive competition that encouraged excellence and innovation quickly degenerates into its shadow version, and there's no way to stop it. All players then have a strong incentive to find still more ways to undermine what few rules remain, and the competition descends into chaos or, worse, into violence. More often than not the descent into destructive competition is characterized by the strong dominating the weak.

This is a dynamic that any parent will readily recognize. If young children are left unsupervised for too long, a healthy competitive game can all too easily morph into a minor but highly destructive fight. Far from achieving the neoliberal ideal of individual freedom and autonomy, the end result is the very opposite: the enslavement of the weak by those best able to undermine the rules.

Even the schoolchildren knew that.

Destructive Global Competition

Neoliberalism gained hold, as we know, during the 1970s, based on an economic vision that enchanted not only politicians and elites but also the ordinary person in the street. It was put into practice through deliberate policy choices on the part of national politicians, notably US President Ronald Reagan and UK Prime Minister Margaret Thatcher. But the central argument of this book is that from around the mid-1980s onwards the implementation of neoliberal policies ceased to be the free choice of politicians and instead took on a momentum all its own. It was as if economic leaders were on autopilot.

Once international competition reached a certain level of integration and intensity, once the global market – and especially financial markets – developed to a certain critical tipping point, the global competitive pressures that this created were *themselves* sufficient to automatically drive governments towards an ever-deeper application of neoliberal policies. The vicious circle of Destructive Global Competition (DGC) had got going to such a point that it became self-sustaining. Once multinational corporations and global investors gained the ability to move capital and thousands of jobs seamlessly across national borders, the genie was out of the bottle and the vicious circle was set in train. Without realizing it governments were then caught in the endless pursuit of their 'international competitiveness' – caught in the game of forever outcompeting each other at cutting taxes and regulations in a bid to retain jobs and inward invest-ment. From then on DGC drew politicians and governments into its destructive vortex, and it is now running beyond anyone's control.

It is this automatic functioning that not only encourages the turning of a blind eye to the destructive aspects of competition; the real danger is that it places the people charged with setting the rules – governments – into a state of paralysis. They are now unable to address seriously the global problems that confront us. It's not that they don't want to act, it's that they *can't*.

A careful reading of almost any serious newspaper offers a wealth of examples of DGC in action. The following examples come mainly from British newspapers, but you can find similar articles in almost any country.

Let us start with a topic that most of us are quite familiar with, that of climate change. The public knows that climate change represents a very serious threat and hopes that governments will implement the commitments they made at the COP-21 Paris climate agreement reached in December 2015. But will they? The agreement reached was hailed as historic, but, crucially, its most vital clauses – especially the adherence to emissions-reduction targets – are not binding. How realistic is it to expect substantive action when the cause of governments' inaction – DGC – remains firmly in place? As the following report from the *Financial Times* explains:

> Governments remain reluctant to address the [climate change] threat because any country acting alone to curb its greenhouse gas

emissions, without similar commitments by other governments, risks damaging the competitiveness of its industries.[20]

Leaving aside those far-right doubts about the existence of a climate problem, any government that wanted to cut carbon emissions substantially could not avoid implementing much tougher emissions regulations and higher business taxes. But any government that did so in advance of other governments would only force its corporations to move production and thousands of jobs elsewhere. Global markets, likewise, would punish any nation that significantly increased its businesses' costs much beyond levels in other countries because this would make its economy less attractive to investors. The 2015 Paris agreement rests on the hope that all nations will move more or less together, so avoiding these risks. But the non-binding nature of the agreement means that all governments are likely to remain extremely cautious.

The fear of losing out to competitors understandably drives all politicians. For them, allowing the national economy to fall behind is not an option: unemployment would rise, inward investment would dry up, the population would suffer and the next election would be lost. Still constrained by DGC and having no certainty that other nations will act, governments are likely to remain limited only to those actions that will not significantly harm their nation's international competitiveness, which in today's integrated global economy means little action or none at all. This manifestation of DGC is rarely recognized, but the few economists that do sometimes refer to it as 'regulatory chill'.[21] Governments are 'chilled', only able to take relatively small steps but not the really large strides needed. Global warming, consequently, is left to worsen.

A similar situation prevails over corporation tax. At a time when corporate profits remain buoyant while the ability of governments to tax corporations in order to provide vital public services is declining, DGC only reinforces the problem:

> Governments vying to attract inward investment are weighing the advantages of cutting business costs . . . [Corporate] Tax rates have been falling across the world over the past quarter of a century . . . This trend is forcing some experts to the conclusion that governments have embarked on a race to the bottom.[22]

In contrast to the static regulatory chill that besets climate negotiations, here we see how DGC often has a dynamic effect. It places governments in a vicious circle in which each is forced to respond in tit-for-tat fashion. If one nation cuts its rate of corporation tax, others are forced to follow. In 2016 Indonesia's President Joko Widodo suggested that it was a no-brainer, pointing out that if Singapore's corporate income tax is 17 per cent and Indonesia's is 25 per cent, businesses will go to Singapore.[23]

In 2013, the destructiveness of this dynamic began to be recognized by some countries, especially France and Germany, resulting in efforts to harmonize corporate-tax regimes across Europe.[24] Such an initiative was dependent on the agreement of all European Union nations, if not of all countries globally. The UK government, like some others, however, had different ideas. In the face of European overtures to cooperate, it remained fiercely opposed:

> George Osborne has set great store by Britain's tax competitiveness, slashing the headline corporate tax rate from 28% to 20% . . . These and other measures have seen a wave of companies shifting their European headquarters or research and development arms to the UK – much to the anger of other member states. The UK has seen an influx of multinationals – among them Aon, Fiat Industrial and Starbucks's European operations – looking to gain tax advantages through the optimal location of the often small number of headquarters staff. Last month the US seed and agrochemicals group Monsanto announced that, should it succeed in taking over Swiss firm Syngenta, it planned to move its headquarters to the UK.[25]

The result, of course, will be that other governments will be forced to join the race to the bottom. Michael Devereux of the Oxford University Centre for Business Taxation foresees that corporation tax may continue to diminish while governments remain locked in competition and fail to find the political will to apply any long-term solution to the allocation of international profits.[26]

One of the key functions of governments – the funding of public services through tax collection – is thus severely undermined by DGC. With corporation and other taxes on globally mobile entities no longer offering adequate sources of revenue, governments have been forced to shrink public spending while shifting the tax burden on to individuals, especially the middle and working classes who cannot easily move elsewhere, and the gap between rich and poor inevitably widens.[27] The growing gap both within and between nations, as we will later explain, has significant consequences for national politics, too, as Donald Trump's 2016 presidential victory and the so-called 'Brexit' referendum to take the UK out of the European Union both showed.

Climate change and fiscal policy are not the only areas affected by DGC. Let us now turn to an entirely different field: human rights, inter-racial equity and economic justice in developing countries. How, we might wonder, could DGC have anything to do with these issues? In the following extract the former South African minister for trade and industry, Mandisi Mpahlwa, explains why the government had to retreat from supporting indigenous black businesses:

> The South African government has exempted foreign companies from having to sell a 25% stake in their local operations to black business . . . The government exempted foreign players because 'we had to be mindful that we also have to position South Africa in a global environment where there is fierce competition for investment'.[28]

Like all other governments, the South African government cannot afford to lose the international competition to attract inward investment, in this instance forcing it to sacrifice the value of racial equality. The tragedy is that, despite having come to power after decades of struggle against apartheid, South Africa finds itself unable to defend even its most cherished aims and values. DGC, once again, is the culprit.

Continuing with the theme of social justice, let us now consider the issue of workers' rights and sweat-shop exploitation, a situation endemic in the fashion industry but one that blights vast swathes of the developing world:

> Asda [part of Walmart] is today offering customers a passable two-piece suit for the price of a round of drinks in a London bar. Bangladeshi student, Shafiqul Islam, said, 'People can't survive on £12 a month, but, if the government protests, Asda and others will go to China or somewhere else.'[29]

By now you get the picture: fear of losing jobs and investment – the fear of becoming uncompetitive – once again leaves governments trumped. The values of human rights, social equity and economic justice are neatly subverted, not by governmental laxness but because politicians have no choice. The only way these countries can stay attractive to corporations and inward investors – the only way they can stay internationally competitive – is to keep their environmental and social regulations to a minimum.

When it comes to one of the most important topics of all, the threat of major global financial crises such as the one the world experienced in 2008, David Harvey explains how, in the years preceding the crisis, DGC quietly sowed the seeds:

> As the financial system went global [in the 1980s], so competition between financial centres – chiefly London and New York – took its coercive toll . . . If the regulatory regime in London was less strict than that of the US, then the branches [of international banks] in the City of London got the business rather than Wall Street. As lucrative business naturally flowed to wherever the regulatory regime was laxest, so the political pressure on the regulators to look the other way mounted.[30]

The severity of the 2008 global financial crisis was extraordinary. As the ex-chair of the US Federal Reserve, Paul Volcker, noted, never before had things gone downhill 'quite so fast and quite so uniformly around the world'.[31] Given just how disastrous the crisis was, considerable speculation arose as to whether neoliberalism might be abandoned or even whether capitalism as we know it had perhaps reached its limit. But such speculation, we contend, is premised on a false assumption that, just because neoliberal policies were implemented deliberately in the 1970s and 1980s, they can just as deliberately be reversed.

This is to completely misunderstand what we are up against. DGC has taken on a momentum all its own, and it cannot be stopped by any government. Operating in a vicious circle, it is just too ubiquitous, too powerful. This is why, despite the crash, the only story in town has been getting back to business as usual. DGC never goes away, as this article that appeared in *The Scotsman* in the wake of the 2008 crisis shows:

> Row erupts as watchdog calls for tax on the City. A fresh row has erupted over 'excessive' banking bonuses after Lord Adair Turner, chairman of the City watchdog, claimed Britain's financial sector has grown 'beyond a socially reasonable size'. His comments caused an

uproar in financial centres yesterday, including Edinburgh, with leading figures and organisations warning that Britain would lose yet another major industry to competitors abroad. John Cridland, deputy director-general of the Confederation of British Industry, said: 'The government and regulators should be very wary of undermining the international competitiveness of the UK's financial services industry.'[32]

The vicious circle of DGC is today an ever-present reality and yet it is sometimes disguised by phenomena that appear to contradict it. Some EU nations, for example, have been able to maintain relatively high taxes and social and environmental standards despite competition from other lower-cost parts of the world. If DGC causes business and jobs always to move to the lowest-cost nations how, one might ask, does Europe survive? And does this invalidate our theory of DGC?

The answer is that national competitiveness is not about any single isolated factor, such as the level of corporation tax, rather it is a complex mix of factors, including not just tax levels or environmental costs but also proximity to markets, availability of skilled labour, raw materials, transport infrastructure and so on. And this complex mix will also vary quite widely from nation to nation according to differing geographic, economic, political and cultural factors.[33]

It is this mix of factors that explains how developed nations, such as the EU states, have managed to survive and remain relatively prosperous. This is because the high cost of the EU's taxes and standards relative to other countries is outweighed by other important factors in its mix, such as the attractiveness of its large, rich and educationally advanced market. On the other hand, for developing nations without such off-setting factors, very low taxes and weak environmental regulations may be the only ways they can attract sufficient inward investment and jobs.

The point, however, is that neither developed nor developing nations seem able to dramatically *alter* their policies towards the much higher social or environmental standards now required to meet steeply mounting global problems. Whether social and environmental protection regulations are racing to the bottom, staying still or rising slightly, then, is not the issue. Because whatever the case, the inescapable reality is that global problems are *still* far outpacing the ability of regulations to keep up, and it is DGC – each nation's fear of becoming uncompetitive – that is holding all nations back.

The lesson is that it's important not to allow occasional anomalies and contradictions to fool us. Just as a river may contain whirlpools, counter-flows and stagnant patches, we don't suddenly conclude that water flows uphill.

A monstrous domination

Once you develop the ear for it, you will hear something familiar in each of the newspaper reports that we have cited – and hundreds like them in newspapers throughout the world. It is a constant, subtle message, as if a tyrant monster were commanding all peoples in all countries:

> Governments and citizens beware! Regulate or tax too stringently or do anything that will make your economy less competitive and you will lose out. Do anything to harm your international competitiveness, and business will go elsewhere, unemployment will rise and your society will suffer!

This monster is, of course, our old friend Destructive Global Competition, and when we fully acknowledge DGC's global dominance we are led to a number of rather worrying initial conclusions:

- The pursuit of social justice and environmental sustainability is fundamentally incompatible with the pursuit of international competitiveness. You can have one or the other but not both.

- The myriad global problems we face are not disconnected. Whether it's climate change, wealth inequality, financial-market regulation, pollution or sweat-shop working conditions, they are all driven, exacerbated and trumped by one single overarching dynamic: DGC.

- It is therefore simply not enough to have great proposals concerning what needs to be done to fix the economy, the climate and so on. Rather, the key issue is how to overcome DGC.

But there is one overriding lesson to be learned. Destructive competition, as we found in the school playground, can only be kept in check by adequate rules and regulations. In the context of an economy, the entity responsible for rule-setting is the state: government. But, as the examples above show, governments have been drawn into the competition, too. Far from setting adequate rules, they're now forced to dismantle them competitively. As Davies points out, 'The problem is that the production and enforcement of rules is now *internal to the game*.'[34]

But what else should we expect? When capital and investment move freely and globally to wherever they can make the highest financial returns, and when governments need these inputs to ensure economic prosperity, what outcome does common sense predict? Common sense suggests that not only will corporations get locked into mutual inescapable competition but governments will, too. How could it be otherwise?

Just when climate change and many other urgent global problems require decisive government action, DGC prevents governments from making any significant move. The conclusion we must reach is that the pursuit of international competitiveness, the very pursuit we are told will assure our prosperity, also turns out to be the source of our collective paralysis.

The game we are all playing is now inescapably a global game. In the absence of cooperation and governance at the global level, the vicious circle of DGC can only undermine lower-level governance structures and ultimately lead us to ruin. Going back to what we learned in the school playground, we can now see how the global market's asymmetry is the problem: global competition is not matched by governance on a similar scale. We have a *global* market but only *national* governance, and the global institutions we do have, as we'll see later, cannot help.

Whether we like it or not, DGC can no longer be arrested by purely national or regional (EU, for example) action. As we shall demonstrate in these pages, only multilevel, cooperative global action can rein it in. Only simultaneous global cooperation can bring global markets back under proper democratic supervision, accountability and regulation, thereby taming the monster, arresting the vicious circle and transforming destructive competition back into its benign constructive twin.

Before we are ready to conceive of any possible solutions to this crisis we must carefully consider how we got ourselves into such a mess in the first place and whether there is any meaning to why we did. To do this we must first take a step back into the very distant past.

2. A New Context for Governance

A great leap forward

Imagine the scene. It is a fine warm day in early springtime somewhere in that part of Western Asia known as the Fertile Crescent about 12,000 years ago. A weatherbeaten tribesman has something in his hand, and he is showing it to a small circle of people of all ages. He has a huge grin on his face.

'You take these seeds, dig them into the ground and add water. Then you just stand back and watch,' says this forward-thinking hunter-gatherer to his rapt audience. 'A few moons later you have food just waiting for you to gather up.'[1]

Half the band mimics the man's smile, but a few old-timers are unconvinced and screw their foreheads into mistrustful frowns. Perhaps they already sense that the new technology of crop sowing is about to change everything. The innovative tribesman's discourse will soon spread abroad, and the new way to take the food supply into their own hands means that people are embarking on an immense technological and social shift.

The consequences and the effects on the society's consciousness of that seemingly simple technological change were utterly revolutionary. The beginnings of agriculture necessitated a more settled lifestyle than hunter-gathering; now investing in a future with predictable food stocks became important. Human society embarked on a dramatic transition from foraging to agrarian societies, from small nomadic hunter-gatherer bands into much larger settled agrarian societies. It was this that made possible the earliest towns and settlements. The new agrarian settlements were capable of producing food in quantity and sometimes even a surplus, which could support far greater numbers of people in societies more structured, diversified and culturally rich.

The development of settled agriculture did not obliterate hunter-gathering or pastoral nomadism, which continued to be practised in marginal lands, even as it is today, but it soon became the dominant economic model that supported trade and architecture and fostered a whole range of allied technical developments. With this change of technology and accompanying lifestyle came a radically new way of thinking about the world, about society and about the future. Some of our evidence for this is found in the remains of religious artefacts and monumental architectural sites dating from the years immediately following the adoption of agriculture in many places from South America to China and India.[2]

Along with a new way of thinking about the world, agrarian societies perforce had to find new ways of organizing their world. It was no longer enough for the tribal women to do one thing and the men another, for the head of the chief family to rule the group, for the shaman to guide them. In the larger groups specialization evolved and hierarchies developed: leaders arose or were appointed or elected; the surplus had to be gathered into storehouses and guarded and administered. Land was now owned, so property rights became the subject of legislation and inheritance; those without land might work on that belonging to others, and their status needed encoding.

The concept of the state began to arise. Individuals would sacrifice freedom to exercise some of their individual choices for the sake of the protection afforded by the larger unit. Citizens were now obliged to contribute to the support of the overarching social unit, the state, and saw it as in their interests to do so. The state's boundaries had to be defined and enforced and sometimes expanded through conquest. Unlike in traditional hunter-gathering societies, relations with neighbours were no longer based on who was a stranger, as Jared Diamond so beautifully explains in *The World Until Yesterday*, but on organized treaties made by the few that had mandatory effect on the whole of society.[3] The requirement to *reorganize* their world is the most important unforeseen effect of radical new technology as it shifts the balance of human societies, even before they are able to predict what the outcome of the changes will be.

New contexts – new gaps

In political terms, such expansions in the scale of governance – from nomadic bands to tribes to small states to nation states – often result from the kind of technological changes we have been describing, because they require humans to radically re-envisage how their societies are organized. The new technology changes the society in such fundamental, game-changing ways that the existing system of governance finds itself undermined and cannot cope. Early signs of this are the inevitable failures of existing governance structures and a loss of faith in those structures among the populace. The hard-to-predict effect of radical technological advances always poses a threat to the existing order and a challenge to envisage anew.

These shifts are so powerful and all-pervading that they create what we call 'a new context for governance'. A new context for governance is a game-changer that forces a society to respond, usually by developing and maturing, but in the interim it can cause much chaos, suffering and malfunctioning while the society is in the throes of trying to adjust. Ultimately, the new context for governance can only be satisfactorily managed by moving to a new, more encompassing *system* of governance that can incorporate and manage the far greater complexity that the new technology has brought about.

A classic shift into a new context for governance occurred through the invention of the printing press by Johannes Gutenberg in 1450. The Middle Ages was a time during which virtually all public knowledge and beliefs were mediated via the Church, thereby securing and reinforcing its powerful position as the exclusive intermediary between God and the individual. The Church dominated the realm of ideas, and the clergy, who represented (alongside nobles and commoners) one of the Three Estates of society, played major roles in the running of medieval kingdoms.[4] But without the Church realizing it, the invention of printing kick-started the end of its monopoly.

By 1500 printing presses were in use all over Europe, and more than 20 million books had been produced. This drove a radical democratization of knowledge that undermined the then-existing political and religious authorities. Printing was a key harbinger of the vast changes to come: the Reformation and, eventually, the European Enlightenment, which together utterly transformed the social and political landscape. From this perspective, the printing press created *a new context for governance* that permeated the society and undermined the established system, eventually to transform it.

The consequences necessitated a radical rethink of how European societies organized themselves. The result was a shift from agrarian societies, which obediently followed the Church, towards larger industrial societies, infused with the new scientific rationalism. It was little wonder that the Church gradually lost its grip as power moved inexorably towards a revolutionary new system of governance, the secular nation state – a development eventually crystallized in a treaty, signed in 1648, known as the Peace of Westphalia, seen by historians as marking the birth of the modern nation-state system.

The printing press was not alone in fuelling this transition, but it was a game-changer. Additionally, the development of firearms, cartography, the nautical compass and sail technology meant that small European nations were able to circumnavigate the globe, dominate the indigenous peoples they found there, create competitive colonial empires and lay the foundations for what we now know as globalization.

We pass no judgement here on the desirability of such game-changing technological developments, such as farming and the rise of city states or the invention of the printing press and its undermining of the medieval religious hierarchy or even today's communications revolution. We are simply noting that they occur and that they constitute an inevitable part of the unfolding story of human evolution. They are to be expected, even if they are not predictable.

In retrospect, there is a discernable and repetitive pattern in what we have been describing.

- First, a game-changing new technology is discovered and it proliferates rapidly.

- Second, the new, dramatically innovative technology has a major disruptive influence on the current way humans organize their societies. In effect, it creates an unforeseen *new context for governance* that undermines the established governance system.

- Next, things get worse, because the society's way of thinking and its way of governing do not match the new context and cannot cope. A gap appears between old thinking (and governing) on the one side and new reality on the other.

- Finally, when the *thinking* of a critical mass of the society eventually catches up, the gap is closed and a new system of governance is brought in. At that point governance context and governance system are back in sync.

- But the story does not end here, because the end of one sequence is only the beginning of the next: evolution marches on.

The observable principle that we see at work here is that the *governance system needs to catch up to match the new governance context*. Otherwise, or until it does, there will be a gap, and such gaps can prove catastrophic if they are not closed relatively quickly. Considering the state of our world today, simple curiosity may be a good strategy if such a situation is suspected. We may want to ask ourselves:

- Is our present system of governance coping well with today's global problems?

- Is our faith in politics and government waxing or waning?

- Is there a gap between the new way the world actually works and existing ways of thinking and governing it?

- If so, can we identify a new context for governance emerging in our present era and how it may be undermining our present system of governance?

It is our contention that globalization in general, and Destructive Global Competition in particular, constitute just such a new context for governance. As a result, and without us realizing it, a yawning gap has opened up between the new globalized way that the world works and the outdated ways in which we still think about it and govern it.

A gun to our heads

George Papandreou, Greek Prime Minister between 2009 and 2011, looks like a man at ease in the modern international world. Born to an American mother and educated in Toronto, Massachusetts, Stockholm and at the London School of Economics, he is an internationally honoured academic. His paternal grandfather was three times prime minister of Greece, so he has high-level politics in his blood. But, not long after he took office in 2009 Papandreou had a remarkable and unsettling personal experience that meant he had to entirely re-evaluate his political take on the world. The shock he experienced was symptomatic of exactly the kind of gap that we have been introducing, between a new game-changing technological reality on the one side and established yet outdated modes of thinking and governing on the other.

Papandreou was present at a meeting of prime ministers in Brussels that took place at the height of the euro currency crisis centred on Greece in 2010. Along with being handed the reins of power came the unenviable task of going to Brussels to inform his European counterparts that Greece's deficit was not 6 per cent of gross domestic product, as the previous Greek government had led everyone to believe, but a colossal 15.6 per cent. As a result, the interest rates at which Greece could finance its debt by borrowing on global markets had skyrocketed, risking a complete default. This, in turn, threatened similar knock-on effects in other Eurozone countries. Ultimately, the prospect of a break-up of the euro was everyone's catastrophic fantasy.

Papandreou's aim was to argue for a united European response that would calm the markets and thereby offer an opportunity for his planned reforms to take effect. But rather than the informed, considered and reasoned debate among the assembled national prime ministers that Papandreou expected, something different occurred, as he himself explains in a riveting TED Talk:

> Picture yourselves around the table in Brussels. Negotiations are difficult, the tensions are high, progress is slow. And then, at ten minutes to 2 a.m. one prime minister shouts out, 'We have to finish in ten minutes!' I said, 'Why? These are important decisions. Let's deliberate a little bit longer.' But then another prime minister says, 'No, we have to have an agreement now. Because, in ten minutes the markets are opening in Japan and there will be havoc in the global economy.'[5]

Obediently, the combined assembly of prime ministers duly rushed to a decision in the brief ten minutes that global markets had allotted them. As Papandreou ruefully sums it up, 'This time it wasn't the military that had a gun to our heads but the markets.'

There are many conflicting interpretations of the euro crisis. Some see it as Europe pulling tighter together to protect its common fate, while others see it as a defeat for the free determination of citizens, particularly for those living in the so-called PIGS (Portugal, Ireland, Greece and Spain). Even though we, the authors, hold differing views on the European question, we are both convinced that the key issue highlighted by Papandreou's experience is how globalization – embodied here in the form of global bond markets – now fundamentally undermines the autonomy of national and EU governments. Rather than markets being subservient to democratically elected politicians, under globalization the reverse is the case: the market tail now wags the governmental dog.

A further example of the inability to respond appropriately to the new context and the pressure-cooker effect it has on governments could be seen in the public outrage over corporate tax avoidance. This first hit the headlines in the UK in 2012, but it has since become a worldwide concern. It was revealed that multinational corporations such as Starbucks, Amazon and Google were paying very little in tax and certainly much less than their fair share. Thanks to their widespread commercial operations across the EU, these companies exploited the differences between various national tax rules and rates to structure their operations so that their profits accrued in whichever nation offered the lowest rate of tax. The public, understandably alarmed, particularly at a time of belt-tightening austerity, called upon politicians to act.

The scandal was well publicized, but what action did politicians eventually take? One logical reaction would have been for the UK government to announce an increase in the rate of corporation tax and, perhaps, a corresponding decrease in personal taxes in order to redress the unfairness. However, apart from calling on the chief executives of these companies to explain themselves before a parliamentary committee and admonishing them to 'play fair on tax', the UK government took no further positive action. Perversely, it took negative action. Instead of increasing the rate of corporation tax it reduced it![6]

A further example occurred in 2012 when the global commercial bank HSBC was found to have broken money-laundering laws. Both the US and UK governments were aware of the breach, and yet they refrained from prosecuting the bank. With the global economy remaining fragile after the global financial crisis of 2008 and HSBC being in a central position, the reason for non-action was to avoid another 'global financial disaster'.[7] While governments have become impotent under DGC, it is clear that the global commercial banks have not only become too big to fail but too big to jail.

What on earth, we may ask, is going on here? If the global market tail now wags the governmental dog, if governments cannot prosecute wrongdoers and if they cannot ensure social fairness by making corporations pay fair taxes something must be very wrong indeed. These illustrations, along with others we have already cited, indicate that a new context for governance is very much with us and that it is undermining the current system of governance. Not only is it preventing national governments from acting as citizens would expect it is often causing politicians to make a bad situation worse. No wonder the public feels frustrated and outraged as politicians struggle to come to terms with the new global reality.

As we saw in Chapter 1 and as the above examples show, we are now living in a new context for governance that has been ushered in by globalization. But the new context is not so much globalization itself but that aspect of it that we earlier identified as Destructive Global Competition.

Unlike Gutenberg's printing press, DGC isn't itself a new technology, but it does arise out of the ability of certain entities – global markets, investors, commercial banks and multinational corporations – to move freely and globally. And that ability is certainly technologically driven: computers, global communications, the internet and so on, are all inherent to DGC's ubiquity and pervasiveness. It is these technologies, along with the deliberate implementation of neoliberal policies, that have brought competition to the global level.

The crucial consequences are that this new globalized reality has overtaken our largely national systems of government and left them in chaos. With governments now competing destructively with each other to stay internationally competitive, there is no governmental entity able to enforce global rules. And it is a fine mess! In these circumstances it shouldn't surprise us that competition's destructive side has come so powerfully to the fore nor that it's now running out of control.

Like Gutenberg's press in the fifteenth century, DGC has initiated a new context for governance that our existing ways of thinking and governing cannot cope with. George Papandreou's shock and outrage at being dictated to by global markets is a great example of how his thinking lagged behind and needed to catch up with the new reality that had overtaken him. But it's not just Papandreou's thinking that lags behind. Ours does, too.

The Myth of the Sovereign Nation

The problem any society faces in acknowledging a new context for governance is that current ways of thinking are invariably slow to catch up with the new reality. Consequently, when we see the evidence, we're likely to dismiss it. 'Old habits die hard', it is often said, and so it is vital to identify the key features of our present outdated thinking habit. Its cornerstone is what we are calling the 'Myth of the Sovereign Nation'.[8]

At the core of this myth is a mindset that nations are always sovereign actors, that governments are powerful and free to decide on their policies and, in consequence, have the ability to solve today's problems. This mindset is deeply ingrained and rests on the experience of the last 350 years, when it was the truth. Prior to the onset of globalization, national governments *were* powerful autonomous actors; they were more or less sovereign. Contrast, for example, the colonial era, in which the newly industrializing nations of Europe freely competed to colonize much of the rest of the world, with today's era, in which all governments seem to have become the puppets of global markets.

Ever since the birth of the nation-state system in 1648 we have become thoroughly inculcated with the idea of powerful governments. Subconsciously, it is daily reinforced by myriad national symbols: pictures of our parliament or congress building, national elections, national flags, national sports teams and so on. In some countries, national flags are waved when an individual has a birthday or arrives home at an airport. It is no exaggeration to say that we perceive the world through national lenses; our way of thinking consequently remains what is called 'nationcentric' – about which we will have much more say later. Not surprisingly, when confronted with an overarching global reality – like globalization or DGC – we are slow to catch on to its effects and think them through. It's as if we're still looking through our old pair of glasses.

Papandreou's shock at having to dance to the tune of global markets demonstrates this thinking-gap perfectly. Despite his international profile and his understanding of global markets, he still believed that as prime minister of a sovereign nation he had a substantial measure of autonomy – that he and his counterparts still had the time to debate and the freedom to decide. But even this highly intelligent man was still thinking nationcentrically; he still believed the Myth. Like someone shocked by an ice-cold shower, he was rudely woken up to the fact that he and his fellow prime ministers were not free and autonomous actors at all.

Worse still, global markets dictate not only the timing of political decisions but their content, too. In the Greek case, if markets were to be pacified and the euro to survive, extremely tight austerity measures would have to be imposed on heavily indebted Eurozone countries, amounting to a fiscal union. Whether citizens would agree to this, or whether they should even be asked, remained a moot point throughout. As far as politicians were concerned, there was simply no choice and no time.

Yet another example of the impotence of national governments has been their inability to halt, let alone reverse, the growing problem of wealth inequality. This problem has been worsening for decades, especially within nations, and it has occurred across virtually all countries, regardless of the party in power – another indicator that suggests there is a deeper force at work and that a New Context for Governance is very much with us.

Inequality has become so pronounced that even the World Economic Forum (WEF) flagged it up as a problem in its 2014–15 *Global Competitiveness Report*. The report noted that the gap between rich and poor was widening in many countries, that youth unemployment was rising, with access to basic services remaining challenging. Even in several fast-growing developing countries it suggested that growth was not making a notable dent in income inequality or poverty and that the vulnerabilities associated with these problems remained entrenched.[9]

It is ironic that the WEF acknowledges the problem while failing to see that it is the very pursuit of international competitiveness that it so strongly supports which prevents governments from taking the necessary measures. At the heart of the problem lies the inability of governments to tax the rich, the multinational corporations and the bankers fairly and to redistribute that wealth in support of the less fortunate. The ability of these globally mobile entities to move elsewhere to escape such taxes of course makes this impossible, so leading to a widening gap between the globally mobile winners and the nationally rooted losers.

Europe has witnessed the dire consequences of a global-market system that produces millions of 'nationally rooted losers'. This is that these people will not stay rooted for long. Mass migration into Europe may have been catalysed by wars in the Middle East, but, as Gideon Rachman points out:

> there are also larger forces at play that will ensure immigration into Europe remains a vexed issue long after the war in Syria is over. Europe is a wealthy, ageing continent whose population is stagnant. By contrast the populations of Africa, the Middle East and South Asia are younger, poorer and rising fast.[10]

Although not directly a consequence of DGC, mass migration can to a large extent be seen as the unintended fall-out from a competitive, win–lose global economy, which, barring mitigating transnational regulatory measures, can only get worse. Mass migration, like the other examples we have cited, will remain impervious to national or even European action.

Only a minority of political commentators were able to identify that the widening gap between globalization's winners and losers, which is driven by DGC, was the key underlying reason for the UK's Brexit referendum result. One was former UK Prime Minister Gordon Brown:

> The elephant in the room is globalisation – the speed, scope and scale of the seismic shifts in our global economy. And the most obvious manifestation of the world we have lost is the hollowing out of our industrial towns as a result of the collapse of manufacturing in the face of Asian competition. These towns are home to a disproportionate share of the semi-skilled workers who feel on the wrong side of globalisation and who opted to vote leave. Unable to see how globalisation can be tamed in their interests, they have, not surprisingly, become recruits to an anti-globalisation movement whose lightning rod is migration.[11]

Here we see how DGC widens the gap between globalization's winners and losers and drives the forces of political disintegration at lower levels. This is a not just a national British phenomenon but one that, because it has global causes, is driving nationalist and independence movements across many countries. In 2016 much the same occurred with the election of Donald Trump in the USA. As nations fail to deal with problems that are beyond their reach, those citizens on the losing end of globalization become disaffected and angry. They punish mainstream politicians by moving to the extremes and, in the case of the EU, constituent regions inevitably start to question the wisdom of staying together in traditional unions.

Predictably, the response of governments to this worsening situation is more of the same. In failing to recognize the new context for governance that confronts them they're driven to evermore desperate attempts to revive an ailing global economy, such as further trade liberalization in the form of agreements like the Transatlantic Trade and Investment Partnership (TTIP). TTIP is a series of trade liberalization negotiations being carried out, mostly in secret, between the USA and the EU aimed at boosting economic growth. However, as many NGOs opposed to it have pointed out, this growth is to be purchased at the cost of granting corporations the right to sue governments if laws are passed that impair corporate profits, and such cases would not be heard in public courts but behind closed doors by secret tribunals.[12] Seeing yet more competition and economic growth as the answer, governments cede still more power to corporations at the expense of democracy, themselves and their citizens. And this is to say nothing of the fact that new technologies such as robotics will ensure that any economic growth is unlikely to be accompanied by more jobs.[13]

The reality is that the free market operates globally at a level above the national. Without any entity of effective global governance to exercise control over global markets, national governments are no longer sovereign – DGC is sovereign. Worse still, the international organizations that we do have, such as the International Monetary Fund, the World Bank and the World Trade Organization, are both run by nation states and thoroughly inculcated with neoliberal doctrine, which dictates that markets should remain as unregulated as possible. The markets have become a super-deity, rather like the fearsome queen of the jungle 'She-Who-Must-Be-Obeyed' in Victorian author Rider Haggard's 1887 novel *She: A History of Adventure*. Alternatively, as Julian Lindley-French, an Oxford historian and professor of defence strategy at the Netherlands Defence Academy, suggests, a new systemic anarchy reigns. Prevailing over all international institutions, it perpetuates the destruction of regulations as the very essence of economic globalization.[14]

Politics in the dark

Papandreou is not alone in finding himself with so little actual power when at the helm of an apparently sovereign ship of state. One can imagine that most politicians still like to believe that they are masters of their own destiny rather than the unwitting subjects of DGC. The way most national politicians declare how they will act decisively on this or that global issue, be it climate change or financial-market instability, certainly has this ring of sovereign autonomy about it. But to many of us it is sounding increasingly hollow. It is as if politicians wish to persuade not only us but also themselves that they still enjoy substantial autonomy and power.

From the outside it looks as if they are snoozing under the spell of an old myth, still to catch up with the new context for governance that DGC has brought about. This effectively amounts to what is popularly known as being in denial. Whatever has caused this state of affairs we are now imprisoned by it. For being in denial about a current reality is like walking in the dark: we cannot recognize what our minds refuse to see, and we cannot negotiate obstacles in obscurity except by stumbling forward.

Awakening from this sleepwalk would certainly cause a rude shock, as it did for George Papandreou, and it certainly switches the lights back on. But they quickly go off again because, as we noted earlier, the existing system of governance has no solution to the new context, so politicians go back to hoping that business as usual will do. The denial gives us politics in the dark, and this is now the problem. By imagining that the current reality is not operating or that it is still manageable under familiar nationcentric government strategies, politicians and economists keep their heads firmly buried in the sand while they become increasingly impotent, the electorate increasingly disaffected and the real problems critical. The result is that, as the poet William Stafford said, 'The darkness around us is deep.'[15]

Hanging on to our Myth

Our deep attachment to the false idea that governments are autonomous actors that remain in control is hard to shake. One reason may be that the consequences of dispensing with it are just too frightening to contemplate. After all, if nations are no longer sovereign and must bow to global markets, who will protect us from all the negative fall-outs of unregulated markets, from climate change, austerity, rapacious corporations and so on? If nations are no longer sovereign, what does democracy mean any more? If whoever we elect has to toe the market-friendly line, why bother to vote? And if, as citizens in a democracy, we no longer have any control over a world heading towards chaos, what is left for us?

It feels as if we are all powerless, and when that happens people generally either do nothing or do the wrong things. So pervasive is this new context for governance that not only can governments take little or no positive action they are often driven to exacerbate the problem by taking negative action. As we saw in the case of the UK government, its need to keep Britain internationally competitive and attractive to footloose multi-national corporations caused it to reduce corporation tax still further, so exacerbating, or at least perpetuating, an already unfair situation. And we saw in the Introduction to this book how former UK Chancellor George Osborne's blatant but understandable *realpolitik* categorically ruled out saving the planet if it meant making his country uncompetitive – and the same, of course, goes for every other government. The result is that all governments remain frozen in regulatory chill.[16]

So what can we do? The image we invoked in the Introduction of the little girl asking her grandfather haunts us. But one thing is clear:

remaining addicted to the Myth of the Sovereign Nation – staying in denial – will not help.

There is, however, another way to look at this.

All we have to do, for now, is to remember that new contexts for govern-ance have happened before and that each time they occurred the scale of governance had to expand in order to cope. This naturally occurring phenomenon has led us from governing ourselves in clan groups and then in larger tribes, then on from tribes to city states, which became still larger and led to today's nation states, which we now take for granted as the end-point of demographic development. But why should it be the end of a process when – through even the briefest look back in history – we can't fail to notice a clear evolution of scale and complexity? Seen in this evolutionary way, globalization and DGC may always have been on the cards. They could well be a prelude – if we play our cards right – to evolution's next step towards ever-larger scales of cooperation and governance. However we look at it, the new context of DGC cannot be avoided or denied if we want to stay in the game. It raises very tough questions that we all have to face:

- Was it only George Papandreou whose thinking needed to catch up, or must ours, too?

- Are we ready to accept that when it comes to global and many national issues our national governments have become substantially impotent?

- Having been brought up to believe in the Myth of the Sovereign Nation, are we ready to accept that this myth, a cherished part of our identity, no longer holds?

- Can we acknowledge that the nationcentric way of thinking may be inadequate, incomplete and incapable of grasping the new global realities?

The Rumpelstiltskin Factor

Our recent process of globalization, like Gutenberg's press in the fifteenth century, has created a new context for governance that our existing ways of thinking and governing cannot cope with. There is a gap. Our merely national systems of governance urgently need to catch up with the new global reality. And yet, the problem is that before our systems of governance can change it is our *thinking* that must catch up first, because the gap is chiefly in our thinking. Our world has fallen into a dangerous thinking gap.

At this stage of our argument, it is becoming clear that we have on our hands a problem that is as much psychological as it is political. Political solutions are, as yet, powerless in the face of new contexts while they are still unrecognized, as we have seen. Our habitual acceptance of the Myth of the Sovereign Nation partially explains our reluctance to shake off our denial. But if we are to deal with this new global context for governance and ultimately overcome it we must start by bringing it firmly into our consciousness. We must admit that it exists – and then we at least have a chance at getting to grips with it. The crucial initial steps involve *identifying* it, *naming* it and *acknowledging* it.

The step of naming an unnamed entity is a key movement upon which properly solving any problem depends and can be surprisingly powerful. For example, in the field of education, before the concept of dyslexia was coined the difficulties certain children experienced in the classroom meant that they were either thought of as stupid or ignored or both. Either way, they did not get the help they needed and the problem wasn't addressed. Once this syndrome began to be named, research could be conducted, special-needs teachers appointed and sufferers were able to find ways of coping and not feeling paralysed by shame. A similar pattern of evolution was visible when autism started to be recognized.

This process of a naming is a crucial step and one that we call the Rumpelstiltskin Factor, in reference to the Grimm Brothers' fairy-tale.[17] In this fable, which appears in countless versions throughout European folklore, a poor miller's daughter gets to marry a prince through the help of a little imp, Rumpelstiltskin, whose name is unknown to her. Eventually Rumpelstiltskin comes to collect his reward: he demands her little baby as his grisly recompense. Rumpelstiltskin agrees to desist if – and only if – the girl, now princess and mother, can guess his name. The vengeful imp knows how unlikely it is that she can come up with his right name, so he dances and sings:

> Today I brew, tomorrow I bake,
> And then the Prince's child I'll take.
> For no one knows my little game,
> That Rumpelstiltskin is my name!

The truth enshrined in this tale is an existential key to knowledge, the kind of wisdom that under the medieval Church's domination over thinking had to be hidden in fairy-stories and put in the mouths of 'the little people', who could not be controlled. Identifying an issue allows it to be named, and naming something takes it out of the closet and permits us to have a *relationship* with it. Once we begin relating to something, we can start to see the problem for what it is, to acknowledge our limitations and our power under these circumstances. Only then do we have a chance of doing something about it. But, until it is named, we have no chance at all.

Everyone knows that today we live in a globalized world, but we have been slow to acknowledge what that means in terms of its competitive effect. We have been reluctant to *name* that effect, and the world is losing out. This is why in this book we have begun by giving names to things which might otherwise seem obvious, taken for granted or missed altogether.

We have needed to name these new super-globalized circumstances and to identify them as a new context for governance. The name we chose for that context was *Destructive Global Competition*. We saw that DGC has forced us to acknowledge that we are still clinging to an illusion, the *Myth of the Sovereign Nation*.

Now self-sustaining and operating beyond any government's control, DGC is the tyrant that is undermining all national and transnational systems of governance and stands in the way of solving many of the world's most intractable problems. While the ubiquitous rule of DGC continues, all governments and all peoples are effectively set against each other in a competitive vicious circle, and there seems to be no way out. And yet society as a whole somehow still remains in denial, as if under a sleeping spell in a fairy-tale.

If we stay asleep much longer Rumpelstiltskin will take the baby.

3. The Blame Game

The economy on the couch

So far we have seen how our present system of governance has been undermined by Destructive Global Competition and that this constitutes a game-changing new context for governance. We saw that, being blind to DGC, politicians and governments remain caught in it and thereby rendered largely impotent. We have identified our attachment to the Myth of the Sovereign Nation as a key factor. Having named DGC as the elephant in the room, we are now in a position to see clearly the nature of the overarching problems besetting the world.

Once the elephant is acknowledged we can start to wonder how we've managed to stay so blind, so asleep. So that we can begin finding solutions that are as game-changing as the new context for governance, we need to understand our complicity in avoiding the acknowledgement of DGC; we must make sure we have got to the bottom of our denial. Crucially, we must try to find out whether this denial is an absolute road-block to any way forward or whether it may simply be a difficult but necessary diversion we have to contend with on the way to integrating a new and unfamiliar reality.

This means we will begin to introduce some psychology into our argument, which so far has been primarily presented in terms of economics and politics. Why, you may be wondering, should we take such an unusual step?[1]

We have already seen that the major problem we run into is a thinking-gap and that actions to address solutions cannot have significant impact until the new context for governance has been acknowledged. We reasoned, therefore, that the current impasse in world affairs can be reframed as a thinking problem. We saw how the familiar world of sovereign national politics has been overridden and how, quite understandably, we cling to an outdated myth, but how desperate that clinging appears in the light of the new context for governance. Our reluctance to abandon the old context is only understandable as a kind of defensive denial towards mentally accepting the disturbing new conditions that all of us are caught in.

Now we need to penetrate this denial in order to see clearly and choose a good way forward. This cannot be done from a basis of politics and economics alone; we need to examine the inner workings of human affairs and for a moment tread a psychological path. Psychology, politics and economics haven't been easy bedfellows. It is more than a century since the discovery of the unconscious mind and psychologists began to map out how human motivation and behaviour are connected. But ever since the European Enlightenment, which was a reaction to the medieval world where all knowledge was guarded as the province of the Church, the various disciplines and sciences have pursued quite separate paths of specialization. This has meant that these disciplines have evolved with distinct bodies of knowledge and haven't really been in dialogue with each other.

The good news is that this has enabled extraordinary advances, which have transformed our lives mostly for the better. The bad news is that the lack of dialogue means that the powerful tools available in one area tend not to be employed in another. Psychology has evolved a potent understanding of human motivation and developed many tools for change, but these have not yet benefited the political sphere. As the late Jungian analyst and scholar James Hillman said, 'We've had a hundred years of psychotherapy – and the world's getting worse.'[2]

In some ways psychology only has itself to blame for remaining an outsider discipline. As fragmented as the Church became, with endless schisms and sects, psychologists and psychotherapists failed to evolve a common body of understanding that could be universally drawn upon. If they had, and if psychology and politics were more in dialogue with each other, commentators would be better able to see through the politics of fear, blame and scapegoating that arise at times of transition in society when people feel helpless and hopeless.

The main reason that we as authors have pooled resources is because we both believe that psychological knowledge is indispensable to seeing our way through the current world political impasse. We need now to combine our economic and political analysis with a psychological one, or we remain like Sleeping Beauty with no hope of cutting a way out of the thicket in which DGC keeps us imprisoned by failing so far to name it.

Powerlessness breeds blame

More prosaically, we need psychological thinking to up the level of political analysis in order to see through some of the ways we react to the problems around us. Otherwise extremism, populism and political apathy, which are clear and present dangers currently, have no real opponents. We can better understand why people invariably turn to nationalism when they feel scared by understanding the mental tricks psychoanalysts call defence mechanisms and which we all employ, such as disowning and projection. These are used when difficult ideas, feelings or roles are banished from our awareness and exported on to other people with whom we don't identify. This is a much more common phenomenon than might at first be imagined and explains why right-wing extremist parties always swell their numbers at such times – especially drawing upon the poor and the marginalized.

Whenever people feel impotent a natural response to make sense of the situation is to make someone else accountable. Blame is the understandable psychological outcome of such impotence. Many traditional communities resort to scapegoating newcomers or outsiders at such times. In the Middle Ages, when the commoners felt overburdened with taxation for the wars pursued by king and nobles, they fell upon the Jews in their towns with terrible savagery. The horrifying excesses of the Second World War similarly arose out of the whipped-up fear and powerlessness that resulted from the difficult peace of the First World War and the Great Depression that soon followed. There is always someone around who can be blamed.

These days, the blame tends to fall on immigrants, mainstream political parties or, in the EU, on the 'faceless bureaucrats' of Brussels. Others of us, resisting the urge to take our anger and helplessness out on marginal communities and wanting a fairer world, feel justified in denouncing our politicians. Or we blame the globally mobile entities – the multinational corporations, the banks, global investors and the rich – who have the power to move their operations or investments around. It is understandable: these are the people who benefit so grotesquely from the globalized world, so they are obvious targets. Besides, so much of our lives seems constrained by the corporate manipulation of our desire, and we both love it and hate it and remain addicted to its products. Moreover, in terms of geopolitics, the big corporations and global investors invariably benefit whenever there is a crisis or a war.

To many of us, it's clear who the bad guys are. And yet, even though this tendency to blame is understandable, is it an accurate apportionment of responsibility? Is it really the fault of the corporate world, or are we just trying to make ourselves feel better?

Corporations R Us

It may at first sound distinctly odd if we start to propose that corporations are not the problem. But what is the reality? Just a little basic economics makes clear that for virtually all corporations, acting responsibly and sustainably would inevitably penalize them by having to pay higher wages and having to conform to more stringent, more costly, standards. The problem, however, is that higher costs, if they are not equally incurred by competitors, ultimately mean becoming a loser rather than a winner and going out of business. In a globalized world where competitors could be anywhere on the planet, any corporation that tries to do the right thing is likely to lose out. As *The Economist* suggests, any firm choosing to go green will merely burden itself with higher costs than its less virtuous competitors.[3]

The overarching problem, then, may not be ignorance or negligence on the part of corporate executives but that DGC makes it difficult for them to act in an environmentally or socially responsible manner, as economist David Korten explains:

> With financial markets demanding maximum short-term gains and corporate raiders standing by to trash any company that isn't externalizing every possible cost, efforts to fix the problem by raising the social consciousness of managers misdefine the problem. There are plenty of socially conscious managers. The problem is a predatory system that makes it difficult for them to survive. This creates a terrible dilemma for managers with a true social vision of the corporation's role in society. They must either compromise their vision or run a great risk of being expelled by the system.[4]

Much the same goes for global investors. George Soros, the successful money magnate who in 1987 famously 'broke the Bank of England', has been the brunt of considerable blame himself. Soros, who now advocates free and open societies, has been able, in retrospect, to reflect on his actions. Here he points out how he like others was caught up in the tide of competitiveness that left him strangely lacking autonomy even as he was benefiting:

> As an anonymous participant in financial markets, I never had to weigh the social consequences of my actions. I was aware that in some circumstances the consequences might be harmful but I felt justified in ignoring them on the grounds that I was playing by the rules. The game was very competitive, and if I imposed additional constraints on myself I would end up a loser. Moreover, I realized that

my moral scruples would make no difference to the real world, given
the conditions of effective or near-perfect competition that prevail in
financial markets; if I abstained somebody else would take my place.[5]

What this suggests is that competition – DGC – is on the whole a much
stronger driver of our increasingly perilous problems than greed. Rather
like a twin-engine aircraft, both the 'greed engine' and the 'competition
engine' pull the plane in the same direction, so it's difficult to tell which
one is pulling most strongly. At present the obviousness of the greed
engine causes us to blame that one. We do so because instances of greed
or malpractice are more visible. Meanwhile DGC, because it operates
largely unseen, is left to do the main damage. Under globalization it is
the competition engine – *the fear of losing out* – that is chiefly responsible
for keeping the plane moving forward. The only justification needed, as
Soros admits, is the grimly reassuring knowledge that 'if I abstained
somebody else would take my place'. Strange as it may seem, investors and
corporations, needing always to keep their profits and their share prices
up, are just as constrained by DGC as governments. Like governments,
any corporation or investor acting ethically is likely to lose out – and that
is not an option.

This analysis should not be mistaken as an apology for reckless,
exploitative or abusive corporate behaviour – far from it. Nor do we deny
that corporations and the rich fund a vast propaganda machine to protect
their interests.[6] Greed and manipulation are, of course, important, but
they are not, we think, key. What we are trying to point out is the unseen
pervasiveness of DGC – the whirlpool in which not just governments but
all corporations and investors and all of us, too, are caught. Initially, the way
we are interpreting the data may go against the grain, but paradoxically it
presents us with more choice than we had perhaps imagined, as we hope
to show later.

Whatever one's view, we are faced with a choice: we can choose to carry
on denying DGC, continuing to play the familiar and easy blame game of
indicting politicians, corporations, bankers and so on; alternatively, we can
accept the all-pervasiveness of DGC, in which case we arrive at a paradoxical
and disturbing truth. On the one hand, DGC prevents governments from
acting adequately, and yet, on the other, it ties the hands of corporations,
too, while allowing them to profit from governments' desperation to stay
internationally competitive. Google and other multinationals highlighted

this double-sided, conflicted and wholly unsatisfactory situation at the height of the tax-avoidance scandal. As Matt Brittin, Google UK's boss, pointed out, 'Google plays by the rules set by politicians. The only people who really have choices are politicians who set the tax rates.'[7]

Mr Brittin's statement is factually correct, even if his innocence sounds rather coy. Even if they don't tell the whole story, his words point to the crucial aspect of the new reality, that, although governments set the rules, the new context of DGC actually leaves them with very few options. Governments can only change the rules to increase levels of tax significantly if, and only if, all other governments agree to do so as well and within a similar timescale. But, of course, they don't because they are all players in the competitive game, and there is no global entity available to enforce tighter rules. To return to our football analogy, there is no global referee, and since governments remain in denial they sadly cannot see the need for one. So DGC remains in control.

In our frustration, we citizens can lash out and blame the multinationals if we wish – it feels good and gives us a temporary sense of meaning, but it accomplishes nothing and nothing actually changes. In the end, we only increase our powerlessness. Alternatively, we can accept the larger reality that any corporation failing to take advantage of lower-cost tax jurisdictions only places itself at a competitive disadvantage to corporations that have no such scruples. For corporations, as for governments, losing out in a competitive global market is simply not an option. Catching up with the new context for governance means accepting that it is not the multinationals or other free-moving entities that are really to blame; DGC is.

Multinational corporations have been the first to wake up to the new reality of DGC. They know what it is, they know how it works and they know how to use it to their advantage. The problem is that in failing to name it, the rest of us – including our media and politicians – remain all but oblivious to it and lag behind. Collectively we still badly need to wake up and smell the kind of coffee that's been brewing.

Normalized denial

Once we see through the habitual, comforting but ultimately useless illusion of blaming, we come squarely back to the problem of the denial of DGC. With its backbeat of blame, this is the theme song of the many ways we hide the truth from ourselves and cling to a familiar reality. We urgently need to understand this denial.

Humans have a natural propensity to delay accepting any new reality, let alone a game-changer like a new context for governance. This is built into us, for it conserves energy and keeps cognitive dissonance – a kind of mental meltdown when the facts do not fit what we perceive our reality or identity to be – at bay. The propensity to deny a reality outside familiar experience is something the brain is wired for and something we all do from time to time. It's a tactic we employ to avoid shock. Denial is therefore an expected stage of a process of coming to terms with the new.

From a psychotherapeutic perspective, denial is a defence mechanism that the human mind can employ in the service of self-preservation or the preservation of a particular idea about ourselves. Denial operates in several different degrees, on a spectrum from being unconscious, where we simply cannot see a reality even if it is in front of our eyes, to wilful blindness or outright mendacity at the other end. So denial is both a potent weapon for survival but also a force against the truth.

Sometimes denial needs reinforcing. As reality inevitably creeps back in we have to deal with the mental discomfort – the cognitive dissonance – this creates in us. But there is one other important, often unrecognized and undervalued, mental trick that seals the denial. This, as we have been hinting, is the use of normalization. Like fish so habituated to water that they take it for granted, we do not acknowledge a game-changing shift that has occurred because the denial of it has become normal. It is normal.

Normalization is a process that renders ideas and habits acceptable, as 'natural' or 'normal', and then taken for granted or established as a part of everyday life. Individuals can normalize their own self-destructive habits even when they are proven to be against their own long-term interests, because normalization works in partnership with denial to hide the truth – even from ourselves.

Normalization, like denial, is a powerful defence mechanism and one that is often overlooked by psychotherapists because it frequently operates in group situations where it is extremely effective and infectious. Operating socially, it weaves a magic spell, an illusion that affects the whole society that is hard to break out of. In such cases it is usually completely invisible and therefore very effective.

The radical French philosopher Michel Foucault highlighted the use of normalization as one of the most perfect means of social control, exerting the maximum control with the minimum expenditure of force. If everyone believes that a harmful situation is normal, they are unlikely to do anything about it. Often, normalized ideas and habits can become a cultural hallmark or tradition, where from an outside perspective they might seem repellent or unnatural. For example, Nick has written elsewhere about how the habit of sending young children away from the home to elite boarding institutions has been completely normalized by the British, where to outsiders the value of children in the home is self-evident.[8]

As an illustration of how normalization affects our topic, let us briefly return to the anger many of us felt at the injustice of multinational corporations not paying their fair share of tax. Although there was considerable coverage and debate on the matter in the UK, at no point was it seriously suggested that the government should raise the level of corporation tax in order to rectify the unfairness. Why this omission? Although from a national domestic perspective closing the advantageous tax loopholes or increasing the rate of corporation tax would have been an obvious course of action, the overarching domination of DGC renders this impossible. At a time when unemployment must be kept low, politicians are afraid to do anything that might cause large employers, such as multinational corporations, to consider moving their operations to some other country. It is the same story with bankers' bonuses.

In this way, the very thing the public wants their elected politicians to do – to raise the level of corporation tax to redress the unfairness – becomes the one thing they cannot do. But this is never mentioned. Why? Because we have normalized the unfairness: we have normalized DGC.

Displacement, compensation and dissociation

Many of us are at times guilty of displacing our anger on to someone who isn't the real cause of it – perhaps on our children or on a colleague – because we've been unable to identify the real cause. Sometimes we ourselves are to blame, but sometimes we only realize in retrospect what was gnawing at us all the time. In reality, however, compensation – the feeling of comfort we experience by displacing blame elsewhere – is never a substitute for dealing with the deeper cause of our anger; blame always leaves us feeling a victim to someone else. Unless we discover what is really going on, both these habits are only temporary solutions for feeling powerless; both end up leaving us just as frustrated as we were in the first place.

It seems to us that in the case of our attitude towards our politicians, we compensate ourselves by blaming them in order to distract ourselves from the painful truth that they no longer have adequate power over free-moving global entities – and neither do we. The upshot is an excessively polarized political scene, which is also normalized. Perhaps the example that engendered the greatest widespread impotent outrage was the global financial meltdown of 2007–8. In Britain we allowed our deeper feelings of hopelessness and powerlessness to be compensated by channelling our anger into a relatively minor, if annoying, issue when, in 2009, widespread abuse of expenses claims by Members of Parliament hit the headlines. This took over public interest from bigger issues about which people felt impotent.

Such local issues operate on us as a distraction, and we displace our feelings of powerless anger so that they land somewhere. Then we can get back to business as usual without being more than temporarily alarmed. To ensure that we keep on ignoring DGC and are not discomforted by doing so, we also allow ourselves to engage in all sorts of material compensations, which are most welcome as economic drivers. The wish to be compensated for some unacknowledged lack is meat and drink to the wheels of corporate consumerism, as the fashion, snacking and techno-gadget industry know to their benefit.

Meanwhile, at the macro level, we remain in thrall to DGC and pay the price.

In the case of multinational corporations, we saw that the price we all have to pay to keep our national level of corporation tax relatively attractive – in a word, competitive – is to forgo the implementation of a cherished value: social fairness. To stay competitive we are obliged to accept that individual citizens and small businesses must pay more than our fair share, while multinational corporations, being able to move across national borders, can pay less or virtually nothing at all.

In an honest accounting system, the price we have to pay for our nation's competitiveness should include what economists call 'externalities', including the loss of social fairness. But, nowadays, this price is never mentioned. We have disowned it or dissociated (an even stronger form of denial) from it. Ignoring it has become normalized, simply accepted as inevitable. At the same time the all-pervading pursuit of national competitiveness has become a monstrous vicious circle in which every nation is playing the same ultimately ruinous game. If allowed to continue, we risk witnessing a veritable 'tragedy of the commons' – a general and comprehensive global breakdown – but no one says a word.

Many of us are very aware of the symptoms of this game, such as global warming, wealth inequality and so on, but we have denied and normalized the common barrier that prevents us from acting on them. The upshot is that solutions such as increasing corporation tax are no longer even mentioned. It is as if we are unable to speak about or even notice that there is an elephant in the room: the problem of DGC and thereby any solution remain denied.

Eyes wide shut

This habit of not speaking about things and banishing them from consciousness is more widespread than we like to think. In the example earlier of dumping our anger on a loved one or colleague, the real cause of the upset has been banished from our awareness. In order to feel safe and comfortable, we dissociate or split off the cause or the feeling that was bugging us all along. In the same way, because of our powerlessness, our society seems to have dissociated the effects of DGC from awareness by denying the obvious. There are many ways we carry out these feats of dissociation and normalization, both individually and as whole cultures, and we do know quite a lot about why people use dissociation. We dissociate because of feelings, realities or identities which we find unbearable. In order to protect ourselves, our minds use an array of defence mechanisms. The defences involve various mental conjuring tricks based on shifting attention and reorganizing objects of perception. Happily, these defence mechanisms have been studied by psychoanalysts for over a century now, and we know a lot about them.

Chief among these is dissociation, or splitting, which are psychological terms for what is usually known as being in denial. Dissociation is the foundation stone of self-protective personality structures which psychoanalyst turned best-selling author Stephen Grosz defines as 'an unconscious strategy that aims to keep us ignorant of feelings in ourselves that we're unable to tolerate'.[9]

If practised over long periods, dissociation can have long-term effects on the brain, let alone on consciousness. Dan Siegel, clinical professor of psychiatry at the UCLA School of Medicine, gives us dissociation's neuroscientific picture:

Dissociation is defined very simply as dis-association – and that means associated things are now literally not linked any more.

> Looking at some of the studies of the brain in dissociation, we can
> see that the brain literally becomes fragmented – it is no longer linking
> its differentiated parts.[10]

Dissociation begins simply, as a self-saving mental trick that any of us may instinctively perform when we are ashamed or embarrassed to make something known, to accept or integrate something. We put it to one side, think of something else; we use forgetting, not referring to, compartmentalizing, denial or deletion in order to assist us in maintaining our internal composure. For example, if you were to ask a friend who is a smoker how many cigarettes they get through in a week, they will very likely give you a number which they think is accurate. When asked to actually count them during a particular week, the smoker will surprise themselves by finding the real number is higher than the estimate. Part of the smoker does not want to acknowledge the extent of their bad habit.

Entire societies can practise communal denial. A well-known, if apocryphal, example of deleting reality occurred when Captains Cook's sailing ships first arrived in the South Pacific in the eighteenth century. Apparently, the indigenous islanders just did not see them. They were unable to perceive them because they had never before encountered such items, and to protect themselves from the shock of having to integrate these novelties that they had never seen before (and would eventually transform their lives) their brains simply colluded in refusing to perceive them.

Do we imagine that we are any more equipped than these islanders to avoid such dissociation? Now that the disciplines of psychology, evolutionary biology and neuroscience have begun talking to each other, there are some voices that suggest not, that today's humans are struggling to keep up with the rapid pace of change and are regularly overwhelmed. The problem, according to evolutionary biologist E.O. Wilson, is that modern humans are subject to more stimulation than our nervous systems were originally equipped for. In an age when we are beset with 'godlike technology' we still possess 'Stone Age emotions' and instincts, while we are still unconsciously governed by 'medieval institutions'.[11]

Today's environment may, in fact, be encouraging our minds to dissociate and compartmentalize as we try to cope with what Harvard Medical School psychologist Deirdre Barrett calls 'supernormal stimuli'.[12] Paradoxically, we may be becoming increasingly prone to dissociating from contexts that we are challenged to recognize in order to protect ourselves, just like the Pacific islanders. This kind of self-defence – from realities that are just too much to deal with – may explain our widespread inability to name DGC and our collusion in denying its existence.

But this does not have to be the end of the story. Even the most powerful defence mechanisms – once acknowledged and identified with – are readily treatable, as Siegel continues:

> Dissociation, while it is one of the most disabling conditions, is one of the most treatable – it is completely curable, and that has been shown.[13]

We can heal ourselves, but, if we do come out of denial, it will mean enduring quite uncomfortable, even painful, feelings that we have been putting off.

Why denial pays

As soon as we fully acknowledge the power and extent of DGC's hold over us, we grasp just how deeply it has kept us all in a state of confusion and denial. Easier said than done, however. It is not just that DGC constrains the actions of governments and corporations, it has also got inside of us. DGC has become an inherent part of the way politicians, journalists and we citizens think, for our environment always influences our psychology. Without advocating Marxism, we can acknowledge Marx's wisdom in proposing 'It is not the consciousness of men that determines their existence, but their social existence that determines their consciousness.'[14]

Since most people around the world are still in denial about the global reality of DGC we normalize it and fail to see that politicians are being asked to do the impossible: to reconcile national interests – keeping their economies internationally competitive, for example – with global interests such as cutting carbon emissions. But because DGC renders these two objectives fundamentally incompatible, and we are in denial about it, politicians are left to persuade citizens (and perhaps themselves) that they *are* compatible when they are not. They are effectively left to mislead themselves (and thereby us) into thinking that, in the age of globalization, environmental sustainability and social justice can somehow be reconciled with economic growth and competitiveness when a brief walk in the daylight reveals that they cannot. Unwittingly finding ourselves smothered by the new context of DGC, yet seeing no other possible context that might resolve it, we are all forced, in effect, to lie to ourselves.

As we saw in the case of George Papandreou, politicians like to believe they are autonomous and powerful, perhaps to avoid the painful reality that they are not. Meanwhile, we citizens buy into this by the psychological trick of projection. We project on to our politicians a power that they do not have, thereby shielding ourselves from the harsh reality that, since our leaders have lost their autonomy, the responsibility for solving global problems now falls to us all. This, however, is a responsibility we do not wish to face, let alone act on. As George Bernard Shaw reminded us, 'Liberty means responsibility. That is why most men dread it.'[15]

To delude ourselves that we do not have to face this responsibility, to compensate ourselves and make ourselves feel comfortable, we deny the reality of DGC, cling to the Myth of the Sovereign Nation and stay stuck in nationcentric thinking, believing that our politicians do have the power when they don't. In this way we remain collectively in collusion, in stalemate and stuck.

Additionally, there is always a hidden psychological pay-off for both sides by staying stuck in polarized conflict and denial. Politicians get the pay-off of still believing they have power and status, and thereby get to keep their cherished identity; meanwhile, we citizens get the pay-off of blaming them when they inevitably fail, and so we get to keep ours. We get to stay pure and free of a heavy responsibility while knowing, deeper down, that it is one we cannot escape and will eventually have to face. Underneath, we are collectively afraid of a future we cannot predict.

A process of grieving

We, the authors, see the world as being on the brink of a momentous transition and yet reluctant to take the next step for fear of falling. It is not surprising, for big and important changes are rarely pain-free.

Many of us will recognize from our own experience that pain and transformation often go together. If we consider rare moments in our own lives when we actually changed for the better – when we actually grew up and took responsibility – we can acknowledge that they were very often painful. They hurt! But with the advantage of age and the ability to look back we can see that pain holds a valuable message. With the greater perspective that maturity affords, we can hope that we are more ready to interpret the pain of change as a sign that there may be a valuable transition around the corner or a new and more exciting stage of our life waiting to unfold.

Faced with a global predicament such as DGC, we can easily go back into denial or give up caring altogether and anaesthetize ourselves with feelgood consumables and everyday concerns. It can all seem too much. The late leadership consultant Stephen Covey explained this kind of crisis by means of his model of the interaction between what he called the 'circles of care' and 'circles of influence'. Sometimes, suggests Covey, our ineffectiveness or sense of impotence is because our circle of influence – what we can actually influence and realistically hope to achieve – appears to be smaller than our circle of care, the kind of things that actually really matter to us. This is understandable, and Covey suggests contracting the circle of care to reflect realistically our actual circle of influence.

Yet to do so in the context of today's global problems, we suggest, is to stay stuck and to pretend that business as usual can suffice. Rather than giving up, there is a process to such life-changing transitions, which depends on the ability to face the pain and grief that arises whenever letting go of the familiar is demanded of us. In order to make it through to a 'new life' depends on having the courage not to turn away, not to creep back into denial. If we can only avoid the temptation of sinking back into denial and compensation, if we can simply sit with the pain and not push it away, we can make it through to the other side.

Whether it be the transition towards accepting the loss of a loved one or the transition to a new way of thinking and governing, the processes are similar and contain similar stages.

The psychiatrist and acknowledged expert on bereavement Dr Elisabeth Kübler-Ross developed a widely accepted model for working with the grief of being bereaved. In a hospital for the terminally ill in the 1960s, Kübler-Ross pioneered the study of death and dying and the impact on those left living. Her resulting model considers the relevant emotions that arise and how these develop into further emotions over five stages. For Kübler-Ross, the stages of the grieving process are:

1. Denial
2. Anger
3. Bargaining
4. Depression
5. Acceptance

Kübler-Ross's model gained widespread acceptance and was eventually applied to a variety of situations involving grief and loss as well as the necessity of giving up attachment to persons or ideas, notably with children in divorcing families, people grieving lost relationships or letting go of substance abuse. Her followers suggest that the five stages exemplify the basic process of integrating any new information that conflicts with previous beliefs.

We propose that these five stages may be as relevant and accurate for the case of a widespread transition to a new level of thinking as they are for individuals. We suspect that our world is putting off acknowledging its loss, that we cannot avoid having to grieve the loss of our familiar world and that a grieving process may have to occur over recognizable stages such as these. In this light, we can see that we inevitably have to get stuck in denial, but it may be just one stage on a recognizable, if difficult, journey. For Kübler-Ross we have simply been at Stage 1 of 5. If this is right, then we have cause for hope.

If we agree to continue such a difficult journey it will take us through the remaining four stages, which, if bravely followed, will allow us to pass out of denial and powerlessness through to the final stage of acceptance. For genuine acceptance, as we'll see later, proves to be a gateway – the solutions to our global problems will not seem as impossible to implement as they do now

In the next chapter we move on to Stages 2 and 3 of this difficult journey to begin finding our way through.

4. Anger and Bargaining on the Difficult Journey

A weekend workout

It's an unusually warm Saturday morning in Finsbury Park, north London. Sally is upstairs in the rambling down-at-heel Victorian terraced house – one of a row of twenty in a neighbourhood that has somehow steadily resisted gentrification – that she shares with her partner of eighteen years, Phil, and their two children. She is trying to persuade her offspring that it would be nice if this weekend they could bring just a little order into the domestic jungles that serve as their bedrooms while she pops out to the convenience store just down the road. Suddenly she hears a familiar noise coming through the open window from the garden below.

'Bloody politicians! How can they be so highly paid for being such *incredible idiots?*'

It's Phil. After a long week teaching at the recently renamed Urban University of North London, which everyone still calls 'the Poly', Phil is indulging in his regular Saturday morning treat – a large cup of milky coffee and a read of the *Guardian* on the garden patio, whenever the weather permits. It's his way of 'relaxing', but, as is often the case, reading the paper has stirred him into a frenzy about 'those stupid politicians'.

He's off again. 'They're the ones we pay to take the goddamn responsibility of solving global problems, but all they do is talk, talk, talk.'

Sally doesn't really mind; in fact, she feels pretty much the same. She could get angry at the mess the world seems to be getting into, with all the things that have been achieved – like idiotic men walking on the moon – and all the things that are left undone that could make ordinary people's lives much better. She is especially cross about the nonsense of closing down the local library to save the local council money while the bankers are being bailed out. But she can't spare the time to think about all that now. All she hopes is that the neighbours, Jack and Stella, who are bound to be out in their garden on a day like this, don't get annoyed by Phil's ranting and swearing.

In fact, Jack, a retired bus driver who has lived in the same house all his life, is pruning his roses and silently hoping his wife will calm down soon. Stella's *bête noire* is not actually Phil but her other neighbours, Lord knows how many unwashed vegetarians – probably all claiming benefits – who occupy the house next door that used to belong to their old chums, now in a home on the south coast. It's the smell of herbs and stewing beans that gets to Stella – who likes 'plain food', as Jack sometimes explains to Phil through clenched teeth – the ones that go to make the veggie burgers that scrawny little bloke delivers to health-food shops on his butcher's bike. Probably on the black, she snorts. 'Typical!'

Whenever they meet on the street Phil tries to chat to 'Katweazle', as the enterprising vegan baker is known, hoping for an ally in this counterculture against the useless politicians. But he won't really bite. 'They're all the same, man,' he chuckles. 'Don't you get it?' Katweazle even considers the *Guardian* an Establishment conspiracy, so why bother? He doesn't. He just gets on with his fringe life and wouldn't dream of voting in the upcoming elections.

Just as she closes the door, Sally hears another explosion.

'Oh my God! F—*ing d—heads*! Politicians, corporate executives, economists . . . *our-economic-f—ing-correspondent*. Do any of them care at all? F— the bloody lot of them!'

Thank heavens he's got his Gestalt group on Tuesday and can do a bit of pillow-bashing and tennis-racket abuse, Sally thinks as she crosses the road.

Emotional recycling

Our domestic vignette tries to illustrate how normal it is to be angry about the state we're in and how people deal differently with their anger about a world that is changing too fast and not in the right way for them. Some bury it in their work; some compensate with shopping. Sometimes people don't show that they are angry when actually they are; they may limit their circle of care and focus on their families, for example.[1] Some displace their anger on to others whom they can't understand, particularly if they are newcomers to their communities, and judge them. Others completely disown the society in which they are living and try to create an alternative one, imagining themselves free. Some regularly explode in tantrums at a world run by fools and motivated by greed.

It is tempting to think that such anger makes no difference, that it's a waste of time, because we are impotent anyway. But anger is important. It embodies values. It is a message that you have *the right* to care, that things matter even if you can't change them. In psychotherapy anger is often seen as the backbone of healing, as the traumatized and abused regularly show us. Anger can give us somewhere to stand, has direction and provides motivation, so it can become the driver to the third stage – that of bargaining.

However, the first three stages of Kübler-Ross's grieving process – denial, anger and bargaining – are interlinked and often move in a repetitive, cyclical motion. We come out of denial for a bit, get furious for the hand fate has dealt us or with the person who has abandoned us, then we plead for things to be different, even when they can't be. Often we go back into denial only to get angry again. In the previous chapter we saw how infectious denial is when it is practised by a whole society, how we can dissociate from a reality that is right in front of our noses – especially when others are doing the same.

The bargaining stage has been especially well observed in children about to go through the catastrophe of losing their united family when a divorce is looming. Making pleas or bargains inside their heads helps them to feel they have some agency, for example, 'If I am really good/do all my homework/keep my room tidy maybe Mum and Dad won't separate.' This helps them keep focused on the hope that the situation might change and distracts from the sadness they'll experience after the divorce. Similarly, confronted as we are with a world gone awry, we start to calculate what we can do about our political situation. We start to bargain:

- What if we turf out the present set of short-sighted, self-interested politicians and voted in a new lot, perhaps 'good guys' like the Green Party?

- Or what if we vote in the kind of person who will make our country great again, shake things up and restore things to how they ought to be?

- Or what if I work to change the unfair electoral system altogether?

- Better still, what if I kiss goodbye to our stupid political system and, like Russell Brand suggests, stop voting?[2]

- Or what if I take action more directly to change the rotten system itself? What if I join an organization like Avaaz, Greenpeace or Friends of the Earth, the kind of organizations that kick politicians' arses?

- Or why don't I save myself the waste of time that politics has become by working directly on corporations, by trying to get them to behave more responsibly?

As we shall see shortly, bargaining proves not to be a solution but just another stage in the process. When it fails to deliver we often go back to anger and sometimes remain stuck there, a bit like Phil in our story. In any cyclical model the trap is to move on to the next stage before completing the preceding one, which encourages cyclic loops that repeat the previous emotion and actions. So when bargaining doesn't seem to be working we may go back into anger or denial. Or we try a different bargain. Getting stuck in permanent anger or repeated bargaining is a kind of flight from reality, not so dissimilar to getting stuck in denial – rather common in cultures where expression of anger is not socially acceptable.

It is perfectly natural to want to adjust our current reality for the best, and initially it seems like it would be far easier to tweak with or negotiate around what we already have. However, to bargain with a New Context for Governance is to hope that we can somehow avoid or find ways of circumnavigating the principle already established, that an existing governance *system* has to catch up with and match a new governance *context*. History shows us that nothing less will do, and yet the temptation to believe there must be some way to negotiate our way out of the tight spot that DGC has us in is enormously strong.

There are two broad avenues such bargaining can take. One is to work through existing national political systems and try to influence them, which we will call the 'inside approach'. The other – the 'outside approach'– is two-pronged: either to work for solutions through non-governmental organizations or directly with corporations in order to change their behaviour. Because many such bargaining efforts represent major commitments of many well-intentioned people, we shall examine each in some detail. First, we look at the inside approach.

The electoral illusion

'Democracy is the worst form of government except all those other forms that have been tried from time to time.'[3]

Winston Churchill's famous remark on Armistice Day 1947 still rings true. It is not so difficult to find fault with the democratic process, especially when party politics, and its short-term perspective ensures that the next election is always the highest priority, which invariably hijacks governments' agendas. But not to have the right to affect events by electing your political representative is undoubtedly much worse. We ought not to take our democratic rights for granted, and yet widespread voter apathy shows that people are turning away from established political processes.[4] Should this be interpreted as a symptom or a cause of democratic failure or merely a short-term blip?

So far we have seen how the economic consequences of Destructive Global Competition affect many areas of life and, most importantly, the loss of autonomy for governments; in this chapter we go a step further to demonstrate how its power extends to the undermining of the very foundations of democracy itself. We propose to begin this by asking you to come with us on an imaginary journey – a night out at the theatre.

Imagine that all our fellow citizens are seated with us in the auditorium, gazing at the stage upon which the drama of democratic politics is to be played out. The entire stage is brightly lit from left to right, and the actors – the leaders of the various political parties – are ranged across it from left to right according to their political stance. Each actor makes his or her passionate speech about what their party will carry out if elected to office, and we in the audience consider the merits of each in turn. Once the actors have said their pieces, through the mechanism of free and fair elections we get the chance to make our free choice, according to our convictions, by casting our vote.

It is this image of personal choice, mediated by free and fair elections, that in Western democratic societies constitutes the deepest understanding of what political freedom means, what democracy is all about. But to what extent is this freedom still true? Let's take a closer look.

As we wait for the performance to begin there is much distraction. Some of the audience are still arriving, forcing others to stand up to let them reach their seats. Programme- and refreshment-sellers advertise their wares as the audience chat to one another in the general clamour. Meanwhile, unbeknown to us all, during the time that we have been waiting something subtle and sinister has affected the stage lighting system. Without us even noticing, the spotlights illuminating the left side of the stage have very gradually faded, leaving it in complete darkness. Only the centre-right now remains illuminated. But the change was so gradual it was imperceptible.

As the two-minute bell rings to warn us that the performance is about to begin, the house goes quiet and we turn our attention to the stage. We do not realize we are looking only at a very restricted portion of the stage. We still think we are looking at the whole stage. Meanwhile, as the curtain rises, our politicians find themselves fighting each other for space, fighting to get into the very narrow, restricted centre-right portion of the stage that is lit. Instead of spreading themselves widely, according to the very different policies their manifestos promised, we find that they are all fighting for the same small area of political space. We, the audience, find ourselves rather disappointed with the boring, repetitive and ineffectual play that ensues. Seeing little difference between the various politicians and their policies, and seeing that they are having little effect, many members of the audience leave the theatre, wondering why they ever bothered to buy a ticket in the first place.

The feeling that democracy has lost its lustre and fails to deliver on its promises is, by now, a widespread complaint that affects citizens in many countries around the world. Either voter apathy or a resort to more extreme political parties are twin phenomena that now stalk all Western democracies. The authors are convinced that DGC makes this inevitable, for it is DGC that has subtly interfered with the lighting system.

Pseudo-democracy

Since the global free movement of capital and corporations forces governments to do whatever is necessary to maintain the international competitiveness of their respective national economies, the policies available to them have become restricted to a very narrow, centre-right, market-and-business-friendly range. Any party in power attempting to veer beyond that range would only make its country's economy *un*-competitive and eventually risk economic decline, which cannot be an option.

In this way, and without us even knowing it, DGC has reduced national democracy to a narrow political monoculture. It is hardly surprising, therefore, that the distinctions between political parties get eroded and that, in every nation, we find left-of-centre parties adopting policies traditionally espoused by right-of-centre parties. This is why, for example, New Labour's Tony Blair was often said to be the best Conservative leader since Margaret Thatcher, or, as former Conservative Prime Minister John Major quipped,

'I went swimming leaving my clothes on the bank, and when I came back Tony Blair was wearing them.'[5]

Under the new ultra-narrow lighting that DGC dictates, politicians and political parties are effectively no longer free to choose their political stance according to their convictions. Instead, DGC dictates it to them. This is what French President François Hollande found to his cost after coming to power in 2012. Having initially attempted to implement the centre-left policy platform on which he had been elected, he soon found France's economy becoming uncompetitive as inward investment dried up and capital and jobs moved elsewhere. Quickly, he found himself compelled to shift his stance to the centre-right. As *The Times* reported:

> After 18 months of stagnation under orthodox socialist leadership, [Hollande] confirmed that he was swinging towards the market-friendly policies adopted over the past 15 years by left-wing parties in Germany, Britain and elsewhere.[6]

It was a similar story in Greece in 2015. The far-left party Syriza was elected to office only to find itself forced to implement a deeply right-wing austerity agenda dictated by global markets and mediated via the troika of the EU, the IMF and the World Bank. The message to citizens ought, by now, to be clear: whatever you vote, you get the same competitiveness agenda regardless. Even if you change the voting system it makes no difference.

Not only does DGC undermine our governments it subverts the very essence of democracy by making any choice of party more or less a Hobson's choice. It is not that there are no differences whatever between politicians or political parties but that the economic policy parameters within which all parties in power must now operate have been severely narrowed. As a result, the electoral choice has turned into 'take it or leave it' – between taking the option to vote or not. Yet, even if we choose not to vote, the result remains the same.

The fact that DGC has rendered left-of-centre policies impractical is an important reason why parties on the centre-left in many countries find themselves in turmoil and riven by division. DGC has driven a wedge between those willing to submit to the competitiveness agenda and those who refuse to. In the run-up to the 2016 US presidential election this was reflected in the split between Democrats who supported Hilary Clinton, the candidate set to maintain the competitiveness agenda, and those who preferred the more left-wing Bernie Sanders, who broadly rejected it. In the UK, at the time of writing, the division is expressed through two factions of the Labour Party, the 'Blairite' centrist pro-business wing and the 'Corbynite' traditional socialist wing. The former insist that the latter are unrealistic and unelectable, while they, in turn, insist the Blairites no longer stand for authentic Labour values.

Both sides are right in their criticisms, but both are also profoundly mistaken in their macro analysis. Electing a Blairite Labour Party, or a President Clinton, would only produce more of the same market-and-business-friendly policies that DGC demands, politics as usual and the world firmly headed on its present disastrous course. Yet if we elected a Jeremy Corbyn, a Bernie Sanders or a Green Party we'd find that they – like François Hollande – would have no choice but to backtrack quickly to policies that keep the country competitive. Whichever road is chosen, DGC sits quietly and confidently at the end of both.

A similar disappointment and sense of betrayal, we suggest, must await those UK citizens who voted to leave the EU, especially the poor and the marginalized who feel they have lost out under globalization. For whether Britain is in or out of the EU or stays within the European Single Market or not, the inescapable reality is that whoever is in government will have little choice but to keep the UK economy as competitive as possible. The gap between rich and poor will therefore continue to widen, while immigration, feeding corporations' need for cheap labour in the service of international competition, is likely to continue much as before. The result is that Brexit voters will end up feeling further betrayed and driven further into the arms of extremist populist parties on the far right.

But it is not only the left that has been split by DGC. A similar wedge has been driven between moderate centre-right parties that espouse the free-market competitiveness agenda and those on the extreme or populist right that appear to reject it. The latter has, in fact, already happened in the USA with the election of Donald Trump. However, despite his pre-election rhetoric against free trade, he may find that he has little choice but to generally uphold it in order to keep the US economy internationally competitive. As one Asian financial-market analyst commented in the immediate aftermath of the election:

Globalisation has taken a certain grip on the world in such a way that reversing that process is almost impossible. No 'protectionist' government will last the 'mile', let alone four years in office, especially not one who is schooled in running businesses.[7]

Electing more extreme candidates, whether from the political right or left, is unlikely to make much positive difference. DGC, as ever, stays firmly in control.

The fact that we have a vote and that elections remain free and fair appeals to our post-Enlightenment rational thinking but it has some serious side-effects. It helps to keep our idealized but illusory image of democracy alive; it keeps us believing that our votes count. It holds the Myth of the Sovereign Nation firmly in place and conspires to maintain the thinking gap we identified earlier. Once we fully let in how DGC operates we realize the truth, that the quality of democracy has been subtly, but substantively, degraded and has been reduced to what we are calling pseudo-democracy.

It is here that the catastrophic error of our deep attachment to the Myth of the Sovereign Nation comes most powerfully to the fore. While we continue to cling to the idea that nations remain sovereign and that politicians therefore continue to hold substantial power and autonomy, we will carry on deluding ourselves that 'if only we vote in the right politician or party, our problems will be solved'. Stay with the Myth and we continue to commit the most fundamental and devastating act of political *self*-betrayal. Only by waking up to the reality of DGC can we start to see democracy for the pseudo-democracy it now is. Only by acknowledging that national party politics can offer no way around DGC – that DGC cannot be bargained with – do we have any hope of genuine political enlightenment and renewal.

Given the new context for governance that DGC represents, it's little wonder that today's modern pseudo-democracies are characterized, on the one hand, by chronic voter apathy and, on the other, by a resurgence of far-right political parties.[8] The invisible force of DGC has comprehensively curtailed our ability to effect solutions to many national and global problems through conventional democratic processes. For, whether we change parties in power or tinker with voting systems, the results must remain much the same: whoever may be in power, and however they may be elected they have no choice but to stay in the narrow area of the stage illumined by light. DGC is in control and cannot be bargained with nor escaped, undermining governments as well as those who elect them.

This situation amounts to what the contemporary German philosopher Jürgen Habermas refers to as a 'legitimation crisis', a breakdown in the ability of the existing, nationcentric worldview and its governance systems to command our allegiance.[9] Not only are governments stuck in a vicious circle that they cannot escape but pseudo-democracy means conventional party politics can no longer help us. Trying to bargain using the inside approach unfortunately turns out to be no bargain at all. The implications are frighteningly clear: our governments are impotent, and so are we.

A European answer?

Unable to resist the pressures of competitive global markets, some politicians still cling to the idea that strengthening the European Union might offer a solution. At a time when the United Nations is struggling to grapple with climate change and the G8 and G20 groups of the world's largest economies are also proving weak, the EU appears to represent the most promising available model for how nations could work together more closely to overcome global problems.

The European solution featured strongly in George Papandreou's TED presentation referred to earlier, in which he graphically describes how 'global markets have a gun to our heads'. Later in his presentation, he goes on to suggest that the solution lies in an expanded and strengthened EU. Likewise, in a television debate that took place in 2014 on Britain's future in the EU, former UK Deputy Prime Minister Nick Clegg recommended the EU for the express purpose of dealing with today's global problems rather than resorting to fantasies about a world of independent nations that no longer exists.[10]

Papandreou and Clegg are not isolated voices, even if, at the time of writing, their message is hardly popular. To many mainstream politicians Europe is still seen, if not as *the* solution to successfully managing globalization, then as an important model or stepping-stone in that direction. Likewise, politicians in other parts of the world hope that other emerging regional associations of nations, such as the Association of Southeast Asian Nations (ASEAN), the North American Free Trade Association (NAFTA) and Mercosur in South America, may follow in the EU's footsteps. But does this regional approach fit the current *global* context? On analysis, there seems to be a glaring inconsistency in Papandreou's argument.

If the 'gun to our heads' is a global gun, as the euro crisis proved, and if, moreover, the entire group of Eurozone nations collectively had to dance to the tune of global bond markets, it follows that even a more tightly integrated EU would not ultimately suffice. For if the gun is global, logically so must be the response. A merely European response, or any response that is *less* than global, will always prove vulnerable to a force that is already global.

We must return to one of our principles here: a governance system that is merely *national* (or regional) cannot possibly match a new context for governance that is already *global*. It is little wonder that under the stress of the already operational new global context for governance many of the EU's key values, especially the free movement of people, are being seriously challenged, which in turn threatens to undermine its members' commitment.

The reality is that whether a nation is in the EU or out of it is unlikely to make much difference because, whatever the case, DGC remains in control. As the Dutch political analyst Joris Luyendijk commented on the UK's so-called 'Independence Day':

> Leaving these decisions to European technocrats means that we effectively hand over control of our society to the corporate lobbies that have direct access to those technocrats. These days global banks and other multinationals operate on a European level while politics still takes place on a national level. The consequence is that big corporations can play off one European country against the other in a regulatory race to the bottom, demanding ever lower if not downright homeopathic tax rates.[11]

If they survive, and if they cooperate, the EU and other regional associations may contribute to bringing global markets back under proper democratic supervision and accountability. But the truly global nature of DGC and the urgent need for action indicate that we do not have the time to wait for a robust global network of such associations to evolve. As the euro crisis, Brexit and the election of Trump demonstrate, neither the EU, the USA nor any regional association of nations are likely to be any match for the new and highly threatening context for governance that DGC represents.

Returning to our stages of grief perspective, it may also be that the faith some place in the EU will turn out to have been a further bargaining tool or even a psychological compensation employed to shield themselves from a highly discomforting reality. While a retreat to a more independent, chauvinistic and protectionist form of governance – like those proposed by right-wing parties such as the UK Independence Party (UKIP) and Donald Trump – seems initially attractive but realistically offers no solution whatsoever, the reality is that since the EU is still too small to match the new context for governance that DGC represents the EU and other regional associations of nations may not offer any effective solution either.

Instead, we believe, a bolder, more global approach is necessary, and the final part of this book will be devoted to setting out our own ideas towards this end.

Tit for tat?

Before we consider the outside approach of working directly with the corporate sector, we complete our review of the inside approach by briefly considering whether a worldwide shift by governments away from today's globalizing trends and towards more protectionist policies might offer a solution. What would be the likely result, for example, if, despite DGC, President Trump were to take a decidedly protectionist stance?

As we have argued, free trade and globalization have left all nations stuck in DGC's vicious circle, so there is a logic to imagining that protectionism – the practice of imposing national tariff barriers to protect domestic industries and workers against lower-cost foreign imports – might offer a solution. Protectionism is precisely what would result if the world were to turn away from the present free-trade paradigm, but would it offer any viable or permanent alternative?

In our view, a more nationally protected world merely promises a different yet equally destructive version of DGC. Free trade and the global free movement of capital lead, as we've seen, to a destructive tit-for-tat down-levelling of regulations or to the governmental paralysis we've called regulatory chill. This maintains the world on its present ruinous path. But a resort by any country to trade tariffs and other protectionist policies can only result in similar retaliation from other nations, since protecting one nation necessarily means disadvantaging others. Without any global agreement as to which tariffs would be deemed fair and which unfair, and without any means to compensate disadvantaged nations, a worsening tit-for-tat cycle of rising tariff barriers is inevitable. This dynamic is one the world has seen before and which has led to many destructive wars in the past.

To paraphrase the nineteenth-century French economist Frédéric Bastiat, if goods are prevented from crossing national borders, soldiers soon will.[12]

By now readers will recognize this tit-for-tat dynamic of raising tariff barriers as simply our old friend DGC, dressed in different clothes. Whether the world chooses free trade or protectionism, the underlying problem is that *neither* would be cooperatively regulated, leaving us subject to DGC whichever model we choose. Changing the mode of world trade, like the rest of the inside approach, turns out to be just another vain attempt to bargain with DGC.

If inside approaches turn out to be false bargains, might not there be more value in trying an outside approach – for example, by eliciting greater social and environmental responsibility on the part of corporations through direct engagement?

Making corporations care

The practice of encouraging greater corporate accountability is sometimes referred to as corporate social responsibility (CSR). In addition to CSR itself, what we are calling the CSR approach includes other initiatives such as socially responsible investing (SRI), shareholder activism, Conscious Capitalism,[13] ethical consumerism, triple bottom-line accounting and many others. We do not underestimate the excellent and valuable work done by sustainability consultants, NGOs and others engaged in improving corporate social and environmental performance. But when it comes to overcoming DGC, what kind of a bargain do we imagine to be achievable? How realistic are our expectations?

By way of illustration, let's go back for a moment to 24 November 2012 when a fire broke out in the Tazreen Fashion factory on the outskirts of Dhaka, Bangladesh. Opened in 2009, the factory employed 1,630 workers and produced clothes for various companies, including the US Marines, C&A, Walmart and others. At least 117 people died and a further 200 were injured, making it the deadliest factory fire in the nation's history but just one of many accidents that occur in Dhaka's dangerous factories each year.

A few months after a spate of such accidents, and despite numerous public pledges from various multinational corporations to clean up their supply chains, the *Independent* reported that little had changed. A BBC television *Panorama* programme investigating the state of the clothing industry in Bangladesh found staff apparently working nineteen-hour days – even being locked inside factories by security guards – making clothes for the cut-price retailer Lidl and being paid around £2 a day. But when reporters visited the Ha Meem Sportswear factory posing as Western buyers, they were shown time-sheets that bore no relation to hours worked.[14]

The garment industry in Bangladesh is a microcosm that demonstrates the limitations of both governments and the CSR approach in the face of DGC. On one side, the government of a relatively poor developing country such as Bangladesh has little choice but to keep safety regulations and enforcement to a minimum so as to keep its garment industry internationally competitive; on the other, the Dhaka factory owners, because they fear losing competitiveness, either against one another or against manufacturers in other low-cost countries, must cut corners or sacrifice safety to keep costs to a minimum.

The multinational corporate buyers, anxious to assure Western consumers of their ethical credentials, finally signed up to an Accord on Fire and Building Safety in Bangladesh.[15] Valuable though this is, it is important to note the last two words, 'in Bangladesh', which show that the accord applies to that country alone. And that, of course, is DGC's get-out-of-jail-free card. Were Bangladesh to become too costly as a result of the improvements to be made under the accord – in other words, uncompetitive – corporations would simply purchase cheaper garments elsewhere.

In this way, laudable national attempts at improving working conditions or making corporations care frequently run aground in response to what is, in effect, a global problem. They demonstrate the present inadequate level of outdated nationcentric thinking at work. The CSR movement has still to realize that DGC has changed the context for governance and cannot successfully be bargained with, so it, too, needs to change its thinking.

Two swallows

This is not a conclusion that advocates of CSR, Conscious Capitalism and the like will enjoy hearing. Seeing that CSR can be successful in individual cases, they are apt to cite research which shows that, over the longer term, corporations adopting a more socially and environmentally responsible business strategy – the so-called 'stakeholder value' business model – outperform those that remain with the more traditional, profit-maximizing 'shareholder value' model.[16] Their assumption, consequently, is that all corporations should – and ultimately will – follow the stakeholder model because it's in their self-interest.

However, in actuality, in any given market sector there seems to be only one major company that makes the stakeholder strategy the centre of its business model and brand image. In the UK cosmetics sector, for example, there is only the Body Shop that takes that approach; in the US ice-cream sector there is only Ben & Jerry's; in the US supermarket sector there is only Whole Foods Market; in contract flooring there is only Interface. Why is this? If adopting a stakeholder approach means improved performance, surely companies would be falling over themselves to emulate one another?

The point that CSR advocates tend to overlook is that while it may be attractive and profitable for one major company in a given market sector to make environmental and social responsibility into a profitable market niche this may only make it harder for competitors to follow rather than easier. The financial investment needed for a competitor to ethically outcompete an already-ethical market leader may be better and more profitably spent by differentiating its products in other ways: by investing in superior product quality, for example, or in branding, in more catchy advertising, lower prices or superior customer service. On this point, at least, the champions of competition like Professor Porter are right. 'Competitive strategy is about being different. It means deliberately choosing a different set of activities to deliver a unique mix of value.'[17]

To take one or two examples of good corporate behaviour to mean that others will necessarily follow is to take two swallows as proof that an English summer has finally arrived! CSR approaches risk creating a false sense of security by giving the illusion of being an adequate compensation for the present lack of the required new system of governance. Bargaining once more turns out to be illusory.

Besides, if adopting a stakeholder approach delivered a competitive advantage in most cases, there would be no need for the CSR approach at all. Market forces alone would already have solved the problem automatically. They would have forced corporations adopting a shareholder-value approach to lose out to those adopting the stakeholder approach and eventually to die out altogether.

CSR advocates, including Professor Porter himself, may, nevertheless, insist that going green and staying competitive are not the mutually exclusive objectives we, the authors, make them out to be. Porter argues that often companies can enhance their competitiveness by developing their thinking rather than fighting higher environmental standards. He cites coal-tar distilling in the USA where 1991 regulations required substantial reductions in benzene emissions. The only solution at the time was to cover the tar-storage tanks with costly gas blankets. But one company, the Aristech Chemical Corporation of Pittsburgh, was spurred by the regulation to develop a way to remove benzene from tar in the first processing step. Instead of suffering a cost increase, Aristech saved itself $3.3 million by eliminating the need for gas blankets altogether.[18]

Fair enough, one might think, but the problem is that Porter's approach is gradualist, as such proposals are called: in other words, too slow. Having forcefully argued that tighter regulations can encourage greater corporate competitiveness through cost savings, in the same article he slips in the caution that governments should

Develop regulations in sync with other countries or slightly ahead of them. It is important to minimize possible competitive disadvantages relative to foreign companies that are not yet subject to the same standard.[19]

And it is here that Porter's argument runs aground. Because, while it may be true that tighter regulations may drive a few companies to save costs, this does not alter the fact that governments, continuing to fear for the competitiveness of their industries, cannot implement anything other than the most timid regulatory changes. Our old friend DGC – here in the form of regulatory chill – confines regulation to a glacially slow pace. Meanwhile, global problems, moving at a much faster pace, are left to outstrip them. The dilemma between going green and staying competitive has not gone away because of the urgency of the problem. Time is not on our side.

The harsh reality is that efforts to encourage individual corporations to behave more responsibly, while laudable, can never be sufficient. The fact that a few corporations individually may be able to behave ethically and may outcompete others in their market does not alter the fact that, collectively, DGC still dictates that in the greater scheme of things the CSR approach cannot be adequate. Like governments, it is not that most corporate executives don't want to behave more responsibly, it's that DGC doesn't allow them to.

Similarly, the ethical-consumer approach by which consumers seek to harness their buying power to pressure corporations towards more ethical and responsible behaviour, is unlikely to be effective either. George Monbiot explains that we may boycott products, but unless we take the trouble of explaining our decisions to the manufacturers of the goods we chose not to patronize the company will have no means of discovering that we made them at all let alone why we made them. Unless our actions are coordinated with those of hundreds or thousands of other consumers our choices are likely to be ineffective. Consumer boycotts are notoriously hard to sustain, and campaigning organizations report that a maximum of one or two boycotts per nation per year seem to work. Beyond that, consumer power becomes too diffuse to be a realistic alternative.[20]

The reality, then, is that there is no real bargain to be made after all. The sad conclusion we are forced to reach is that, ultimately, everyone on the planet is undermined by the new context for governance that DGC represents. Not only does DGC frustrate all attempts at meaningful reform that come from inside the established political system, it also severely limits those, like the CSR approach, that seek to work outside the political system. Neither approach offers a satisfactory way out of the trap.

A crisis of agency

The second strategy of the outside approach is to seek solutions through non-governmental organizations (NGOs), especially those that campaign for global justice, such as Greenpeace, Friends of the Earth, Avaaz, Occupy and others. Many dedicated and inspired people help keep hope alive through their tireless activities, as the following report by Kirsty Wright, senior campaigns officer for Global Justice Now, shows:[21]

I have spent this week at the World Social Forum in Tunis. Run by a group of activists with no office or paid staff, the World Social Forum has still succeeded in bringing together thousands of activists – some reports say as many as 70,000 – from around the world to discuss where we're at in the quest for real solutions to the poverty, inequality and injustice we see in the world today. One of the key questions I've been focusing on here is around how we should move forward in the struggle with climate justice, given the deepening climate crisis has been mirrored by ever worsening outcomes of the UN climate talks.[22]

The World Social Forum (WSF) is a major global event that has been running annually since 2001 as a counterpoint to the World Economic Forum held in Davos. First held in Porto Alegre, Brazil, and in many other locations since, the WSF serves as the rallying point for the world's many thousands of non-governmental organizations and activist groups that we call the global justice movement (GJM). Sensing the redundancy of conventional party politics to deliver solutions to today's problems, the numbers of people joining or supporting NGOs over recent decades has increased dramatically. These people do not lack values or strong motivation, as Wright demonstrates:

> As well as the launch of the Global Campaign to Demand Climate Justice, which will be holding a month of action on dirty energy in October, there has also been a specific 'Climate Space' at the World Social Forum for the first time . . . It's a long road ahead but one that should not be walked alone, as we link the climate struggle with those of other social movement struggles around hunger, employment, the debt crisis, democracy, water and privatization.[23]

The GJM has played a vital role in bringing many urgent global problems to the public's attention and is pioneering many different and important solutions. However, its rapid growth sometimes appears more like an instinctive reaction to the redundancy of established political systems than a considered response. This is inevitable, since people turn to NGOs in disgust at the inadequacy of the established political system. Strong feelings therefore motivate and mobilize the GJM but at the same time blind it from spotting how its own approaches are also fundamentally undermined by the new context of DGC.

The GJM's *modus operandi* could be simplified to a wish such as this:

> If only we lobby governments hard enough, if only we shout loudly enough about errant corporations and if only we raise enough public awareness, in the end governments will accede to our demands.

Lobbying, protesting, petitioning, blaming (and sometimes shaming) tend to constitute the core of the GJM's approach – and we all have a right to express our outrage in such a way. It is an understandable and often attractive approach, but by now the reader will recognize it simply as Stage 2, anger, a move that won't necessarily result in any lasting change. Columnist Michele Hanson recounts her own endeavours:

> Most of my chums have spent their lives protesting. You name it, we've done it: sit-downs, boycotts, donations, marches and rallies. We're still

doing it online: signing letters, petitions and more protests, against rape, violence, detention centres, culls, cruelties, racism, pollution, corruption – a torrent of nastiness that never seems to end. No wonder some of us are feeling a bit worn down.[24]

It is important work, but its efficacy is not assured. Hanson continues:

I'm not rabid. I just want things to get a bit better. But they don't, so I've given up. I've wasted my life. Everything I fought for has failed. The world has only lurched further into everything I didn't want.[25]

By now the catch will be familiar: while DGC and the limitations of the Myth of the Sovereign Nation remain unacknowledged, protest will never be enough to do the job. Because it is focused on the wrong target. The painful reality is that DGC does not allow the targets of our protests – governments and corporations – to respond adequately. As we have seen, DGC allows them to respond only to the extent that their competitiveness will not be significantly harmed. Such a response, we saw, falls far short of what is necessary to make any significant impact on global problems.

The realization that protest is a journey without end or has become substantially ineffective is beginning to be recognized by a few radical activists, even if they have not yet fully understood the decisive role that DGC plays. For example, with the benefit of hindsight, Micah White, one of the initiators of the Occupy Movement, argues that it may be comforting to believe that Occupy splintered into 'a thousand shards of light', but in reality it failed to live up to its revolutionary potential. It was unable to end the influence of money on democracy, overthrow the corporatocracy of the 1 per cent or solve income inequality.[26]

In order to get back up to speed we all have to realize that the existence of DGC and the desire to solve global problems pull in opposite directions: you can have one or the other but not both. The overarching and inescapable fact is that, for any nation, the implementation of social justice and environmental sustainability necessarily means that business costs and regulations have to increase, thereby placing national competitiveness in jeopardy. As a result, no amount of pressure or protest is likely to drive any government to accede to the movement's demands. Neither can blaming and shaming corporations have anything more than a temporary effect.

For the GJM, a move towards Stage 5, acceptance, would mean acknowledging these limitations. But first it would entail Stage 4, depression: the grief of acknowledging that its *modus operandi* has no realistic chance of success. Little wonder that the GJM is no better placed that the rest of us, reluctant – as we argue – to come out of denial. Some politicians have even articulated this unpopular reality loudly and clearly, including former UK Prime Minister Tony Blair, who was in no doubt that the reality of the politics of climate change is that no country will be willing to sacrifice its economy in order to address the challenge.[27]

Most citizens, and especially the GJM, are reluctant to hear this heartless message. The realization that the GJM and wider society avoids is that the mother of all problems is not global warming, rapacious financial markets, lax governments, pollution, fracking,[28] corporate power or any other single issue about which people are rightly concerned. The problem that has to be solved is DGC, because this is what prevents us from tackling *any* of these issues.

Unfortunately, in failing to name DGC, the GJM tries in vain to bargain with an invisible foe but has no answer to DGC and no way around it. To accept this reality would be a bitter pill because it would mean a complete shift in its operational structure – and therefore its identity. And identity, as we'll now see, is the biggest psychological problem of all. -

5. Identity and Belonging

Nick's story

The old barn had been swept and cleared out and a huge trestle table set up in its middle. Ringed with rush-bottomed wooden chairs, the table stood right beneath the ancient oak truss that supported the roof clad with random stone tiles known as *lauzes* in that part of south-western France. The small glasses that we had used for our wine were now filled with coffee, and the chatter in the room had begun to die down. I leaned back on my chair and surveyed the scene. The seated company were drawn from three families of the locality as well as a couple from the city an hour's drive away. Most were in their sixties apart from the farmer's daughter, her husband and their two girls, who gave every appearance that they would rather be at home. Everyone else seemed to be in their element.

And then there was us. Although an arthritic knee had recently accompanied my fiftieth birthday, I was feeling quite a youngster in this gathering and delighted to be included in the day's *vendange*, the grape harvest. But not because I was particularly fond of wine or the kind of country lunches that were served before we would empty the giant wooden bins perched on the trailers into a prosaic concrete fermenting tank. I was deeply touched that my wife and I – foreign and urban as we were – could be included in a ritual so ancient and natural and so different from what we knew from our own backgrounds.

Looking up the table, I could not help smiling when I noticed where my wife was sitting – right at the edge of the women's area and at the beginning of the men's. These gender divisions were so unfamiliar to us, but they had formed naturally and without comment. Would she enjoy being part of this feminine experience or would she feel boxed in by the sexist arrangement? I wondered.

For my part, I decided to say nothing about my gluten intolerance or my alcohol avoidance, for to make a fuss about the heavy bread and pungent wine that formed the backbone of the meal would have been churlish. It would certainly highlight my own difference in this community that I felt glad to be temporarily welcomed into. My wife appeared less concerned to be the only woman drinking the dark, rather sour wine, fruit of the last year's labour, from the label-free glass bottles that enlivened the dining table.

Who am I?

Belonging to a group is a fundamental human need. Belonging to one's own family, tribe or nation gives us context, stability and orientation. In many ancient societies, banishment – the forfeiture of the right to live in the community where one belonged – was used as the ultimate sanction; it was a punishment worse than death. The extension of a sense of belonging is similarly powerful. The pleasure of being included within a group when we are strangers can affect us deeply, which is why many societies consider hospitality to outsiders a high art and sacred duty. To be accepted as part of a gathering of others when we come from different backgrounds is a tangible privilege; but being different in such a setting really highlights one's own identity.

Alongside our need to belong, and closely connected with it, is our essential impulse to create and cherish an identity. Identity is the central question in human psychology and affects all of our thinking and behaviour. Equipped with our self-reflexive neocortex (the new-brain) the human animal is always searching for identity. Our minds are, as it were, constantly asking the question 'Who am I?' It is almost impossible to switch this function off. Our minds always have some answer, for they are endlessly associating our identities with qualities. For example, each time we look in the mirror we inevitably generate an automatic commentary on who we see and therefore what we are, whether not bad for your age, or ugly, fat or having a bad-hair day. Our sense of identity is formed of adjectives that describe what we believe ourselves to be and where we come from.

This choosing of identity is the most human of problems. Even though they have intelligence, it is unlikely that animals have identity crises. It is hard to think of a dog or cat thinking to themselves: Am I really a dog/cat? What does it mean to be a dog/cat? The Ugly Duckling had an identity crisis, but Hans Christian Andersen had devised an allegory for humans to reflect on. In fact, some of the deepest spiritual enquiries consist of intense sessions of asking this 'Who am I?' question repeatedly of one's self. It is said that either madness or enlightenment can result.

Identity is both simple and complex. It is partly given, such as our sex at birth, our original language group or the religion into which we were born, and partly developmental, as in our age, social status or eventual country of residence. It is also partly a matter of choice, since we can move to another country and consciously identify with that culture, or we can support a certain football team because it is local to us or we like the colour of the strip, and we can convert to another religion because we like their ideas or our partner belongs to it. Sometimes there are crossover-identity or belonging groups; for example, women from different cultures may have lots of thoughts about what men are like that transcend their cultural differences; similarly the old may recognize similar feelings about the younger generation, whether they were born in Andalusia or Azerbaijan.

How does it feel?

Identity is a touchy subject because it regularly produces very strong feelings. Identity is a mental property, but our minds are not just computers. Because of the self-reflexive quality of that evolutionary marvel the new-brain, our minds are constantly making commentaries on our experience, and these commentaries are dominated by emotions. Whenever our minds create identities we also have feelings about them: how we feel about our current age is a universal example but one that also shows how ephemeral this process is.

This is known to psychology as the 'mind-feelings loop', which works in a cycle, in this way: thoughts about something are influenced by feelings (even when there is an absence of visible emotion), which then influence our thoughts again, about which we have further feelings. An example of the mind-feelings loop could be when a person stands up to address a group in public, dries up and wonders what has happened. Immediately internal answers come, 'You have nothing to say' or 'You're stupid'. Such answers then produce even more feelings, which grip the mind and undermine its creativity – about which there will be even more feelings.

Our minds are rather easily dominated by the 'lower' emotions: anxiety, neurotic shame, fear and disgust. When we are temporarily gripped by fear or if we inhabit a long-term low sense of self-esteem we can make rather radical choices to bring about a new sense of identity or belonging (or both) as an attempt to ease the emotional discomfort. An extreme example on an individual level is someone who does not feel comfortable in his or her body and who might opt for gender-reassignment surgery.

On a societal level, someone who does not feel particularly valued in their community may displace their identity issues into some commercial brand or leisure group identity. Advertising and marketing take full advantage of this, so that those who wear a T-shirt displaying a little crocodile feel perhaps they belong to a more valuable group, and those who wear a particular scent feel more beautiful, or those who support a particular football team feel more powerful. The Romans knew long ago that the circus was a way to displace the people's dissatisfaction with their lot, and sport has traditionally taken its place alongside religion – 'the opium of the people', as Marx called it – as a focal point for identity and belonging.

The psychology of belonging

Just so there is no misunderstanding at this point, we are not saying that there is anything wrong with loving one's country, religion or football team. We are social beings. We all need to belong in order to feel safe and valued and not alone, and so we love what we belong to. The problems of belonging identity arise when it becomes too rigid, when we over-limit our identity rather than enlarge it in order to embrace the multiple identities that are possible for us. And the limitation of identity is exactly the issue that the ideas in this book are concerned with. It gets particularly problematic when we need to defend an identity at the expense of other identities that are perceived as being in competition with it. Even though quite a banal occurrence, cleaving to one identity and making this 'good' while making others 'bad' – such as foreigners, immigrants or those of a different religion – has a much darker side to it and can become pathological.

Here is an example, remembered by Nick, of how identity issues can tug us in opposing directions, between feeling we belong and excluding others:

I was once offered the chance to watch my favourite football team, Arsenal, at close quarters. I had bagged prime seats for a Champions League game at the brand-new Emirates Stadium in north London. We got to sit right at the front. Great! The experience of watching my team so close up was remarkable. Whenever a great roar of surprise or joy arose from the 75,000-strong crowd I could feel it literally rattle my chest. It was fantastic to chant along with the rest and feel that massive surge of identity and belonging expressed in sound, sweeping me away and freeing me from all my usual inward musings.

I struggled a bit when the crowd roared 'You're rubbish!' at their opponent's supporters after Arsenal scored their first goal. They clearly weren't rubbish; they had defended well and were unlucky to concede a goal. But the real difficulty for me came when the crowd began to fire up the home supporters by means of a chant about their local north-London rivals, who weren't even at the ground: 'If you 'ate

Tott-en-ham, stand up!' At this point I really was in a dilemma, because the only football game I had ever been to with my father as a child was at Tottenham Hotspurs' ground, White Hart Lane. I did not want to identify with Arsenal by demeaning Spurs.

But the group energy of the whole crowd was too formidable and too *frightening* to resist. So, reluctantly, I got to my feet with all the others so as not to stand out from the crowd and draw attention to myself. I had allowed myself to be coerced by the aggressive side of the human need to belong and to carry an identity.

Last refuge of a scoundrel?

How do these needs to belong and identify influence us in the socio-political arena?

When someone is feeling threatened by the economic or demographic changes happening in their community – such as those occurring in many localities under globalization – they may experience that their identity is under threat. They may then react to immigration by adopting a strong chauvinistic identity at the level of nationalism. These are exactly the people that anti-EU political parties across Europe and populist parties elsewhere seek to recruit. When unconscious fear is consciously whipped up and manipulated it can easily morph into violence against those who belong to a different identity group, as the world discovered to its cost in the 1930s. Perhaps this is what Samuel Johnson was referring to when in 1775 he uttered his famous remark that 'Patriotism is the last refuge of a scoundrel.'

The psychology behind fear-based chauvinism is clear, although typically masked by the value of loving one's country: if the underlying fears are not given place and consciously expressed they will remain in the unconscious and cause havoc. This is because of the prime law that governs depth psychology: *whatever is unconscious ends up controlling our behaviour*. Unconscious fears, which are a facet of our human frailty and vulnerability, in the end, if they remain unconscious, are given command of individuals' (and thereby society's) destiny, because they are afforded the power to dominate behaviour.

A parallel problem to defensive nationalistic chauvinism, and a major one in today's world of global migration, are the identity issues of those who do not feel fully accepted in the country to which their family has emigrated and with which they do not fully identify. The link with our anxieties over terrorism is clear, because there is a chance such people might embrace radical fundamentalism in order to have an identity big enough to compensate for their feelings of powerlessness and isolation.

Alternatively, these stirrings have the potential to degenerate into widespread social unrest within nation states. Cultural historian Andrew Hussey has studied the problems of disaffected young Muslims in the *banlieues* (suburban ghettos) of French cities and the riots that have been erupting cyclically in those areas. France has both the highest proportion of North African immigrants and arguably the most rigidly codified national identity of all modern Western societies. There is a massive reluctance there, suggests Hussey, to acknowledge 'the devastating psychological effects of colonialism'. In consequence, many young Muslims have begun to question their newly acquired identity and in the process to hate France. Hussey attributes this to the legacy of colonialism which, he argues, has destroyed all sense of authentic identity in them and goes as far as undermining their sense of self to the extent that they don't feel that they properly exist any more.[1]

The human experience is one of having multiple identities, but those of gender, religion and nationality are among the most defining (and therefore the strongest), giving the greatest sense of belonging and resulting in the greatest polarity when they clash. Despite their potency, such identity problems and the strong feelings they throw up have the capacity to become avoidable disasters. They can, as we saw earlier, be healed, but without the benefit of seeing the whole picture the authorities will be likely to overreact and go headlong into control mode.

As the negative effects of Destructive Global Competition worsen, this is inevitable because, as we now know, the existing system of governance can have no answer to the new context for governance. Meanwhile, migration fuelled by global wealth inequality and the resulting intercultural tensions can only get worse. So, until our identities are able to expand to embrace the need for cooperative global governance, we can only expect national governments and their forces of law and order vigorously and violently to protect private property, vested interests and the status quo. This action is wasteful, since it is applied in the wrong direction: it is like a doctor treating a symptom rather than a cause. While the causal problems remain denied, governments cannot avoid being ranged against *symptomatic* behaviour.

As we have seen, the human psyche inevitably employs defence mechanisms such as denial whenever a rigid and limited identity seems under threat. Clinically, whenever such mechanisms in an individual are identified as creating rigid control of behaviour, immediate and long-term psychological treatment is recommended. Societies are not under the same scrutiny but have similar reactions. The only remedy for a larger identity to be embraced is to allow an acknowledgement of what has been denied, accompanied by a grieving and reparation process. This is difficult but necessary.

At the other end of the spectrum, a *carte blanche* anti-chauvinism diversity policy, multiculturalism, which denies the fears of traditional indigenous people about incoming settlers, is equally ineffective. Having the tendency to push people into accepting a new situation too soon, such approaches risk inspiring a backlash and playing into the hands of the far right. It is no coincidence that at the time of writing France's far-right political party, the Front National, is making enormous gains, as are similar parties all over Europe. Worryingly, it has changed its discourse into one of appealing to the masses whose anxieties have not been sufficiently listened to in the postmodernist agenda that has been hoisted on to a very conservative country.

It appears that we humans have two rather different forces that govern our identity. One is rather static: an incontrovertible need to belong and a tendency to want to maintain fairly fixed identities in order to have a stable sense of who we are and therefore function well. But the second force, testified to by evolution, also acts on us: we also have a *dynamic* capacity to expand our identities and increase our circle of belonging and thereby jettison fear-based identity compensations such as national chauvinism.

Shortly, we are going to see exactly what humans might have to come up against in shifting to a fresh identity, but what is evident is that we make this leap when, and only when, we already feel that we belong sufficiently, feel secure enough, adequately valued and listened to. But we are now in a position to see how strong unconscious identity issues keep us bargaining with DGC when it is well past its sell-by date.

With us or against us

On 17 September 2011 around a thousand protesters gathered in downtown Manhattan and started walking up and down Wall Street. A few hundred stayed overnight in Zuccotti Park, but at least eighty were arrested after they forced the closure of several streets. Occupy Wall Street had begun. On 15 October 2011 thousands of protesters staged demonstrations in 900 cities, including Auckland, Sydney, Hong Kong, Taipei, Tokyo, São Paulo, Paris, Madrid, Berlin, Hamburg and Leipzig. Similar protests occurred in London outside the Stock Exchange; the police tried to thwart it, but soon nearly 3,000 people were gathered outside St Paul's Cathedral and 250 camped overnight. In Frankfurt 5,000 people protested at the European Central Bank, and in Zurich, Switzerland's financial hub, protesters displayed banners proclaiming 'We are the 99 per cent!' Headlines soon pushed this powerful identity soundbite around the world.

Having a strongly defined identity is very useful and helps us to navigate the world successfully. But one of its limitations, which strongly applies to this political analysis, is that it can powerfully restrict how to *think* about the world. Psychotherapists have come to understand that within our main identity we can possess a variety of subsidiary identities known as 'sub-personalities'. One of the strongest – and therefore least flexible – turns out to be an identity produced and maintained by being stridently against something. When such a sub-personality becomes overly dominant to the point of becoming a central identity, a therapist might suggest that the person operating in this way had been hijacked by a 'rebel sub-personality'.

The rebel sub-personality is an odd beast. It appears to be on the side of freedom and against oppression, but whenever it gets crystallized as an immovable point of reference in the psyche its limitations become very apparent. Since it needs to maintain its identity as 'good' or 'free', and what it is rebelling against as 'bad' or 'repressive', it has quite limited range, which, in practice, means severe restrictions on its creativity. On close examination it turns out actually not to be free at all, for it needs to be in a two-way relationship with another, which is the bad one. It is, therefore, eternally in a game, a kind of dance, always needing a wall to bounce off or there is no game. It is always a game of two, because without the game there can be no identity.

This kind of identity dynamic impedes those who wage a war on terror, just as it does those who battle the Establishment or the 'structural elite'. In this light, we can see that for the global justice movement to recognize and name DGC would be extremely difficult, because it would utterly change the game of 'free rebels' against 'oppressive tyrants' and deflate the strength of its identity. But such an inclusive, non-judgemental recognition remains a challenge for the GJM because it does not fit with the need to identify itself as the good anti-group.

In order to maintain a good identity we use the same psychological trick as we examined earlier in the case of denial – dissociation or splitting. Because we want to see ourselves as good, we put those aspects of ourselves that we find shameful on to another person or another group. With such splitting we effectively diminish our self-knowledge.

The logic of dissociation operates like this: to sit comfortably in the identity 'I am good' means I have to maintain the identity 'I am not the one who is bad'. In consequence, someone else must be that for me, or carry that identity for me. As we saw earlier, dissociation is the foundation stone of self-protective personality structures. Surprisingly, dissociative defences – such as objectification, projection and compartmentalization – unconsciously dominate the most humane anti-Establishment thinker as it does the hyper-rational Establishment supporter. For while the green movement calls for one-world awareness, in actuality the psychodynamics are rooted in an us-and-them mentality, with green good and the other bad.

As long as we need to have someone else to carry a dominating bad identity, we are stuck in a polarized psychodynamics of unconsciously needing them. This is very important for our case. The classic GJM activist maintains a trouble-free identity, free from the discomfort of cognitive dissonance, by expressing outrage at the bad authorities, the bad corporation, the bad climate change and so on. This way, an identity of 'I am not the one who is wrecking our world/in it for myself/only concerned with profit, etc., but they are' can be maintained, but only by means of projecting the disavowed identity on to another.

Psychologically, it does not matter that the activist may enjoy the fruits of globalization such as mobile devices and the internet, for the need to identify the other as the NOT ME by employing these defence mechanisms means that the brain is in partial shut-down mode. The thinking platform, therefore, appears highly energized but, in fact, loses flexibility and creativity.

The postmodernist trap

If these identity and belonging issues are challenging or beside the point we invite you, the reader, to examine the ways that you yourself identify within this 'for-and-against' polarization of political views, which powerfully affect identity and therefore thinking styles. We think such an exercise worth while, because we have had to go through and had to reflect on similar processes ourselves. The results are often surprising and sometimes a bit shocking!

This us-and-them mentality is very common but functionally very static. It prevents the GJM from recognizing the overarching realities we have been pointing to, for its style of thinking is embedded in its worldview. This is prevailingly *postmodern*; in fact, the tendency to define one's self as against something is one of the features of postmodernism, the worldview that tends to dominate academia these days.

Postmodernism is – by definition – a reaction to the *modernist* approach to life; it is a highly charged critique of that which it sees as being domineering, anachronistic and favouring the haves over the have-nots. Its strength lies in its ability to take multiple perspectives and to see through the rigid social structures of our traditional society and deconstruct the power dynamics that used to be taken for granted. The most marked features of postmodern thought, therefore, are the deconstruction of power, the promotion of diversity and equality, the consequent suspicion of all hierarchies and a rejection of big-picture meta-narratives (such as the one we are presenting in this book). Beginning to think this way was an utter revelation that changed the face of sociology and politics – if not economics – from the 1970s onwards.

However, once a world conditioned by a new context for governance is recognized, the limitations of this thinking style become apparent. Both postmodernism and its adversary modernism are rooted in the kind of rational, linear either/or thought processes that characterized the Enlightenment and rely on nation states as autonomous actors that ought to bring either progress or justice or both into actuality.[2] In their extreme or highly committed forms, like all identities, both have recourse to the same psychodynamic processes to maintain and reinforce their identity. We have touched on some of the defence mechanisms of dissociation, as well as the secondary defence of normalization. But other facets of dissociation further bolster them, such as *projection, compartmentalization* and *objectification*. These shortcomings are not the GJM's alone but are, in fact, shared by the institutions it routinely criticizes.

The hallmark of postmodernism, however, is the rejection of the notion of hierarchy. In practice, this turns into an unshakeable identity edifice to house the GJM: all global problems are seen as myriad and equal, so no single issue is permitted to claim more importance than any other, for that would be hierarchical. Likewise, solutions must be myriad and equal, too, as witnessed by the oft-repeated phrase 'There are no single solutions.' In this way, the GJM's postmodern perspective proves calamitous, compromising its ability to achieve unity and effectively preventing it from coming together around a single plan of action. This is echoed in the clarion call to 'Think globally, act locally', which, although nodding towards more systemic global thinking, still reduces everything to local fragmented action. The result can often be 'You take your solution and go your way, and I'll take my solution and go mine.' Ironically, the only beneficiaries are the vested interests that benefit from DGC; while the GJM remains fragmented and diversified into many single issues, DGC stays quietly in unified global control.

Anecdotally, a colleague of ours who was once consulting to a leading worldwide NGO told us that it was impossible to structure meetings because of the inability of executive members to prioritize topics. In a not dissimilar vein, here is how one commentator described proceedings at the World Social Forum:

> The diversity of opinion and approach is both a strength of the Forum, as well as its principal weakness. The Forum derives strength from this diversity as it provides the opportunity for a very large number of movements and organisations to come together, each feeling that their views have a place in the open space of the Forum. At the same time the diverse trends and opinions lead, often, to a sense of frustration that the Forum is not able to hammer together a consensus regarding both a strategic understanding and tactics to be applied.[3]

Supporters of the GJM may protest that the movement is well aware of DGC or at least of that aspect of it that resembles a race to the bottom. The difficulty is that the postmodern denial of hierarchy prevents the GJM from prioritizing DGC as an issue that trumps all others. Instead, it is relegated to just one other global problem alongside all the rest and so remains effectively invisible. While DGC quietly ensures that the world stays firmly headed towards potential catastrophe, the GJM is content to bargain with its symptoms, believing that the small concessions it occasionally wins might one day amount to an overall victory. Occasional short-lived concessions thus become a psychological compensation for the movement's fundamental impotence. They are just enough to keep the movement believing that bargaining might work when a walk in the daylight reveals that it cannot.

From depression to acceptance

Little wonder, then, that global problems remain unresolved, a stalemate. And small wonder that we, for our part – along with governments, corporations and protesters alike – keep cycling around the first three stages of grieving: in and out of bargaining, anger and back to denial.

Now we can see how the next stage – depression (or grieving) – sets in. If we really acknowledge our impotence we would naturally become depressed. There is not very much we can say to help you through this stage, but it is important to be on guard against what looks like this stage but is in fact a retreat from life. Depression is sometimes thought of by psychotherapists to be anger turned inwards, so getting depressed might not be the depression stage but could be withheld anger. Alternatively, it could be resignation, which is a kind of a bitterness, a giving up, and cannot lead to action based on the realistic appraisal of a new, if unwelcome, context, which is what we get by truly going through the depression stage. Holding grief has value. This demands commitment, however, whereas bitterness is a turning away. The poet Robert Bly once suggested that when sadness is unavoidable, bitterness may be kept at bay by holding what he calls a 'grief-pipe' between the teeth; using an image recalling a Native American peace-pipe, the poet hints at the determination needed to come through the process to its eventual peaceful outcome.[4]

If grieving is faced, without cycling back through the previous stages, it can create space within the psyche, and this can become transformative. It becomes a reflective opportunity for us to let in the freedom stage – acceptance. In fact, depression as a path to freedom is well known in psychoanalytic theory. As far back as the 1920s Melanie Klein suggested that traumatized young children could be observed going through cycles of hate, envy, blame and splitting, which she named the 'paranoid-schizoid position'.[5] The observed infants only reached an end of it when they gained what she called the 'depressive position'. Eventually, she proposed, pining for what was lost or damaged by hate would turn into an urge to repair. The world would be more richly and realistically perceived as a realistic ego developed. Maturation, she argued, was therefore closely linked to loss and mourning.[6] Over the years her schema, like the Kübler-Ross model with which it seems to have much in common, has been applied to all manner of human processes, notably in couples therapy.[7] Many models of the creative process echo the need to fall back from activity into some sort of switching off, which often feels like giving up, before a new solution emerges.

However, readers may still be unconvinced that there is any value in depression. If you are finding our invitation to cast off an old way of thinking rather unattractive, it may be because of cognitive dissonance or it may be because the reality is just too terrifying. Don't worry, 'this, too, shall pass', as the Sufi mystics suggest.

Rumpelstiltskin can help. Like many mental phenomena, the recognizing and the naming of a new reality is a simple and powerful way to overcome its hold on you. You can then feel the feelings, accept the reality and be ready for a new platform from which to act when it appears. As history suggests, the only appropriate response to a new context for governance is neither denial nor anger nor bargaining but acceptance, and acceptance means going through the grief-and-depression stage. We have to accept the reality of DGC and pseudo-democracy and shift to a new level of thinking and a new system of governance.

By healthily seeing things as they truly are, we gain the opportunity to re-engage at another level. Using the helpful distinction posed by consciousness theorist Ken Wilber, we can set about the task of vertically transforming the paradigm or system to a new, higher level rather than simply horizontally translating it, which is just more bargaining, moving the same problem to another but similar place.[8]

Letting go

By now readers will be able to hum our theme song: a prerequisite to finding a new and more powerful way of thinking and acting is that we must fully accept our powerlessness in the face of DGC. Although we, the authors, recognize this as an essential step, we are under no illusion that it is easy. Initially, it seems to be counterintuitive. It may feel like capitulating, like giving up the fight for global justice, forcing oneself to tolerate an intolerable situation.

And yet there are good reasons why such a process has to occur. The human mind resists giving up on known realities, and this seems to be a hard-wired self-preservation feature. However, students of the creative process have regularly observed that before a new insight or solution to a problem can arrive there are stages of frustration, which only pass when a giving-up or surrender stage has reluctantly occurred. This is probably why Archimedes was unable to solve some of the problems of physics until he relaxed in a nice hot bath.

Similarly, from clinical experience, we psychotherapists know how emotions can dominate a person's thoughts so that they are unable to see a new or more appropriate reality until they have fully let go. This is down to our old friend the mind-feelings loop. While our minds are dominated by the normal but clinging emotions of hope, frustration, fear or resentment, we are rarely able to think clearly or creatively. Our thoughts – and our ability to think new thoughts –are dominated by these emotions. Until we have been able to grieve and access a much deeper range of feelings, we often stay stuck.

With the recent discoveries coming from the field of neuroscience, and particularly the more widespread understanding of the nervous system, thanks to the availability of data from fMRI scanners, we are now beginning to understand the physiology of such processes. The widespread difficulty in letting go of a well-known but painful situation may well be because the left hemisphere of the brain, which prioritizes detailed short-focused attention over the bigger picture, has a tendency to dominate perception at times of stress. Often a letting-go process is needed where the deepest human emotions, those of grief, acceptance and surrender, start to open the heart and allow the body to relax, de-stress and activate the parasympathetic side of the autonomic nervous system, permitting the right hemisphere of the brain to evaluate much broader contexts.

Accepting the reality of DGC and relinquishing our attempts to bargain with it will involve such a letting-go process. This will be a challenge, but it is not one that we really have much choice in; it is the vital shift that a new context for governance demands of us all, sooner or later.

Accepting one's powerlessness, like accepting the death of a loved one, is never easy. It is therefore worth taking time to feel our way through this. It may be helpful to remember the mythological phoenix that first had to die and turn to ashes before it could be reborn. Similarly, a genuine and complete acceptance of our powerlessness in the face of DGC can unveil a profound paradox, one that opens us to a powerful new way of thinking. And this can effect a transformation.

The empathy test

We have arrived at acceptance. What does genuine acceptance mean and what does it feel like?

Perhaps the best way to approach it is to try to place ourselves in the shoes of those we usually blame for the state of the world and see how they think. If I were a disillusioned citizen, for example, or a global-justice activist who had invested much of my identity in confronting politicians and corporations, how would I behave if I suddenly found myself in the shoes of a corporate CEO? Would I be able to accede to the demands that activists like me have been consistently making on multinational corporations? Let's try it.

Imagine you are now a corporate CEO. What does it mean for you to behave in a way that fully respects society and the environment? It would be to act against your own interests and quite perilous. It would mean that your company's costs would dramatically increase, causing it to lose out to competitors who may not share your ethical values or who operate in less costly parts of the world.

Your company would lose profitability, and its share value would plummet. Eventually it would be taken over or go out of business. Long before that, you would lose your job, only to be replaced by someone with fewer scruples. Your attempts to act responsibly would thus be futile. Knowing that behaving honourably would be to act against your company's interests and your own, what would *you* do?

Similarly, what if I found myself in the shoes of a prime minister or a president? Would I be able to impose tighter regulations on markets and raise taxes on corporations and the rich when this would only result in them moving to other, less regulated countries? Now let's try that scenario.

You are a national prime minister or president. As soon as you try to impose tighter market regulations and put up corporation tax – in fact, as soon as you even float such an idea – the markets would react badly, seeing your country as business-unfriendly. Markets would start to slide, your currency would lose value, while capital and investment would immediately go elsewhere. In no time this would harm your country's economy, increase unemployment and you would most likely lose the next election.

Knowing that this would be to act against your country's best interests, let alone your party's, what would *you* do?

Once we realize that we would be forced to behave in much the same way as those we habitually blame, we have to face that continuing to blame them would be misguided. However, if a major part of our identity or worldview has been based on our strident view that 'if only those idiots would see reason and care about the planet, etc., etc.' then letting go of this worldview will now mean undergoing a kind of a death process. If I have to let go of my cherished beliefs, it feels as if a sense of who I am and what I stand for has to die.

Once I have submitted to this dying process, my empathy and my new thinking reveal a new insight: while there will always be some unscrupulous and selfish players, it is less the case that politicians and corporations are unaware of global problems or have no desire to do anything about them but that DGC prevents them from acting meaningfully. My belief in my own superior position, I now recognize, is bogus and must be relinquished. Let it die.

One world

As empathy overcomes blame and new thinking allows the Myth of the Sovereign Nation to die away, we find ourselves transformed. We now realize that we are all caught in a powerful global whirlpool of which we have only now become fully aware. Until now we could not understand why all the fish were swimming around in such odd destructive circles; we thought there was something wrong with the fish – and blamed them for it. It is hardly surprising that we could not notice it before because, as Einstein once said, 'What does a fish know about the water in which he swims all his life?'[9]

But now we have acknowledged the ever-present reality of DGC, now that we see the whirlpool in which all the fish – which, of course, includes us, too – are helplessly caught, we can stop blaming each other and start to focus on the real culprit. In this new atmosphere of non-judgemental acceptance of each other, we acknowledge that the problem is *systemic*: all of us are DGC's prisoners.

Although it is true that the rich and the globally mobile increasingly and disproportionably benefit from DGC while the poor become increasingly dispossessed, we must remember that this does not mean they have the power to halt it. No individual person, corporation or nation has the power to do that. To believe that any restricted group is in control of this process or could reverse it is to underestimate what we are up against. The fact is that capital has gone global, and a new context for governance is upon us. Any blame is therefore misdirected; it is futile, like wanting to lock the stable door once the horse has already bolted, and only plays into DGC's hands, diverting us from acknowledging the new context and thereby acting on it.

The realization that the *system* is at fault rather than any individual or group means that we are all in the same boat – one in our vulnerable common humanity. This is a profound psycho-spiritual insight, and allowing it to penetrate us leads to an entirely different level of collective awareness and responsibility. Perhaps it is best summed up by Mahatma Gandhi's remarks:

It is quite proper to resist and attack a system, but to resist or attack its author is tantamount to resisting and attacking oneself. For we are all tarred with the same brush and are children of one and the same Creator, and as such the divine powers within us are infinite. To slight a single human being is to slight those divine powers and thus to harm not only that being but with him the whole world.[10]

Accepting the reality of DGC entails a radical forgiveness both of each other and ourselves. It means finally renouncing the blame game and taking joint responsibility for finding solutions. It is a vital psychological move, because without it we will find that we remain subconsciously attached to the old ways of blaming and believing that bargaining with DGC might work. Accepting DGC means that there is no longer an in-group and an out-group, no longer an us and them and no longer a 99 per cent versus a 1 per cent. The new reality is that there is just one humanity. We are the 100 per cent.

Pragmatically, accepting the reality of DGC does not mean that all the many campaigns to raise awareness of global problems and injustices should stop, nor that we should stop supporting them. Rather, it implies something far more important: that we should stop *believing* that these campaigns can do the work needed while DGC remains active. So, even as we continue with what we call 'bargaining strategies', our attention, now fed by our hearts and our souls, must instead focus on one single key issue: how to disarm and overcome DGC.

This is where we will turn shortly, but first we need to find out how our thinking can transform alongside our feelings.

6.   A New Thinking Platform

Heeding Einstein's advice

Before we are in any position to deal effectively with Destructive Global Competition, a transition to a new way of thinking needs at least to have begun. The first humbling step may still be difficult. Placing ourselves in the shoes of those we once blamed, we find we have to let go of blame and integrate the fact the Myth of the Sovereign Nation has ceased to be relevant. Because it has lost its power, it is now a myth and can no longer guide us in future. As we begin to acknowledge fully the all-pervasiveness of DGC and the super-mobility of capital, we accept that national governments are no longer the autonomous powerful actors we used to count on. We now recognize just how beholden they are to DGC and, even though they still remain important, how powerless they are to overcome it. Nations have ceased to be sovereign – DGC is sovereign.

Even though we do not know exactly what the new political order will look like, we can predict that national politics has to undergo a profound transformation. It is not that national politics is finished but that its role is now far less important than we thought. Sovereignty has become only a rallying cry, like those who want to make countries 'great again' or 'stand on their own two feet'. In our globalized interdependent world such cries and the movements that utter them can only now be seen as desperate and regressive acts of denial or bargaining with DGC. National politics will survive, but it now must adapt to the more modest and realistic role of determining and implementing those decisions, laws and actions that can still be taken at the national level while coordinating ascent to those that need to be taken at the global. It may even be that politics at a community or local level will interface more with the global.

Once we have digested this painful reality, it becomes easy to see how stuck in an outdated worldview we have been. We begin to notice how addicted most of society and the media still are to this perspective and how shallow and partial it has all become. Western society's thinking remains at a *nationcentric* level, which, although it brought enormous benefits, has created massive expansion and consequent global problems. But recently it has engendered huge polarization. The national political scene at once evokes boredom and apathy in many young digitally connected people while, at the same time, fear drives the old industrial working classes –

globalization's losers – into the hands of far-right extremist parties, which poses an enormous risk of serious civil strife.

The emerging truth is that both modern and postmodern habits of thinking are outdated. We remember that Einstein warned us that we can never solve major problems with the same thinking that created them in the first place. We are now entering a new era where what we once knew as 'the Truth' no longer serves us. Rather than try to name it as something else – post-postmodernism or the Information Age, for example – we would do much better to consider its central truth: our old way of seeing the world has become outdated and harmful, and what is now clearly required is *the ability to think and act in a way that is as free from national borders as DGC and super-mobile capital is.*

Higher levels of thinking, which operate at a post-nationcentric level, do exist and can be engaged. These levels are what we call 'worldcentric' levels. A worldcentric thinking platform has a much wider perspective than traditional, modernist and even postmodernist ways of thinking about the world. It offers an entirely new context-informed identity, enlivened by a more encompassing way of understanding and thinking. Returning to our earlier metaphor, where modernism and postmodernism see only the fish, worldcentrism also sees the whirlpool that encompasses them.

Worldcentrism embraces a genuinely global and systemic view. Thus it allows us to understand the dynamics of the whole and therefore think creatively about its future. Like a climber on a mountaintop who enjoys a more panoramic view than he did on the way up, a worldcentric perspective has the capacity to take account of the broader global context – including destructive phenomena such as DGC. Only worldcentrism, consequently, has the potential to overcome them.

Worldcentric thinking might not sound immediately attractive to all readers. Some, reacting to history, will hear alarm bells sounding. But worldcentric thinking is not to be confused with ideas of global imperialism or with the current impotent status of the United Nations or its forerunner the League of Nations. In fact, both of these bodies were and are expressions of nationcentrism, only empowered to do the bidding of the nation states that created them.[1] Nor should fears about any overarching world parliament or a controlling world government be invoked. Worldcentric thinking is not about any structural undertaking, it is an aspect of *consciousness* that is available to all but only recently becoming possible for human beings as we evolve. Worldcentric thinking is an *inner* facility that is the counterpart to the outer forms of global technologies such as the internet and even DGC, and it has been waiting for us to embrace it.

The evolution of thinking

Over the last fifty years some philosophers, social scientists, psychologists, biologists and theologians have investigated the idea that it is not only physical matter that is subject to evolution but consciousness itself. As history rolls on, the ability of mankind to hold increasingly complex thoughts and perspectives is evident from many sources, artistic and literary as well as scientific. The way we think is itself evolving, and our brains may even be on the way to adapting to our new potentials.

The notion of evolving consciousness may be new to some readers. It has certainly taken a back seat to the focus on the evolution of material forms, as most scientists are still dealing with the ramifications of gene theory and so on, while politicians and economists – as we know to our cost – have been too blinded by the beacon of neoliberalism to notice what else is going on. To explain more precisely how thought is evolving, researchers in the field have begun to categorize various levels of thinking, which themselves evolve in humans during the developmental lifespan. Some of these frameworks aim to be all-encompassing models and aim to comprise all the thinking levels that have evolved up to this point in human history. Many describe the development of thought in human beings and how this interfaces with our psychology, ethics and behaviour.

It is not our aim here to create a new model of the development of consciousness but rather to point out that these frameworks are now becoming increasingly relevant as the need to make a transformative shift to a new thinking platform becomes clear. There are several very useful models that have been the lifetime achievements of various philosophers and social psychologists, including those put forward by James Mark Baldwin, Jean Piaget, Thomas Kuhn, Jürgen Habermas, Lawrence Kohlberg, Carol Gilligan, Robert Kagan, Clare Graves, Robert Pirsig and Ken Wilber, to name but a few key figures. So we are not attempting to reinvent the wheel here. Our own particular contribution to this science is to illustrate how *identity* is compromised (and potentially expanded) in this process and how human organization, which includes economics and politics, is forced to respond to changing environmental conditions and technologies and in particular to new contexts for governance.

So far in this book we have suggested that our civilization has moved through various different stages, usually brought about by technological changes, and that these transitions have radically altered our perspectives and our need to reorganize ourselves in relation to the environment and our changing needs and desires. We briefly considered the shift from hunter-gathering societies to agricultural; we did not refer to the Age of Empire or the Dark Ages, but we thought how the world changed in the Middle Ages, throwing off the stranglehold of Church control via the new medium of printing. We alluded to how this expansion of freedom of thought continued into the Renaissance, the Reformation and the Age of Exploration, which kicked off the era of colonial expansionism and finally blossomed into the Enlightenment, which birthed the industrial and scientific revolutions. The advances in complexity of the accompanying worldviews meant the rapid emergence of the modern period, followed by the current postmodern worldview to revise the faults of its preceding era.

Many historians and psychohistorians have looked for patterns in the evolution of human activity and the way we see the world. The American economic historian and critic of capitalism Brooks Adams, born in 1848, believed that commercial civilizations rose and fell in predictable cycles out of the interplay between the human-driving emotional impulses of greed and fear.[2] Greed fostered the commercial spirit of lending and borrowing, which, he says, eventually undermined the Roman Empire from within and engendered scepticism, which turned the Romans away from their gods and their military traditions, causing them to rely on mercenaries to administer the empire. At the end of the Dark Ages, fear-driven imagination ruled the cycle, turning people to the superstitious veneration of Christian relics and belief in miraculous absolutions. This led to the restricted thinking of the early medieval period and the cultish fundamentalism of the Crusades before the rise of Western mercantilism turned people back to trade and the revision of established religion. Following the money, Adams noted how the centres of world trade shifted first to Constantinople, then to Venice, whence to Amsterdam and then London. In 1900 he predicted that the baton would pass to New York.

A recent groundbreaking overview of the mutual relationship between thinking and history comes from the British scholar and psychiatrist Iain McGilchrist.[3] He attempts to track the history of civilization through a different human interplay: the two distinct and different modes of seeing that our brains use. McGilchrist charts the repeating cycles that are dominated by the conceptual reality favoured by the left hemisphere of the human brain and the gradual return of those of the right. The left's perspective involves a narrowing in on detail at the expense of larger perspectives and gives rise to materialism, competition and military and engineering achievements. The perspective of the right hemisphere, however, which manages to take over in periods such as the classical period of Greek drama or early-nineteenth-century Romanticism or the 1960s, takes in the big picture and the web of relationships. It seems to favour climates in which the arts and cooperation tend to flourish.

On the other hand – in everyday life and in politics – when we think about different people or cultures, both today and through history, we tend to assume that their differing worldviews remain relatively fixed. 'People are different,' we say to ourselves with a shrug. We resign ourselves to the conflicts that these differences inevitably entail: political right versus political left, traditional religious societies versus secular modern societies, globalizing corporate modernists versus egalitarian postmodernists and so on.

As Samuel P. Huntington suggests in his influential book *The Clash of Civilizations*, we tend to see different ways of thinking and different cultures as distinct, disconnected and unchanging, as if they were hard billiard balls that conflict and clash. However, if we dare to take a longer view of human history we see that individuals and whole cultures gradually evolve from one level of thinking to the next. We notice, too, that there is a definite and predictable sequence to these changes. In this way, levels of thinking can be viewed as less like billiard balls and more like turns in a spiral that individuals and whole societies pass through.

To make sure we are looking in the right direction, we must take a look at how other experts have attempted to map changing worldviews, ways of thinking or levels of consciousness – we use these terms interchangeably, even at the risk of imprecision – that have been shown to evolve in individuals and in whole cultures over the course of human history. We are looking for a universal overview – even if very general – of how different people and cultures think, including the direction in which their way of thinking is likely to evolve over time, in order to help us understand the big leap forward we have to make in our thinking and what built-in obstacles there may be. For this reason we turn now to developmental psychology: how human thinking itself changes and evolves.

Thinking about changes in thinking

The great daddy of developmental psychology was the Swiss clinical psychologist Jean Piaget, who was born in 1896 and died in 1980. Piaget conducted pioneering research in how children develop their cognitive capacities over time. In particular, Piaget's model of development accounts for cumulative thinking based on earlier identifiable building blocks. Through repetition of research, Piaget demonstrated how children progressively enlarge their understanding by acting on and reflecting on the effects of their own previous knowledge. In this way they learn to organize their knowledge in increasingly complex structures. Piaget's system, called 'genetic epistemology', attempted to address what he later called 'the central problem of intellectual development'. His model evolved into a global theory of cognitive-developmental stages where individuals exhibit identifiable patterns of thinking and cognition in predictable periods of development contained in a hierarchical structure.[4]

Clare W. Graves was a professor of psychology in Schenectady, New York. He built on the work of Piaget, but he was also influenced by Max Weber, Abraham Maslow and Jane Loevinger, and his research and writing focused rather on the processes of human psychological maturation. His main interest was not in early development but how humans evolved new 'bio-psycho-social coping systems' to solve existential problems and cope with changes in their environment. Graves saw that coping systems were related to evolving human culture and individual development and could be traced at the individual, cultural and even species levels. He proposed that our brains would adapt and evolve to our changing world, that man's nature was not a set thing; it was ever-emergent, an open not a closed system.[5]

Graves argued that humans respond to external conditions by thinking and creating systems in a hierarchical framework subject to both progression and regression. Movement would continue in leaps, bounds and descents over time to stretch human consciousness into further expansion, as he explained:

> Briefly, what I am proposing is that the psychology of the mature human being is an unfolding, emergent, oscillating, spiralling process marked by progressive subordination of older, lower-order behavior systems to newer, higher-order systems as man's existential problems change.[6]

In his emergent cyclical levels of existence theory, Graves modelled this spiral of progression in eight distinct levels of increasingly complex systems of context, meaning and values. Hierarchically ordered, these levels of thinking were subject to change and influence, and, following Piaget, the values of each level could be identified as responses to solving the problems of the previous level. As these value systems were established, groups, societies and cultures would create structure, which individuals would integrate. Graves distinguished between shifts from one level to another that occurred either incrementally or through a breakthrough; the quality of the latter kind of change is what we today, after Thomas Kuhn, might call a 'paradigm shift'.

Each of Graves's first six levels of thinking builds its distinct status on having seen through and rejected the shortcomings of the previous level. Graves called them 'First-Tier' levels, by virtue of their narrow perspective, which recalls McGilchrist's left-hemisphere analysis. We will explain each of these levels in a little more detail shortly. The move from First-Tier to Second-Tier thinking, however, recalling McGilchrist's more global context of the right hemisphere, involved what Graves called a 'leap' in perspective. Second-Tier levels, which we refer to as worldcentric, have the huge advantage of being able to see the entire system in context so they can incorporate the values inherent in previous levels, discard their defects and create a new *non-polarized* synthesis. However, First-Tier thinking does not easily yield to Second Tier, precisely because of the magnitude of the leap required.

It is this tension between First- and Second-Tier levels of consciousness that caught the excitement of the authors. It helped explain how the need to move to a new context where cooperative global governance, in order to address global problems such as DGC and climate change, appears absolutely logical, common sense and obvious, and yet how so many well-meaning people just couldn't see it and, in fact, reacted negatively to the idea. Using the lens of Graves's schema it became clear and simple: this new context for global governance can *only* be seen from a worldcentric Second-Tier perspective, whereas the nationcentric First-Tier perspective remains polarized in a them-and-us, either/or dialectic and cannot even behold the new idea, because it exists at a different and higher level. First-Tier thinking imagines its level to be the pinnacle of creation and is therefore resistant to making any leap at all; the Second Tier is far more flexible and creative because the possibilities of implementing the new idea via values and structures already existing in other levels is a pragmatic reality.

As we have indicated, in this book we are not in search of a new way to model the whole of human experience nor of a theory on which to construct our argument. But we are convinced that the economic and political changes necessary at this crucial time in world history rely on the ability of enough people in the world to change their thinking and identify the major obstacles to addressing global problems so that we can all get on with solving them. Graves's model, and especially how subsequent theorists have developed it, could be a very useful tool to help us see how changes in thinking actually function and how they get stuck.

Thinking on an ascending spiral

First articulated in the 1960s by Graves, the idea of placing emerging consciousness on an ascending spiral (or double helix as he originally suggested) has since been further developed by several theorists, initially by two of his students, Don Beck and Chris Cowan, who applied it as Spiral Dynamics to business management and leadership development.[7] Next it was updated by the consciousness theorist Ken Wilber, dedicated to mapping all of human psychological and spiritual development possibilities, who has adapted it into his heavily researched All Quadrant, All Levels (AQAL) model that constitutes the intellectual foundation of the Integral Institute in Boulder, Colorado.[8] By taking the research of other theorists, including Graves, into account, Wilber's AQAL framework suggests that values or worldviews – the aspects of consciousness we are mostly concerned with in this book – comprise only one of many lines of human psychological development, albeit an important one. For the purposes of this book, we are interested in how the evolving spiral of worldviews shows how increasing complexity of context seems to be a natural part of human development in which the wider perspective offers a more mature understanding of human affairs and thereby potentials for problem-solving.

The usefulness, for our purposes, of any model or framework that identifies stages and levels of consciousness is based on it satisfying enough of the conditions set out below:

- It should bridge the gap between how humans operate as individuals and how they operate in groups, societies and cultures.

- It should span both the development of *interior* emotional and cognitive faculties as well as the *exterior* fields of organization and action, such as the economic and political activity we are thinking about in this book.

- It should systematically show how individuals progress through a series of shifts in understanding, meaning, values and behaviour in their developmental history.

- It should make the connection that human culture moves along a comparable development track, since societies are made up of individuals at varying stages of consciousness.

- It should show that when a sufficient number of individuals attains a certain level of consciousness a contextual shift can occur.

- It should show how a succeeding level absorbs but also negates the meaning of the previous failing level by going further in perspective and complexity.

- It should help us understand how when levels of meaning and context begin to fail at one level there is a resistance to shifting to the next, which is attempting to encompass and go beyond it.

The ascending spiral works very well in this context, so we will present its different stages or levels in order to see what may be relevant for our argument. The eight levels are as follows, labelled according to what seems to us the most useful combination of names applied by some of the theorists we have mentioned previously.

First-Tier levels

1. **Survival**/ Archaic/ Instinctive
2. **Tribal**/ Animistic/ Mythic
3. **Warrior**/ Power/ Dominant/ Egocentric
4. **Traditional**/ Authoritarian/ Conformist
5. **Modern**/ Technocratic/ Rational/ Meritocratic
6. **Postmodern**/ Egalitarian/ Pluralistic

Second-Tier levels

7. **Early Worldcentric/** Systemic /Functional /Integrative
8. **Late Worldcentric/** Holistic / Global but stratified

The Ascending Spiral of Worldviews

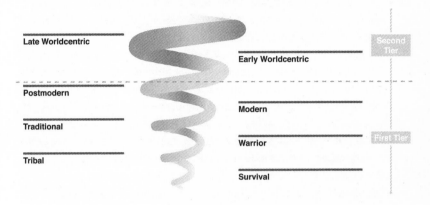

The levels that most concern us in this book are Modern, Postmodern and especially the Second-Tier shift to Early Worldcentric, where worldcentric thinking begins to come into play. But first we will briefly sketch out the whole spiral movement as it has evolved over the course of human history.[9]

- *Survival*
  Our fundamental worldview is about basic survival. For early humans the need for food, water, warmth, safety and sex predominate. The sense of individual self is barely present and thinking is near automatic; the social structure would be loose bands of people bent on survival; their economic mode would have been hunter-gathering. Basic needs call all the shots. Psychologically, the worldview of a new-born infant or a highly traumatized person is at this level.

- *Tribal*
  Now consciousness becomes Tribal, and the self is experienced as a part of the group. Basic survival needs being met, this worldview is enlivened by meaning that comes from outside the group – spirits and mystical signs, interpreted by shamans. The spirits are to be obeyed, as are the tribal

chief and elders. Rites of passage, seasonal cycles and tribal ceremonies define the life-cycle. Thinking is animistic, enshrined in blood oaths, curses, ethnic beliefs and mystical superstitions. Economically, the mode is foraging. Today, Tribalism can be experienced in rural parts of developing countries as well as in ghetto street gangs, football supporters and corporate loyalty.

- *Warrior*
  Here the self continues to awaken and now feels its own power to influence and control its environment. The world is full of threats; predators abound and are to be overcome and subdued. This consciousness is rooted in will, pleasing oneself and dominating others. It demands respect, dictates to others and does what it likes. In European historical terms its heyday was the age of the great empires subduing those who were 'other'. In the developing child it is the 'terrible twos'. Its thinking is egocentric, its *modus operandi* exploitative.

- *Traditional*
  In reaction, a sharp tug on the reins is needed. A worldview of respect and authority. Now life has meaning and purpose, as defined by a higher power or absolutist religion or cause. The personal self is sacrificed to a higher cause or to salvation via the One and Only Truth. Good and bad within the psyche are projected externally into archetypes: God, the Devil and their representatives on earth. Society is rooted in order; a strict code of conduct is absolute, for eventually obedience and discipline will bring their reward. Thinking is absolutistic – all or nothing, black or white.

  Traditional social structures tend to be rigid, hierarchical and authoritarian. In extreme form, fundamentalism abounds; in moderation it is about belonging. Economically its mode is agrarian. Politically it is expressed in conservatism and patriotism, 'for God, King and Country'. Today, China would be an example of such a national society, even though it is changing fast. Psychologically a developing child conforms, whether to rules, parents or school, because he or she needs to belong.

- *Modern*
  Conformity is eventually relieved by individuality. The Modern mindset sees that the world is to be mastered through strategy, self-interest

and competitiveness. The European Enlightenment was the first large-scale emergence of the Modern way of thinking. It was the harbinger of the nation state, democracy and the social contract, while supporting colonialism and the expansionism of the industrial age. The rational egoic self is self-interested but with its capacity for logic is able to put itself in the shoes of others. Under the banner of 'Progress', however, nature and other cultures are resources to be exploited through science and technology. Its thinking is linear, either/or, subject–object, concerned with achievement, self-advancement, competition and success through merit.

- *Postmodern*
  A new sensitivity now emerges in reaction to this self-centredness, believing that all beings and interests deserve inclusion and respect, and that all viewpoints should be heard. Equality is a given, and everyone must be freed from dogma, greed and domination; hierarchies of any kind are to be deconstructed. By eliminating hierarchy, Postmodernism seeks harmony, care and sharing, aligning itself with those of like mind but against those it perceives as antithetical. Its thinking is seen in multi-culturalism, political correctness, environmentalism, global-justice activism, Occupy and Web of Life theories. Economically the mode is post-industrial and informational. The trap for the Postmodern level is the belief that its worldview is the last word in sophistication; its mantra is 'Nobody tells *me* what to do!'

A transition point for new eyes

The transition from the Postmodern to the Early Worldcentric level is also the shift from First to Second Tier, from nationcentric to worldcentric thinking, and a much greater leap than any of the previous transitions, according to all spiral theorists. As Graves explains:

> After being hobbled by the more narrow animal-like needs, by the imperative need for sustenance the fear of spirits and other predatory men, by the fear of trespass upon the ordained order, by the fear of greediness, and the fear of social disapproval, suddenly human cognition is free. Now with his energies free for cognitive activation, man focuses upon his self and his world.[10]

In ancient times, the difficulty built in to transitioning from one major contextual level to another was recognized, but it was expressed in different – mythic – terms. Levels of consciousness were seen as different worlds or domains. These were patrolled by specific guardian deities, often female, such as the sphinx in ancient Egypt. To get past the sphinx, the hero – one who was on a maturational journey, according to the ethnologist Joseph Campbell – had to answer a riddle.[11] In our current situation this doesn't mean we have to get good at crosswords but that we have to get rid of dualistic or polarized thinking.

The move to Second Tier means that we relinquish an identity where others have got it wrong or 'nobody tells me what to do', as in the Postmodern, and instead integrate the wisdom of all the previous levels, which we may have once rejected, with the insights of the new. So powerful is this shift in awareness that it is no wonder that the ancients represented the threshold as being guarded by figures of power. And, if the transition from First- to Second-Tier thinking is the major shift in awareness that is now needed – as the authors believe – it is no surprise that we run into problems here. Our world being stuck on its destructive path and unable to find a way out seems like a testament to the difficulty of making this huge leap from First to Second Tier, from nationcentric thinking to worldcentric thinking. In fact, the Postmodern level appears to be where the spiral movement gets stuck. It may be that this is a built-in *reculer pour mieux sauter* stage, pulling back before a leap forward, but it is why we devoted considerable space in the last two chapters to show why the global justice movement represents a particularly difficult-to-understand obstacle to further evolution. Our hearts are fully with its aims, but because it cannot properly acknowledge the reality of DGC its thinking remains stuck and it thereby struggles to get to the worldcentric thinking platform that the next stages introduce.

The Postmodern level, in fact, tends to have difficulty with the whole idea of levels. Since its level of consciousness is based in the deconstruction of power dynamics and is distrustful of anything that resembles a hierarchy, this is perhaps no surprise. Often when groups broadly at a Postmodern level are presented with an Early Worldcentric perspective they will baulk and cause a regression by reinvoking values such as diversity, gender equality, peace and other versions of plurality. What the Postmodern level struggles to see is that these values are included in the Early Worldcentric level but do not *define* it, and therefore such objections can constitute a distraction, particularly when there is some powerful conflict emerging or when some Traditional elements such as order, structure and discipline might be required. The Postmodern group thereby resists the difficult transition to the next level by staying in its known and familiar territory, and this ends up blocking further progress.

With the advent of the Early Worldcentric level, the Postmodern rejection of hierarchies gives way to a realization that hierarchies are naturally occurring phenomena and can now be differentiated: some are healthy while others are not. The most important hierarchy it becomes aware of is the spiral of consciousness itself. Whether explicitly or implicitly, the Early Worldcentric level recognizes that each level is a valid, if partial, way of viewing the world. Life is now recognized as a kaleidoscope of natural hierarchies, systems and forms. In contrast to Modern and Postmodern, whose mode of thought is either/or, Early Worldcentric makes the move to both/and. Its thinking is systemic and inclusive; flexibility, spontaneity and functionality predominate.

Here it should be emphasized that Early Worldcentric and, to a lesser extent, Late Worldcentric levels are only now beginning to manifest in the world, so it is harder to be certain about their characteristics, which are unfolding as we write. In order not to risk predictions beyond our immediate area of expertise, we will restrict ourselves to advancing some examples of how we see these levels manifesting in the political world in terms of global problems and how they each seek to solve them. For the sake of brevity, we'll refer to the Early and Late Worldcentric levels simply as 'Early' and 'Late'.

Second-Tier political awareness

Being aware of the spiral, Early sees the different levels that people and cultures find themselves at and seeks to work with them in ways that will help them evolve. Its focus, however, tends to be on the *individual*, be it an individual person, corporation or country. Seeing the different thinking levels that are in play, Early seeks to align them cooperatively to produce optimal outcomes. In terms of global problems, where Postmoderns focus on fighting the system, those at Early seek to work with the system to obtain better outcomes. Examples can be seen in corporate social responsibility, chaos theory, social enterprise, Conscious Capitalism,[12] organizational and sustainability consultants, Paul Ray's 'cultural creatives'[13] and Don Beck's work supporting transition from apartheid in South Africa.[14]

In contrast to Early, the Late level moves beyond an individualistic focus to encompass the collective dimension. It sees the whole world as a dynamic organism. Drawing on the same awareness of the spiral, Late thinking is intuitive and its perspective is global and cooperative. Unlike the First-Tier levels (and to some extent Early)[15] the Late is capable of recognizing collective global phenomena – such as DGC – and can devise global solutions where these are necessary. Its thinking is holistic, and yet its solutions are stratified in ways that take each of the prior levels properly into account. It is the first level, consequently, that is fully worldcentric. Examples of Late Worldcentric thinking are few, but would include the writings of Ken Wilber, Otto Laske and theologian Pierre Teilhard de Chardin.

As far as politics at this level are concerned, we are on new ground. However, the main difference between Early and Late, as we see it, is that whereas Early seeks to transform the individual person, corporation or nation Late seeks to transform the world. This would not resemble the past attempts by domineering empires, the Church or neoliberalism but in the sense of what Wilber calls 'the prime directive',[16] a form of cooperative global governance that respects and honours all cultures simultaneously *in their own context*, whatever their stage of development, by ensuring that each is not just respected but equitably supported by a cooperatively governed global economy that is genuinely fair to all.

The blind spot of an *individual* focus on the values make-up of individual corporations or nations is to miss seeing the collective global dynamics. For example, someone at Early may be aware that in a particular country Postmodern multiculturalism and diversity norms may be starting to threaten a healthy sense of Traditional national identity and that this is something that may warrant redressing, perhaps by reducing immigration. But only someone at Late would recognize that the collective global dynamic of DGC makes this phenomenon inevitable across virtually all countries, since a drift towards nationalism and the far right, as well as a general disillusionment with mainstream politicians, are not restricted to a few individual nations but a transnational trend.

Thus, no amount of values-alignment work within an individual nation can possibly have any lasting beneficial effect *unless* the global dynamic of DGC is also addressed. We will shortly present a campaign that offers such a potential.[17]

Dynamics in the spiral

Having described the levels in the spiral, there are important points to note about how the levels relate to each other and how they manifest in both individuals and whole societies. We briefly list the most important:

- *Not what but how*
  The levels do not determine what people think but how they think. A devotee of one fundamentalist religion, for example, is operating at the same level of consciousness (Traditional) as the devotee of another fundamentalist religion. The conflict between them is not one of *context* but one of *content*. Their ways of thinking are simply different versions of the same level.

- *Levels unfold in sequence and cannot be skipped*
  Research suggests that both individuals and whole societies tend to ascend the levels in the sequence shown in the diagram. Moreover, since each level arises in reaction to its predecessor, no level can be skipped or avoided. Individuals and societies must pass through each in sequence, even if some may be navigated more swiftly than others. However, since the pace of change is accelerating exponentially under globalization, Late Worldcentric may follow upon Early Worldcentric very rapidly indeed.

- *Each higher level transcends and yet includes its predecessor*
  Each new level of thinking represents a new, more encompassing way of looking at and understanding the world. Each new turn in the spiral includes more and sees deeper and wider than its predecessor. But a new level doesn't replace its predecessor, it incorporates it. It takes into account the important truths of its predecessors and yet it also goes beyond them to offer its own more complete perspective. Thus, using Wilber's invaluable terminology, each new level transcends, negates and includes its predecessors.[18]

- *No individual nor any society is at just one level*
  Because each level transcends and includes its predecessor, whatever the level we happen to be at we still have access to all the levels beneath our current level. As we go through them they become part of us.

Although we tend to operate from the *highest* level we have attained, we still have access to prior ways of thinking and may still resort to them, especially if we feel threatened or under stress.

- *Evolution up the spiral is not a linear lock-step affair*
Progress up the spiral is neither inevitable nor linear but characterized by periods of stasis and regression as well as by moments of swift progress. However, movement appears to be directional towards ever-larger perspectives, greater cognitive sophistication and increasing circles of care, compassion and embrace.

- *Each level has its healthy and its unhealthy aspects*
Just as any technology can be used for good or ill, each level in the spiral has its healthy and pathological sides. For example, *healthy* Traditional includes loyalty to friends and family, a measured pride in one's cultural and national identity, tolerant religious faith, respect for the law and so on. *Pathological* Traditional, on the other hand, can be seen in religious fundamentalism, xenophobia, the patriarchy and an inability to tolerate difference. Readers may recall that we touched on some of the pathologies associated with Modern and Postmodern in earlier chapters.

- *Levels evolve in response to changing life conditions*
A new level of thinking doesn't simply emerge from nowhere but develops in response to changing life conditions. This is one of the messages inherent in Einstein's advice that present problems need new thinking, because each level not only solves the problems of the previous level it creates its own new ones, and these new conditions, in turn, spur the emergence of the next level. An ever-evolving spiral of consciousness is the result.

This is precisely what is happening to us all right now. New life conditions have emerged under globalization – in particular, the new context for governance we call DGC. The present level of thinking cannot cope because it is too partial and too limited – too nationcentric – to understand what is occurring. But these unhealthy limitations do have a purpose. As Robert Pirsig reasoned in his model of competing patterns of value, their excessive *static* quality tends to invite a chaotic dynamism that finally stimulates the development of the *next* more encompassing level.[19]

However, in times of transition and stress we humans tend to be motivated by our basic fear of change and our hard-wired distrust of strangers, and we then *regress* down the levels. As global wealth inequality drives the mass migration of people from the developing to the developed world, citizens inevitably blame their Modern/Postmodern governments for allowing it to happen and not addressing their fears. Failing to see that DGC is the real culprit, they then move their support to right-wing parties, which cater better for the worldviews of the lowest four levels. The need to move to more global awareness is thereby powerfully resisted despite it being the only level at which the problem can ultimately be solved.

From the perspective of the spiral, the life conditions of globalization are severely undermining the Traditional level in virtually all nations, since DGC subjects national identities and cultures to severe threat. Familiar Modern/Postmodern governance strategies, both of which are nationcentric, have no answer to the new context for governance that DGC represents. The only solution resides in moving up to a new, Late Worldcentric system of governance, a new form of global governance capable of delivering a global economy that is genuinely fair to all, that allows citizens in developing countries to make a decent living on home turf. Only in that way can mass migration be brought within sustainable limits, allowing those at the Traditional level to regain stability. Only then can a healthy sense of national identity be restored and preserved for *all* countries and their cultures everywhere. In contrast to the flawed Postmodern concept of multiculturalism, we might call this 'simulculturalism'.

- *Different people, as well as different societies, have progressed further than others*
  Because of their differing historical, geographical and cultural circumstances, different societies around the world have moved up the spiral at different speeds. Those that evolved faster came to dominate other cultures and will have hindered their evolution in important ways. These differences and interactions account for the differing worldviews we see in different parts of the world today, which inevitably give rise to conflicts between them.

  Nor should this come as much of a surprise, viewed in the context of global psychohistory. In *Guns, Germs, and Steel* Jared Diamond explains how geographical differences across the world happened to favour European societies, enabling them to develop more quickly than other societies, leading to technological advances that facilitated European colonization of much of the rest of the world.[20] Since the way people think is inextricably linked to their material and economic development, Western societies progressed up the spiral more swiftly than societies elsewhere. The ruthless colonization of the so-called 'New World peoples' will also have traumatized those populations and delayed their progress up the spiral.

Nevertheless, a society's position on the spiral is no reflection of its intrinsic value but rather of its complexity. Just as we recognize that some children may be more developmentally advanced than others, this does not mean we value them differently. The identification of a society's level simply helps us to better understand the way it views the world, what its present needs are and what will best help it to evolve further. Despite its progress-oriented history, Western societies are equally able to lose dynamism and to get stuck, hence the main thesis of this book so far.

- *Conflicting worldviews*

A particular feature of people or societies at any of the first six levels on the spiral (First Tier) is that each believes its own particular perspective – its own level – to be the only valid one. Hence societies holding a Traditional worldview tend to see Modern societies as decadent, while Modern societies see Traditional ones as repressive. Meanwhile, Postmodern environmentalists tend to see Modern corporate globalizers as the problem. Each of the first six levels effectively sees all the others as wrong-headed. Only its view is right. Little wonder there is so much conflict in the world.

At the same time, while different levels of consciousness conflict as they invite differing perspectives, this doesn't necessarily prevent their peaceful coexistence. For example, the USA is a society that, like most developed nations, spans Traditional, Modern and Postmodern levels. People on its west and east coasts may be more likely to have a Modern or Postmodern worldview, whereas a higher percentage of those in its southern and inland states hold a Traditional worldview. Despite this wide divergence that produces competing political views, they all coexist more or less peacefully within one nation and one national identity.

It is only at the Worldcentric levels that these conflicts start to resolve themselves, as we are now in position to realize how each level is a valid and valuable part of the whole spiral. We realize that each level holds both an element of truth as well as its own particular limitations, with its healthy and unhealthy aspects.

- *Towards ever-larger circles of care, compassion and embrace*
  As individuals and whole societies gradually progress up the spiral, another trend reveals itself. Each new level represents an expansion in the circle of care, compassion and embrace. As we ascend the ladder, just like on a hike up a mountain, the view gets wider and more inclusive, and the more we see, the more we care about and seek to manage. From the *ego*centric levels of Survival, Tribal and Warrior, concerned only with self, to the ethnocentric Traditional concerned with the group or religion, to the *nation*centric levels of Modern and Postmodern concerned with the nation, we eventually move to the *World*centric levels where concern shifts to all life and to the entire globe.

  Potentially, humanity may yet attain a Third Tier, the Cosmocentric, but for now it is the threshold between nationcentric and worldcentric, between First Tier and Second Tier, that offers today's challenge. We face the necessary 'death' and inclusion of one and the difficult birth of the next, with all the fear and trepidation that this difficult yet vital evolutionary transition entails.

- *The pattern of transformative change*
  Consciousness theorists suggest that transitioning from one level to another tends to involve a series of recognizable and often painful steps, which together amount to a transformation. It may not surprise readers to know that these steps closely resemble Elizabeth Kübler Ross's five stages of grief that we have used to bring us to this point in the book.

Concerns about the idea of ascending levels

For those readers struggling with the hierarchical framework of the spiral model, it might prove helpful to imagine the different levels as concentric circles or spheres, each one enfolding the previous, like the layers of an onion – a more 'feminine' model (as the Integral thinker Indra Adnan proposes) than a ladder of progress.[21] However, the difficulty can be assuaged by realizing that the hierarchy is not one of power or role but one of *context*, that is to say, like climbing a mountain; the higher you go the more you get to see. Gaining a new context means that the data we see is the same only we see more of it and in greater perspective. So we then acquire, as it were, new eyes with which to see the same world. And, in fact, this changes everything.

The fact that different individuals and societies have evolved at different speeds and so find themselves at different levels may seem controversial because it implies a value judgement, and some readers may sense an unpleasant whiff of an old-fashioned elitism. In fact, understanding how these different levels of seeing the world can coexist in individuals and societies – in us, as in you, the reader – turns out to be a tool of compassionate empathy that can have an important contribution to make on worldwide coexistence and cooperation.

To offset any anxiety about elitism, this awareness of levels of consciousness gives us an enormous advantage as well as a special responsibility, a depth of field that explains why we inevitably fail to recognize the new thing that is happening and enables both perspective and vision. Best-selling author and Franciscan friar Richard Rohr suggests that all maturation processes, including psychological and spiritual growth, happen in stages that are subject to a dynamic that he calls 'falling upward'. In this process, existing stages are not always discernible, Rohr argues, because one can only discern and understand the earlier stages from the wider perspective of the later stages.[22]

This is exactly the same mechanism operating in the ascending spiral of levels. Such a wider and higher perspective seems to us to be precisely what is needed for political direction and what is so lacking in most approaches today, where we have become used to a lowest-common-denominator perspective. So it is to worldcentric citizenship and forms of action that we turn next.

7. Criteria for Worldcentric Political Action

A brand-new civic identity

As we have seen, the psychological need to identify and belong carries social consequences, both positive and negative. In the context of global problems, how we understand the world and see our place in it radically affects how we participate in our society, and this is also subject to change. So embracing a new way of thinking at a worldcentric level affects how we experience ourselves at all levels. Now we can go beyond the well-known mantra of the Postmodern level – 'Think globally, act locally', a way of thinking that flattens our field of action to a mainly local dimension – and move to the worldcentric multidimensional mantra of 'Think globally, act globally (and nationally and locally)'. Whereas Postmodern's oppositional either/or thinking often pits global against local, Worldcentric's both/ and thinking sees how global affects local and vice versa; solutions are therefore needed at all levels and become complementary.

This expansive movement in identity is part of the benefit of the new thinking platform. Earlier we observed how over the course of evolution human social units have increased in size; accompanying this has been a necessary evolution in how we identify as belonging in our society, which we call our 'civic identity'.

Civic identity is about that aspect of our values and worldview that we term 'citizenship'. It is based on how we understand the world and its problems as well as our role therein, including our rights – what we are permitted to be – and our responsibilities – what we are required to contribute. But it has a further dimension, which these days is becoming increasingly important. Functionally, our civic identity rests on our own personal assessment of whether cooperation and governance are required to solve societal, environmental or economic issues at a particular level – local, national or global. Most people in Western countries take a local and national civic identity for granted. We have no difficulty whatsoever in recognizing the functional necessity of local and national governance, and we readily participate in elections on both those levels.

This book's aim is to awaken in us a third, *global* level; to realize that some form of global cooperation and governance is functionally necessary. Not to be confused with politics, civics is fundamentally about the *perception*, by citizens, of a need for governance. Politics, on the other hand, is what happens *after* governance (or formal government) has been established at any level. In that sense, civics is prior to politics.

How does our civic identity affect the way we approach our everyday world? If our level of civic identity happened to be relatively shallow – that is, at say an *ego*centric level (Survival, Tribal or Warrior) – we would understand the problems we encounter in purely immediate personal terms. For example, imagine you woke up in the morning to find a storm had blown the roof off your house. How would you react if your level of civic identity were merely egocentric? Since you would understand the problem only in personal or local terms, this is how you would see the action or governance required: I need to fix my house with a stronger roof.

If, on the other hand, your level of civic identity were at a deeper ethnocentric level (Traditional), your understanding would extend to include those who belong to your locality, tribe or religion. In that case, you and others in the local community would feel moved to act on that level, and the local government or the tribal or religious authorities might then strengthen building regulations or customs. If your civic identity were at a still-deeper *nation*centric level (Modern or Postmodern), you would see the problem in even broader terms. So you might additionally campaign to get your government to legislate to reduce the nation's carbon emissions. And if your civic identity was at the even deeper and broader *world*centric level, you would understand the vicious circle of DGC and so, in addition to all of the lower-level actions, you would focus most of your attention on how DGC could be overcome and how a form of effective international cooperation could be achieved. Being now focused on realistic cooperation (rather than on competition or idealistic cooperation) means that while you still hold out for universal freedoms, you welcome *more* governance in the world, as a tool towards global self-regulation.

Just as consciousness levels are highly uneven across the world so are levels of civic identity. Being partitioned into 200-odd nation states, we might conclude that most people are at a nationcentric level of civic identity. But this is not so. Despite national partitioning, vast numbers of people especially within developing countries, still remain at a broadly ethno-centric civic level. They still identify primarily with their tribe, religion or locality. As the Arab Spring revolutions suggested, these societies are still struggling with ideas of national-level governance and democracy. This unevenness is reflected in the World Values Survey which showed that 47 per cent of survey respondents identified primarily with their locality, while a further 38 per cent identified with their nation. An overwhelming 85 per cent of the world's population thus hold either an ethnocentric or at best a nationcentric civic identity.[1]

To be writing a book about global cooperation in these unfavourable circumstances might seem far-fetched, but, as we mentioned in the Introduction, it doesn't take many people to change the world and it never has. It only requires a critical number, which some suggest may be as little as 10 per cent of an overall population. This is why awakening a global civic identity in a small yet critical number of people is so important. Those at a nationcentric level, still holding the Myth of the Sovereign Nation as their civic identity, need to let go of it and shift to a worldcentric identity. But, as we saw, our outdated attachment to that Myth is what stands in the way.

From worldcentric thinking to worldcentric action

With the identification of worldcentric thinking new vital questions come into view:

- What forms of practical action does this new way of thinking disclose?

- What kind of actions could possibly overcome the death grip that DGC has us in?

From the new worldcentric platform we are able to recognize new guidelines towards answers to these questions, including:

- If we accept that DGC is a truly global phenomenon beyond the control of any government, the only way to overcome it is through *world*centric – that is, *global* – action.

- Some system of coordinated international action that includes all, or virtually all nations, seems to be unavoidable.

- All nations would have to be able to implement policies to solve global problems without fearing that capital or corporations might move elsewhere.

- If all nations moved together on certain critical policies, no nation need lose out because capital and investors would have nowhere to run.

- No nation need fear becoming uncompetitive, and DGC would be outsmarted. We would all win.

The idea of virtually all nations acting in concert may at first sound outlandish and inconceivable. This is because it is a Second-Tier thought. However, accepting that it is essential to our civilized survival is part and parcel of the difficulty we face in accepting any new context for governance, the challenge that inevitably confronts us when we have to discard an outdated yet familiar way of thinking and adopt a new worldview, a new identity. It is the challenge inherent in Einstein's advice: that present problems will only be solved with new thinking and the new and more encompassing forms of action that it discloses.

Five minutes left

Throughout this book we've been arguing that the current model of competition has reached its limit and only global cooperation can overcome the hold that DGC has over us. Only global cooperation can deliver a reasonably just and sustainable world. But if DGC's vicious circle were to be broken, what would global cooperation actually look like and what would it be able to deliver?

As we enter what Einstein might have called this book's final five minutes, we consider two issues: first, the potential benefits of global cooperation and, second, the criteria that a transformative programme of worldcentric political action would have to meet in order to achieve it.

Let us start with the potential benefits. Here we propose ten concrete benefits that a more responsive form of global governance could bring to our world.

1. Global warming could be brought within sustainable limits and the global commons adequately protected for the future.

2. Multinational corporations, the financial sector and the rich could be more fairly taxed and regulated, so reducing inequality and restoring national public finances to health.

3. The global financial system could be reformed to serve the needs of the real economy rather than the economy serving the financial system.[2]

4. Global governance, if designed cooperatively and appropriately, could reduce intercultural and international tensions, reduce inequality and migration and so substantially remove the causes of terrorism.

5. Just as cooperation in Europe has today made war between EU states unthinkable, the same would become more likely on a global platform, reducing the risk of large-scale conflicts.

6. Consequently military spending could be dramatically reduced, releasing enormous sums for health, education and development in developing countries. This, in turn, could help curb population growth so gradually bringing it back into balance.

7. Global governance could ensure that the full environmental impact of goods and services was properly reflected in their cost. Externalities, as economists call these impacts, would thus be internalized.

8. Wealth could be redistributed more equitably across national borders on a debt-free basis, so supporting good governance and stronger economies in the most deprived nations.[3] This would allow people to make a decent living in their home countries, dramatically reducing economic migration and associated intercultural tensions.

9. Following a graduated approach that takes the particular needs of poorer countries into account, much higher environmental, social and governmental standards could be implemented worldwide.

10. Global governance would enable the localization of economies and cultures everywhere. For example, global taxes could be raised in ways that make long-distance transportation much more expensive and thus favour local production and consumption. Since such a tax would be applied globally, no one's competitiveness would suffer.

These benefits are largely the benefits of scale. Strangely enough, they have – in principle – much in common with those that societies in the late Middle Ages started to enjoy once they stopped competing and fighting with one another and transformed their small states into larger nation states. Because together they were safer and stronger; together they were more prosperous; together they were greater than the sum of their parts. The same goes for humanity today as we find ourselves facing the transition to global cooperation.

Ten boxes to tick

If these ten points describe the potential, what criteria would define a worldcentric form of global politics that could set the process in motion to deliver these benefits? What are the boxes that a successful campaign for global cooperation would have to tick?

From the broader worldcentric perspective that we gain from our new vantage point on the top of our hill, many of these now appear self-evident. But it's worth briefly enumerating them before we move on to consider the Simpol campaign in the next chapter. We've distilled them down to ten essential criteria.

1. Global and simultaneous

Economic globalization is now so advanced that merely national solutions can't work any more. Worse still, destructive competition between nations – what we've called DGC – runs the show. If its vicious circle is to be broken, appropriate reforms must be implemented globally so that the scale of governance matches the scale of the economy. Nothing less can possibly suffice if we're to have a just and sustainable planet. Only then will our governance system be back in sync with the new governance *context* that DGC represents. But since we have no institution of world government capable of implementing solutions globally – nor do we need one, as we'll show next – we will require all or sufficient nation states to do so instead.

If all or sufficient act together, global coverage can be achieved. And to avoid every nation's fear of DGC's first-mover competitive disadvantage, nations will have to implement the necessary reforms *simultaneously* on the same date and at precisely the same time.

If this sounds too outlandish, it could be that nationcentrism may still be lurking in your psyche. Try to remember that it only sounds outlandish to the extent that we have not taken the new globalized reality fully on board. Accept that reality and you start to see global and simultaneous implementation as perfectly logical and necessary. We can freely acknowledge that it represents a huge challenge, but the point is that it's no longer one that *phases* us. We know global cooperation is necessary. We know it's difficult. We just need to get on with it.

In fact, throughout history global and simultaneous implementation has always been the basis for governance. Any new national law, for example, is customarily implemented globally, in the sense that it applies to the whole national territory and not just to part of it. Also, it is implemented simultaneously, since it comes into force on a given date. Take the British practice of driving on the left side of the road. If Britain were to decide to switch to driving on the right, it would hardly implement this only in one part of the country but not others. If it did, you can imagine the result. Rather, it would be done globally and simultaneously, as it was when Sweden made that change at precisely 6 a.m. on 3 September 1967. As we'll see in our final chapter, cooperation in biology has been the same, too. Global and simultaneous implementation, we'll discover, is literally as old as the hills.

That's because it works.

2. Citizen-powered not state- or UN-dependent

The need for global, simultaneous international action brings us to consider the existing global institutions, such as the United Nations (UN), the International Monetary Fund (IMF), the World Bank (WB) and the World Trade Organization (WTO). If global action is necessary, our initial assumption might be that these are the institutions that ought to take on the task. But can they?

At first glance, the global remit of these organizations might appear to indicate that they are worldcentric. But a closer look reveals the UN to be too deeply constrained by the nation-state system it is inescapably a part of. To deliver the kind of global reforms needed, the UN would have to be in a position of some authority over nation states. But the reverse is the case, because the only powers available under the UN Charter are the powers of sanction and the use of force. These powers, however, are not exercised by the UN as an autonomous independent entity but by the Security Council – that is, by the USA, Russia, China, France and Great Britain who are the Security Council's five permanent members. The only powers the UN has are not even its own powers at all.

This leaves the UN caught in a contradiction. If it were ever to gain a sufficient measure of autonomous authority over nation states, then nation states – and especially the most powerful ones – would first have to voluntarily cede their existing authority to the UN. But, as repeated failures to reform the UN have shown, any change likely to compromise the power and authority of the Security Council is vetoed by one or other of its permanent members.[4] In a competitive world the most powerful nations insist on maintaining their autonomy, a situation that could be regarded as yet another manifestation of DGC. Despite its worldcentric ambitions, the UN remains – through no fault of its own – too heavily beholden to nation states, subtly but decisively nationcentric. While the UN certainly deserves our support, we'd be unwise to rely on it to deliver the kind of reforms needed.

The same problem applies to the IMF and the World Bank. They are governed not by the UN nor by any equal international consensus but by their principal shareholders who are, once again, the world's most powerful nations.[5] Worse still, these institutions do not govern the global economy but mainly react to it. And given that their thinking currently remains hijacked by neoliberal orthodoxy, it's hardly surprising that whenever things go wrong they inevitably prescribe yet more competition rather than less: more austerity, more deregulation, more privatization and so on.

The WTO, on the other hand, has a more consensual structure, since it is governed by its 200-odd member-nations equally. But, in practice, only the most powerful nations are able to use its rules and dispute-settlement procedure to protect or project their interests. Beyond that, the rules embodied in the WTO only serve, arguably, to regulate fairly a global trading system which, because it already structurally favours the most powerful national economies, provides merely a veneer of fairness.

The problem is that the WTO only governs *trade*, so the vital factors of society, especially labour and the environment, are left out of its remit. While the destructive competition that is endemic to the WTO's trade-liberalization agenda systematically favours capital over the interests of labour and the environment, the resulting social and environmental crises, such as economic migration and global warming, are left to nation states to deal with. But, as we have seen, DGC comprehensively prevents governments from regulating adequately.

It is difficult to see, then, how the UN or the other existing global institutions could evolve to a position from which they could drive nation states to deliver the necessary reforms in a manner that could be described as fair or acceptable or in a way that is accountable to citizens. They are simply too beholden to nation states and especially to the most powerful ones. Meanwhile, nation states, as we've seen, are in turn strongly guided by global markets and DGC. This combination not only ensures that global problems keep on worsening, it reminds us just how forlorn is the hope that either the established global institutions or the world's nations could ever solve global problems if left wholly to their own devices.

This is why *citizens* must drive a new form of worldcentric politics. The campaign must give us citizens sufficient power to *compel* our governments towards cooperation. Like it or not, we must take responsibility for solving global problems, and our campaign must give us that power.

3. Immediate universal self-interest

It is obvious that solving global problems such as climate change is in everyone's best interests, which is why environmentalists struggle to understand why governments find cooperation so difficult. The problem is that it's not in nations' *immediate* best interests.

The obstacles are twofold. It's not just that DGC would cause a competitive disadvantage to any nation that moved significantly in advance of others, there is also the problem of winners and losers. The fatal flaw is that, presently, the world is trying to solve global problems *one* single issue at a time. But take almost any issue, such as carbon-emissions reductions, and we almost always find that there are some nations that win and others that lose. The big polluting nations would have the most to cut and therefore the highest costs, so they'd have the most to lose. The result is that there is no incentive for them to cooperate. Small wonder we see only inadequate progress.

The solution is to negotiate two or more complementary issues together so that nations that might lose out on one issue can gain on another. Imagine, for example, that alongside a negotiation to reduce carbon emissions, governments had also agreed to negotiate a global-currency transactions tax.[6] The billions of dollars that even a fraction of a per cent levied on all currency trades would raise could then be apportioned so that the losers on the climate part of the agreement were compensated. In that way action could, in principle at least, be made to be in every nation's immediate interests. It would make them *want* to act *now*.

We're not suggesting this would be easy. All we're pointing out is that, apart from fairly exceptional circumstances such as the Montreal Protocol that succeeded in banning ozone-depleting chlorofluorocarbons (CFCs), the single-issue approach is designed to fail. The reality is that we will not get substantive international agreements that are adequate and actually stick unless they are in every nation's immediate interests, and that cannot occur unless agreements incorporate *multiple* issues. This, then, is another criterion that a worldcentric global political campaign would have to meet.

4. Not 'one-size-fits-all' governance

A common concern about the idea of global governance is the fear of monolithic uniformity: all nations and peoples having to conform to the same 'one-size-fits-all' global laws and regulations. But this need not be the case, nor should it be. Just as governments at the national level apply many devices such as exemptions, redistributions and compensations in order to differentiate between the varying needs and abilities of different parts of the nation, the same can and should be the case at the global level. Many national laws, such as income tax, are also progressive and ensure (or ought to!) that the rich pay more and the poor pay less. Global laws and regulations could be designed in a similar fashion. An international agreement could thus include various provisions to ensure a proper differentiation between nations according to the needs and abilities of each.

Moreover, global revenues need not necessarily be levied on citizens but could instead be raised from financial markets and from the now possible higher corporation taxes. These could be used especially to assist poorer nations on a debt-free, interest-free basis even if certain safeguards might need to be built in. Various compensatory measures, then, could be negotiated as part and parcel of an overall global agreement to ensure that the particular needs and capabilities of each nation were taken properly into account. The result would be diversity within a broader uniformity from which all nations would benefit.

5. Legally binding and enforceable

Designing international negotiations to provide the best chance of all nations winning is not only vital for action it is also necessary, because any agreement worth its salt needs enforcing on an ongoing basis. The trick here is to remember that if an agreement is seen by each nation to be in its *interests*, so each nation will also see the agreement's enforcement as in its interests, too. This is a further reason why a multi-issue policy framework is so important. The necessary verification and enforcement measures could then be included as an integral part of any agreement. In addition, in order to make any agreement legally binding upon each nation, each would need to pass the necessary legislation at a national level, specifying the internationally agreed date and time for it to come into force.

6. Accommodate non-democratic nations and be accountable to citizens in democratic states

When most of us think about global governance we almost automatically think of an elected world parliament or something similar. This is because of our nationcentric thinking habit that leads us to take whatever is our image of *national* governance and project it up to the *global* level. But there is little chance that non-democratic states such as (at the time of writing) China would be willing to agree to an elected world parliament. Allowing its citizens to participate in such elections would only invite them to wonder why they don't enjoy the same rights at the national level. Such notions of democratic world parliaments do not take non-democratic nations properly into account, and in order for it to work all or sufficient nations must be accommodated.

This is why a global and simultaneously implemented agreement offers a much more appropriate alternative. If you can achieve an *agreement* and can enforce it cooperatively, you don't need a world parliament or, indeed, any other new institution at the global level. Besides, an agreement can more easily accommodate both democratic and non-democratic nations. While democratic nations might decide to participate in the agreement as a result of their own internal democratic processes, non-democratic nations can do so by the simple decision of their government.

Vital though it is to achieve international consensus, there is another important criterion to be met. This is that citizens – at least those in democratic countries – must have a *binding* say in the policies to be implemented. To involve solely the world's governments in the design and implementation of global policies without input from or accountability to citizens in democratic countries would be to invite a top-down global autocracy – exactly the scenario some New World Order conspiracy theorists fear.[7]

We also need to ensure that the views of citizens in highly populous democratic nations, such as India, are not permitted to overwhelm the views of citizens in less populous ones. If this were not addressed, citizens in small democratic nations would effectively have no influence at all. An appropriate balance could be achieved initially by citizens of each democratic country engaging in their own national democratic process to formulate the policies they desire to be globally agreed and implemented. Next, when it comes to trying to achieve agreement on those policies at the international level, this would then be subject to the *equality* of all nations, whether they are democratic or not.

Clearly, this would effectively give greater weight to the votes of citizens in smaller democratic countries. But this seems to be the only practical way that accountability to citizens in democratic nations can be assured while equally including non-democratic nations, that equality among nations being, after all, inherent in the concept of all nations agreeing to act simultaneously.

Under this global governance arrangement, then, all nations would be respected on their own terms and none would be ignored. Meanwhile, citizens in democratic nations would have a binding influence on the policies to be implemented.

Some of us in democratic countries may initially see such a proposal as a betrayal of global democracy, as somehow compromising the ideal of every adult on the planet having an equal vote. It's worth remembering, however, that when democracy first emerged with the European Enlightenment, it did not emerge in the more developed form we in the West are familiar with today but in what was then only an embryonic, workable form. Many centuries were required for it to evolve into its present manifestation. In much the same way, we could imagine that strict global democracy – one equal vote for every adult on the planet – might only evolve some time *after* global governance of the kind we are proposing here had been achieved. But today such arrangements would, for reasons we've outlined, be extremely premature as well as unviable.

7. National sovereignty: the subsidiarity criterion

Another important criterion to be met by our global governance campaign is that it must respect the principal of national sovereignty. Only issues that *cannot* be decided nationally should be decided globally. This is vital to reassure individual nations and their peoples that their autonomy is preserved and is not limited any more than absolutely necessary to solve global problems. Whatever still works at the lower, national level would thus be safeguarded, while what doesn't work, or cannot be solved, would be taken up and dealt with at the global level by the global agreement we're describing. We therefore need a clear, practical subsidiarity criterion for distinguishing between national policies and global policies.

Here we encounter a surprise. This requirement, we find, is inherently satisfied by the logic of the need for simultaneous action. A satisfactory distinction between national and global policies is already accomplished if we differentiate policies that need *simultaneous* action from those *that don't*. What belongs where becomes evident if we apply the following question, the subsidiarity criterion, to each policy proposal:

Would the unilateral implementation of the policy measure (i.e. its implementation by a single nation or by a relatively small group of nations) be likely to have an adverse effect on the nation's (or group's) competitiveness?[8]

If the answer is *no*, then the policy concerned is clearly one that individual nations or restricted groups of nations can happily implement independently, as they mostly do today.[9] Policies in this category could include those such as national housing policy, health and education policy or culturally defined issues such as capital punishment or abortion. For policies where the answer is *yes*, on the other hand, these policies – and only these – need to be dealt with at the global level because only simultaneous implementation can overcome the barrier that destructive global competition represents.

Accordingly, policies are differentiated into two distinct categories: *unilateral* policies or *simultaneous* policies. Unilateral policies effectively belong to the national context, while simultaneous policies belong to the nascent context of global cooperation we are describing. The simultaneous mode of policy implementation thus represents, potentially, the new, higher, more authentic level of worldcentric civic-political complexity, humanity's next evolutionary step, which is the new level of cooperative global governance.

Far from curtailing national sovereignty, implementing policies simultaneously would actually enhance it. Currently, individual nations would *like* to implement many policies, but their fear of losing out to others means they are unable to. By making such policies feasible again, simultaneous implementation would enhance national sovereignty by bringing a greater range of possibilities back into our hands. Indeed, the application of the subsidiarity criterion would enable all sorts of global problems to be dealt with in a far more effective high-impact way, giving us all greater relative autonomy: greater power and flexibility as we proceed together into the future.

8. Neither NGO nor political party

We come, now, to perhaps the most interesting and challenging criterion of all. Earlier we saw how bargaining does not work, whether it is attempted from inside or outside the established political system. This means that there is no point in devising a global political campaign on the model of an NGO such as Greenpeace, Avaaz or Occupy. Protest and the CSR approach, important though they are, cannot do the job. Unless it occurred simultaneously in every country, even a bloody revolution would be useless. Capital would instantly exit countries where the revolution took place only to carry on elsewhere exactly as before.

Equally, as we saw in Chapter 4, the problem of pseudo-democracy means that party politics is an idea past its sell-by date, so starting a new ethical political party, changing the voting system, or other inside approaches won't work. Even transnational political parties have little chance of success because it is highly unlikely that enough national branches of any such party would ever be simultaneously in office in enough nations to permit them to coordinate their policies.[10] Even if it found itself in power, any national branch of a transnational party would be unable to escape its prime responsibility to protect its national interest. With few of its sister-parties in power in other countries and with global markets being highly competitive, it would find itself having to subordinate its global aspirations to the prime objective of pursuing its own nation's interests, caught in DGC's vicious circle, just as all existing parties are today.[11]

A genuine and effective worldcentric political campaign cannot, therefore, be a conventional NGO or a political party, and yet it must somehow be able to wield considerable political power, because, as we saw in Criterion 2, it must offer citizens a powerful way to drive their governments towards global cooperation. It must put *citizens* back in the driving seat. The ability of those of us in democratic countries to compel our governments towards cooperation is absolutely crucial. As implementers of change, governments remain key, but today they are beholden to global markets and DGC and not to the people.

This means that it's simply not enough to have great proposals concerning which reforms are needed to fix the economy, the climate or the voting system and so on. Paul Mason has fine recommendations for suppressing monopolies and socializing the financial system,[12] Thomas Piketty proposes progressive global taxation on capital,[13] the global justice movement has various prescriptions for sustainability and the UN always has a raft of development goals. But all of these approaches fail in their avoidance of how they could be implemented. The unifying precondition is that we have to have a means of *getting such reforms implemented* in a globalized world. In other words, we *first* need a means of rescuing governments from the clutches of DGC, from vested interests and from pseudo-democracy and for driving them to cooperatively implement the needed measures.

This means that, despite everything, we are forced to reconsider the inside approach. We simply *must* find a new and potent way to use our hard-won democratic processes to drive governments towards global cooperation but in a completely new, transcendent worldcentric way. Here the central conundrum any would-be worldcentric political campaign has to solve is this: in order to drive national governments towards cooperation it must somehow interface *directly* with our right to vote but *without* being a political party. Where does this leave us?

On first appearances, it seems we have utterly checkmated our own argument. But in the next chapter we'll see that, in fact, the opposite is the case. This is because worldcentric thinking transcends this dilemma. We are *already* radically free, and our votes, if used appropriately, are already unimaginably powerful – we just need to recognize it. And in the next chapter, we will.

9. A cooperatively developed policy platform that avoids the inclusion of harmful policies

In the previous chapter we saw that nations and peoples across the world reside at quite different and conflicting levels of consciousness. It is therefore to be expected that they will hold different views and will likely disagree about which policies they see as being most appropriate for global implementation. A worldcentric political campaign would need to overcome these divergences.

National societies broadly residing at the Traditional level, for example, may wish to see the global implementation of the death penalty or of shariah law, while nations or societies at a Postmodern level might wish to ban aeroplanes to stop carbon emissions. Clearly, these are extreme examples. Nevertheless, the problem we face is how appropriate global policies can possibly be arrived at when participants hold such divergent perspectives. Although the differing values of each national society need to be heard and taken into proper account, we somehow need to end up only with Early or Late Worldcentric policies, policies that would be beneficial for all and which take the whole world into account.

Why should this be so? Privileging the Worldcentric levels may at first appear contradictory to the principle of fairness, or it may seem elitist and undemocratic, but prioritizing those levels is both necessary and appropriate because, as we suggested earlier, they benefit from a special quality possessed by none of the preceding levels. Whereas each of the preceding First-Tier levels generally sees only its *own* perspective as valid and so rejects the others, the Worldcentric Second-Tier levels are the first that recognize, honour and integrate *all* of the previous levels. They are, in effect, the only levels that are genuinely worldcentric, the only levels capable of devising global policies that would be genuinely beneficial and acceptable to all.

This doesn't mean that some grand committee of worldcentric 'wise elders' should develop policies. Rather, as we'll later see, the Simpol proposal permits beneficial, worldcentric global policies to be arrived at entirely consensually and – paradoxically – with the whole world's participation and involvement.

10. A tag that builds global trust

Before any kind of international negotiation could take place, the people and their politicians will need to trust each other. So will governments. The building of sufficient international trust is an absolute prerequisite to implementing significant global agreements and sticking to them. All parties will need to know who they can trust to participate in any agreement and who is still in doubt.

In his book on the evolution of cooperation in human societies, *Ultrasociety*, Peter Turchin explains why trust is so fundamental and argues that symbolic tags play a crucial role in building it. Our distant ancestors relied solely on face-to-face cooperation among a circle that included only relatives and friends. Anyone unknown was a potential enemy, so an important evolutionary breakthrough was the capacity to tag cooperating groups with symbolic markers such as language and dialect, styles of clothing and ornamentation or tattoos as well as behaviours like participation in collective rituals. Symbolically tagged cooperative groups allowed humans to increase the scale of cooperation beyond the circle of those personally known and to encompass whole tribes or nations.[14]

At the global level, the building of sufficient trust, to the point at which binding agreements can be negotiated and simultaneously implemented, is likely to be subject to the same criteria. Our worldcentric political campaign must therefore include a marker – a tag or a brand – that distinguishes those people, politicians and governments who support it from those that don't yet support it.

It doesn't take many people to change the world

Before we present the Simultaneous Policy (Simpol) campaign, which we suggest meets the above criteria, let us first address another of this book's claims: that changing the world need not take as many people as we think. On this, we agree with the dictum widely attributed to Margaret Mead: 'Never doubt that a small group of thoughtful, committed citizens can change the world; indeed, it's the only thing that ever has.'[15]

This may feel counterintuitive, perhaps because we live in an age of massness. Mass global communications, mass media, mass consumerism and so on contribute to our feeling isolated and powerless, that we don't matter. But what does history tell us? It turns out that many of the key transitions we have alluded to were inaugurated not by masses of people but by a relatively small group. The Enlightenment, for example, stemmed from the emergence of a handful of creative individuals in Europe who were operating at the Modern level. Ken Wilber notes that the emergence of Enlightenment thinking can be seen as what he calls a 'probability wave'. Such developments are inevitably inaugurated and channelled by a group of leading intellectuals, he argues. As with any profound social transformation that represents what he calls genuine 'vertical' transformation, this group has already been riding the edge of an emerging probability wave – a new way of thinking. It is likely then that such opportunities for transformation that herald a higher level of thinking and governance are led not by the many but the few.[16]

Simply put, new levels of consciousness, such as the Modernist

Enlightenment are inaugurated not by masses of people but by a relatively small group. That group represents what we today call 'thought-leaders' rather than those with highest social advantage. New technologies, such as Gutenberg's printing press, as we saw, kick off the process, which leads to a new context for governance. Then philosophers such as Bacon, Descartes, Locke, Voltaire and Newton help to bring in the necessary new thinking. It was this relatively small group, and not the wider societies in which they lived, that instigated the Enlightenment.

It is only after some time that the new worldview, driven by the effects of emerging technologies, eventually beds in and spreads throughout the culture. Such transformations probably involve what Malcolm Gladwell calls a 'tipping point'. Wilber speculates that when just 10 per cent of the population arrives at a new worldview a tipping point is reached after which the new way of thinking proliferates rapidly throughout the entire society.[17]

New technologies and new thinking aren't the only drivers of such transformations. As we saw in the previous chapter it is also the prevailing life conditions that help. In our global era, the deepening crises of climate change, financial disasters, resource scarcity, mass economic migration and so on are all life conditions that are helping to push us towards the next level of thinking and governance. Global technologies and their effects – including DGC – are already with us.

However, as we've been arguing, it's our *thinking* that badly needs to catch up. If Wilber is correct, an approximate 10 per cent tipping point is likely to apply now for the worldcentric worldview to proliferate rapidly, so we need to build towards 10 per cent of us adopting the new world-centric thinking.

This is why *you*, the reader, matter.

New thinking is critical, but even that is not enough. To change the world, a new system of governance needs to be brought in. Until it is, no amount of new thinking will change anything, so we also need a new worldcentric *political practice* – a new political paradigm – that is powerful enough actually to effect the transformation.

A new and potent worldcentric political practice is what calls us now, and in the next chapter we will suggest what this might look like and present an early example that is already in action.

8. The Simultaneous Policy

Turning the tables: John's story

It's a bright spring day in Blackheath, where I live in south-east London. It's early morning, and the plentiful squirrel population is busy darting up and down the trees. All seems well with the world – and then my doorbell rings. I open the front door and, quickly focusing on the caller standing in front of me, I notice she sports a large red rosette. I'm instantly reminded that a general election is due on 7 May, just a few weeks away. By all accounts it's going to be a close-run thing, and all the party candidates are chasing every last vote.

'Good morning, Mr Bunzl,' the local Labour Party candidate cheerily greets me with a smile. She has a pile of leaflets at the ready. 'I just wanted to ask whether I can count on receiving your vote on 7 May.'

Suddenly wide awake, I'm prepared for the encounter.

'You know what,' I begin to build my response, 'I'm actually a little fed up with the inability of party politics to deal with the really big global issues. So I'm going to be voting for any politician within reason that has signed the pledge to implement the Simultaneous Policy alongside other governments. Whichever candidate signs the Simpol Pledge gets my vote.'

I have had my say, and we both retreat within a moment of silence.

My campaigning visitor seems momentarily confused – taken aback even – at this reversal. Everyone takes for granted that it's us, the voters, who have to do the choosing, and our choice is supposed to be between politicians. It is not *politicians* who have to choose whether to support a particular policy. Whatever is going on inside her, she seems to be clocking that whatever she was about to say about Labour's manifesto won't make much difference.

'Er, what actually is the Simultaneous Policy?' she eventually enquires, hoping it may be something she can support in order to gain my vote.

I smile, hand her one of my Simpol leaflets along with a pledge form for politicians to sign and wish her a pleasant day, content that I have handed the choice back to her. As she walks back down my front-garden path, she has only one issue to consider: whether or not to sign the pledge to implement Simpol. If she does, she won't be taking any risk because of the condition of 'simultaneous implementation', which is built into the pledge and which we will explain below. On the contrary, she will gain the prospect of gaining my vote and the votes of the growing number of other Simpol supporters in her area. Should she refuse, she risks that I (and other Simpol supporters) will very likely vote for one of her rivals who chose to sign instead, in which case she could lose her seat.

The tables have been turned.

The case for Simpol

In the last chapter we saw that in order to drive governments to cooperate we will need a campaign that not only operates internationally but is rooted in our already-existing rights, as citizens, to elect our own representatives. Such a campaign cannot, we said, be a political party and, as John's experience above suggests, neither does it need to be. In fact, turning the tables in the way described is based on three fundamental realizations that arise from what we have covered previously. It is on these founding realizations that the Simultaneous Policy campaign rests:

Simpol's founding realizations

1. Party politics has become substantially meaningless.
2. We must create our *own* global-policy platform.
3. Simultaneous implementation makes Simpol a no-risk proposition.

1. **Party politics has become substantially meaningless** because Destructive Global Competition means that voting in a conventional manner by choosing between political parties has become a choice that is no choice. We are left with pseudo-democracy because the policies of whomsoever we vote into power inevitably have to conform to the parameters set by DGC. Once we get over the desperate sense of powerlessness that this evokes, we find ourselves paradoxically liberated. Knowing that party politics has become substantially meaningless in terms of solving global problems, we get some good news: we need not lose any more time creating new political parties or continuing to exercise our pseudo-choice between existing parties. Instead, we are radically free, free to turn the tables.

2. **We citizens must therefore create our *own* global-policy platform** because, as we have seen, DGC makes it impossible for politicians to do so. Politicians may *say* they can reconcile social justice and environmental sustainability with staying internationally

competitive, but, as we have seen, these two aims are mutually exclusive. Remaining confined to the narrow policy parameters set by DGC, politicians simply cannot deliver, and they cannot escape the dilemma.

From this it follows that we citizens are free to develop our own set of global policies. In fact, it is not so much that we have the option to develop them, we absolutely must. Since our governments are beholden to DGC, no one else can. And since any effective platform of policies must be implemented simultaneously – by all or sufficient nations – it must be a 'simultaneous policy'.

3. **The condition of simultaneous implementation makes supporting Simpol a no-risk proposition** because politicians of whatever party can freely support the campaign knowing that its platform of policies would only be implemented *if and when all or sufficient other nations support it, too*. Until then, politicians can carry on with their usual policies, as DGC determines that they must. Signing a pledge to implement a set of policies on the basis of simultaneous implementation thus presents them with no risk whatsoever and no conflict with their party's existing policies.

This is why the campaign we are describing is called the Simultaneous Policy – Simpol. Simpol, in fact, has two principal aspects. First, it is a *policy*, a range of policies to solve global problems. Second, it is a political *process*, a process by which we citizens can drive our politicians and governments to implement the policy. Later we will look at what policies Simpol might contain and how they may be developed. But first we take a look at Simpol as a political process.

The Simpol campaign was launched in the UK in 2000. Still small and run by volunteers, it has been steadily gathering political support by encouraging its small but growing number of citizen-supporters to turn the tables in the way John described in his story at the beginning of this chapter.

In the most recent national election in the UK in 2015, supporters of Simpol-UK, the UK branch of Simpol, succeeded in getting more than 600 candidates from all the main UK political parties to sign the Simpol Pledge. Thirty of these signatories were elected as Members of Parliament (MPs), and many have left their comments on why they back the policy on the Simpol website.[1] Signatories to the Simpol Pledge declare their agreement to implement Simpol's range of global policies, subject to those policies eventually being formulated and internationally agreed, and subject to all or sufficient other governments also agreeing to implement them simultaneously.[2]

How could Simpol-UK's relatively small number of supporters achieve such a big result?

Using our votes to take back our world

The answer lies in a new, powerful way of voting that Simpol has been pioneering and which its supporters are adopting. Here's how it works.

When you sign on to the Simpol campaign in the run-up to an election, your national Simpol organization sends a message on your behalf to all the candidates standing in your constituency (as electoral areas are known in the UK) informing them that you and other Simpol supporters will be giving strong voting preference to politicians or parties that sign the pledge to the probable exclusion of those who don't. In this way, with support for the campaign growing, Simpol is becoming a powerful voting bloc, putting strong electoral pressure on politicians.

The message that you and other Simpol supporters are sending to politicians is clear. On the one hand, signing the pledge does not represent a risk for them, because the implementation of Simpol would occur only at some future date, only once its package of policies had been agreed and only if sufficient governments around the world had signed up, too. And yet, on the other, they need to sign the pledge if they want a chance of getting our votes. Politicians who sign it therefore attract the Simpol voting bloc, the potentially vital additional votes they may need to win their seats. But, if they *fail* to sign, they risk losing those votes to other candidates who may have signed instead. And if that happens they could *lose* their seats.

To sum up: for politicians, Simpol is a win–win. Signing the pledge at this stage represents their support for Simpol only *in principle* and is thus a no-risk proposition. A politician who fails to sign, by contrast, risks losing those votes to political competitors who have signed, and that could spell political disaster.

A cynic might think that politicians would only sign up to gain our votes only to cancel their pledge after the election. But there would be little point in this since Simpol's implementation cannot take place *until all or sufficient nations* are on board, so, until implementation occurs, there is nothing for a politician to go back on. Cancelling their pledge therefore makes no sense. If a politician *did* cancel their pledge, the national branch of Simpol would publish it prominently on its website so that no Simpol supporter would ever be likely to vote for that politician again. Once made, then, cancelling the pledge is simply not in a politician's interests. And when it came to the point when all or sufficient nations were on board and implementation could proceed, world problems would, by that time, likely be so critical that no one in their right minds would be likely to hesitate. By then, implementation would have become in everyone's interests anyway.

For citizens, supporting Simpol is rather like having two votes: one that operates at the global level and the other at the national. Signing on to the campaign, accompanied by the email that your national Simpol organization sends on your behalf to all the candidates in your constituency or to your MP, represents your *global* vote. Then, on election day, you get your *national* vote, too, just like everyone else.

It is important to stress that Simpol supporters do not give up their autonomy as voters. Their commitment is only to give *strong preference* to candidates who have signed the pledge to the *probable* exclusion of those who don't. Each supporter thus still retains the ultimate right to vote as they please.

The domino effect

The combination of a no-risk pledge and the fear of losing if they don't sign can create a domino effect among politicians. In our recent experience in the 2015 UK election, there were some constituencies in which when one candidate signed the others quickly followed. In fact, once *one* major candidate signs, the others have little choice, especially in closely contested seats.

In the highly marginal constituency of Weston-super-Mare in the far south-west of England, for example, the Conservative Party candidate had already signed the pledge at a previous election, so his name already appeared on our website as a pledged politician. Then, as campaigning got under way in 2015, and perhaps realizing that one of his competitors had already signed, the Liberal Democrat candidate signed on 3 March. A day later the Labour candidate signed, too, and the day after that the Green Party candidate also signed. With the sole exception of the UKIP candidate, we had a full house. The result? For Simpol it was already clear, even though the election was still two months off: whoever won the seat

Simpol won regardless. Another MP would be added to the growing number of those in the UK and elsewhere who are pledged to implement its global-justice agenda as soon as sufficient other MPs and governments sign on.

Much the same domino effect occurred in Scotland during the European elections in 2014. Catherine Stihler, one of the Labour candidates, was first to sign the pledge on 1 May. A few days later, perhaps seeing that she had signed, one of the Scottish Nationalist candidates, Alyn Smith, followed suit. Finally, another Labour candidate, David Martin, got in on the act, too. All three are now Members of the European Parliament (MEPs) and pledged, alongside some other MEPs, to implement Simpol alongside other governments.

The Simpol campaign doesn't merely work in the run-up to elections. In every country, as each new supporter joins the campaign, we immediately inform their representative parliamentary member, regardless of whether an election is imminent or not. On a few occasions, just one supporter is sufficient to encourage the sitting MP to sign the pledge. On 18 August 2015, for example, Jonathan Edwards, the Plaid Cymru (Party of Wales) MP for Carmarthen East and Dinefwr, signed the pledge after a single supporter in his constituency had joined the campaign. In fact, while Simpol presents politicians with a powerful carrot-and-stick incentive to sign the pledge, this is far from always necessary. Even MPs sitting in safe seats have signed simply because they think Simpol is a good idea and worth supporting.

Simpol's approach also appears to work well in proportional-representation electoral systems. In the Irish general election in 2016, for example, fifty-three candidates from most of the main parties signed the pledge in the run-up to polling day. Of those, fourteen were elected to the Irish parliament, the Dáil.

Electoral regulations in some countries do, however, give some cause for caution. In Canada, for example, politicians are legally banned from signing pledges in the run-up to a national election if they restrict the MP's freedom of action.[3] At first glance this might appear to scupper Simpol's strategy, but there are a number of factors to take into account. First, Simpol's pledge makes clear that it is only a commitment *in principle*, so it is doubtful whether it would contravene such bans at all. Second, even if it did, since such bans usually only apply in the immediate run-up to an election, Simpol's campaign could instead focus on gaining support from politicians between elections rather than during them. Failing those options, a more loosely worded declaration of support could perhaps be used as an interim measure until citizen support became so strong and irresistible that political parties effectively had little choice but to include the pledge as an integral part of their party's policy.

As national Simpol campaigns develop, they seem to be organizing themselves in a way that reflects each nation's particular political system. In the UK, for example, the management of the campaign is underpinned by supporters at a local-constituency level who choose to become active on an ongoing basis. They do this by organizing themselves into local Simpol groups, each based in their respective parliamentary constituency and focused upon gaining increasing citizen support. This means that support is being continuously built between elections so that each time an election occurs politicians know that the block of Simpol supporters in their constituency is growing ever larger and, consequently, that it is in their electoral interests to sign the pledge.

Testament to the worldcentric thinking that lies behind Simpol is the fact that it has the potential to transcend and include party politics and nation states. As a result, it has gained support from citizens and politicians from right across the party-political spectrum and from many different countries. While the campaign is most developed in the UK, campaigns are already developing elsewhere. The UK, however, could be regarded as a kind of pilot test, providing a taster of what might be possible when large numbers of citizens join the campaign.

Important to note is that Simpol does not require the support of a majority of a national population to be successful. In first-past-the-post electoral systems, such as in the UK, the USA and Canada, it only requires the *critical number*, that number being whatever is the margin of support between the main competing candidates or parties – a margin which, as the electoral experience in Weston-super-Mare showed, can be extremely small indeed. For example, some readers may recall that support between George W. Bush and Al Gore in the 2000 US presidential election was so finely balanced that it hung on just a few thousand votes in Florida. Now let us imagine what might be possible if Simpol were soon supported by some thousands of supporters in that state and in other key US states. If overall public support between the two main candidates or parties in a future election were as finely balanced as it was in 2000, it would take only a relatively small block of Simpol supporters – potentially just a few thousand in each of the key states – to make it in the vital interests of both presidential candidates to sign the pledge.

In countries with proportional-representation systems, on the other hand, gaining support may be somewhat harder. Nevertheless, all electoral systems are based on competition between political parties, so given increasing support from citizens, Simpol ought to prove effective regardless.

With many parliamentary seats and even entire elections around the world often hanging on a relatively small number of votes, it's not difficult to see that the number of campaign supporters needed could be surprisingly small. This helps us recognize the disproportionate power we citizens already possess to ensure that our governments cooperate to implement a global-justice agenda. This disproportionate power demonstrates that it need not take as many people as we might think to change the world.

Simpol's extraordinary power and the fact that it does not require a majority highlights the vital need for it to have sufficient democratic legitimacy were it ever to be implemented. Its Founding Declaration consequently specifies that implementation can only proceed once a majority of citizens in each democratic country – be they campaign supporters or not – had first given their consent.[4]

In considering the likelihood of Simpol enjoying the support of a majority of citizens in each democratic country, it's important to understand that global conditions are very likely to deteriorate further in the coming years. Equally, it is likely to become increasingly apparent that present bargaining strategies are inadequate. As a result, support for the campaign is likely to grow stronger. By the time any global negotiations or national referendums took place, it is to be hoped that a majority of citizens in democratic countries would have become Simpol supporters in any case.

As this process unfolds, it is important to bear in mind the role that the Simpol brand may play in helping citizens, politicians and governments to distinguish between their peers who support the campaign and those who remain to be persuaded. When citizens advertise their support for the campaign or when politicians and governments sign its pledge, they effectively tag themselves publicly as global cooperators. They are saying to the public, to their peers and to the whole world, 'I'm ready to negotiate and implement Simpol as soon as you are.' They publicly affirm to their peers, 'I will if you will!'

The cooperation imperative

Anticipating a deterioration in global life conditions and working in alignment with that evolutionary trajectory is important because transformations usually occur as a result of such pressures. Necessity being the mother of invention, the global situation is likely to worsen to such a degree that global cooperation will start to be seen not so much as an option but as an imperative. It's important, then, to see the Simpol proposal against the backdrop of this growing cooperation imperative.

The power of worsening circumstances to produce cooperation is often surprising and should never be underestimated. A recent example was the global financial crisis of 2008 during which all the world's major central banks acted simultaneously to cut interest rates by 0.5 per cent. As the London *Financial Times* reported, this action was 'unprecedented' and a 'historic piece of coordination'.[5] Although they were not part of the plan, the newspaper further reported that the People's Bank of China 'moved almost simultaneously' to cut its rate as well. Like any vicious circle, a worsening world predicament means that the incentive for global cooperation can only intensify. And, when it does, simultaneous action is key.

In fact, barring a complete global collapse, the adoption of some form of global governance is all but inevitable, because it will be the only way for us to survive. As we saw, to avoid complete chaos the scale of governance must be brought into sync with the scale of the economy: governance *system* must match new governance *context*. The danger, then, is that if we citizens do not use a campaign such as Simpol to intervene swiftly to ensure that global governance is shaped according to our needs, governments and global corporations will surely shape it according to *theirs*. As US politician Mike Enzi sagely observed, 'If we fail to ensure we're sitting at the table, we'll be on the menu.'[6]

What Simpol uniquely provides, then, is an appropriate organizing framework for global governance to occur, but in a way that is driven and shaped not by governments or corporations but by citizens.

Using our votes in the way Simpol suggests is entirely consistent with our recognition and acceptance of pseudo-democracy. Rather than choosing between the manifestos of the existing political parties – promises that in the light of DGC we know to be largely empty – Simpol supporters instead make politicians compete with each other to support Simpol. In that way meaning and purpose are instantly restored to our votes while their power is brought to bear at the global level. Simpol, then, like many game-changing innovations, embodies a paradox. It allows citizens to turbo-charge national party-political competition to produce its very opposite: international *cooperation*.

Making ourselves genuine world citizens

The harnessing of our right to vote is a critical feature that distinguishes Simpol from initiatives that propose a world parliament, direct global democracy or other forms of global governance. Since none of those initiatives uses existing electoral processes to achieve their aims, they of course cannot be implemented unless national governments give their *consent*. Such initiatives thus place the ultimate authority for global governance with nation states rather than with citizens. Simpol, by contrast, offers citizens in all democratic nations a way we can use our votes to *compel* our governments to consent, a way we can make it in their electoral interests to cooperate globally.

Simpol thus puts citizens back in the driving seat in a unique and highly creative fashion. Not only does it allow us to drive our politicians and governments towards cooperation, that power equally confers upon us the opportunity to determine Simpol's policy content. As we earlier noted, Simpol isn't just a new way to use our votes, it's also a platform of policies, even if their precise content is yet to be decided. We will consider shortly how this might take place.

For the moment, the point is that Simpol solves the central conundrum we referred to earlier. It puts forward no candidates at elections, so it cannot be described as a political party. Instead, it allows citizens to use their votes powerfully to drive *existing* politicians and parties to support it. Simpol, then, is neither political party nor an NGO but a kind of hybrid initiative, one that works *through* the existing system while not being a part *of* that system; a unique evolutionary novelty that makes it, arguably, the first genuine legally binding form of global electoral politics.

The phrase 'world citizen' is often used today, but the factor that actualizes citizenship, whether locally or nationally, is our *legal right to vote*. Without it, citizenship at any level remains merely a forlorn aspiration. We may feel ourselves to be world citizens, but until now we have had no legally binding means of expressing it. Until now, at the global level, we have had *no agency*. It's precisely this opportunity that

Simpol offers us: the opportunity to use our national, legally binding votes to make ourselves *genuine* world citizens.

Simpol offers a logic of surprising potential. What we see being pioneered in the UK is that a disproportionately high number of politicians and governments in democratic countries could be motivated to global cooperation by a relatively low number of citizens. In this way a powerful process towards binding global governance could be catalysed, even while so few citizens yet possess a worldcentric civic perspective. As citizens at other levels of thinking see how Simpol re-empowers their votes, and how voting itself can regain real meaning, they are likely to be drawn to the campaign, in turn leading still more politicians and governments to sign on. If what has been achieved in the UK continues to be replicated elsewhere, a powerful, dynamic *virtuous* circle can be set in train, potentially leading many governments in democratic countries to sign on.

Cooperating with non-democratic nations

Non-democratic nations are unlikely to be among the first nations to support Simpol. But, as citizens in democratic nations mobilize and as their governments are gradually driven to declare their support, the international pressure on all other nations would grow. Under such circumstances, non-democratic nations would have a strong incentive to participate.

For example, rather than taking high-interest development loans from the IMF or World Bank, revenue raised from global taxes – perhaps on the rich, on transnational corporations and on financial markets – could be redistributed to these nations on a debt-free basis.[7] This could provide the necessary funds for the healthcare, education and infrastructure that these countries so desperately need. In this way the governments of poorer nations, many of which are non-democratic, would have a strong incentive to cooperate.

A global cooperative agreement such as Simpol could also provide a solution to one of the most contentious issues between nations in the north and those in the south: the substantial subsidies provided to farmers in the north. These subsidies destroy the competitive advantage of southern nations and so prevent them from exporting their agricultural produce, making it virtually impossible for people in these countries to raise themselves out of poverty. But Simpol could change this. For example, one of its policy measures could be globally agreed quotas for each agricultural product. Each nation would be permitted to subsidize its farmers to produce those products up to that agreed level. In that way the need of northern nations to keep their land productive and their farmers in business would be satisfied.

All quantities *above* the agreed quotas could be traded freely, so allowing southern nations to exploit their competitive advantage. Further win–wins would also accrue. Not only would all the world's agricultural land become maximally productive to feed the world's population but the increasing affluence of southern nations would make them into increasingly attractive markets for manufactured goods produced in more developed countries.

Desirable though binding global governance may be, there is always the risk that so-called rogue nations might still refuse to cooperate. Here it's worth remembering, as Professor Ian Goldin reminds us, that not all global issues require every nation's participation.[8] Many problems could no doubt be solved by the simultaneous action of a much smaller group. But for policies requiring the participation of all, or nearly all, nations, there remains the legitimate concern that some non-democratic nations could still prove uncooperative.

In considering this possibility, we can acknowledge that today's entreaties to international cooperation are usually sponsored or heavily influenced by individual nations and are consequently tainted by the hidden hand of narrow national self-interest. Simpol, by contrast, is a proposal that comes, instead, from citizens, not from any nation nor from any existing international institution but from an objective, third position which has no hidden agenda and seeks only the common interest of all. This is an important factor unlikely to be lost on rogue states, a factor which makes it more likely that their willing cooperation may result. But if, despite this, a few rogue nations still refused to cooperate, no doubt the vast majority of nations could agree suitable provisions designed to isolate them in such a way as to ensure that they could not undermine the agreement.

It is also worth remembering that although the *populations* in some non-democratic developing countries may broadly reside at Warrior or Tribal stages of development, their *governments* at least are more likely to be at Traditional or higher. That is, at levels that are perfectly capable of seeing what it is in their rational self-interest. This means that a pragmatic global agreement such as Simpol, which is based on self-interest and reciprocity rather than on a value such as democracy, is more universally appealing and therefore stands a better chance of success. Also, as we pointed out earlier, differing levels of development do not necessarily preclude the possibility of a certain degree of unity. Just as different levels conflict and yet still cooperate within a nation, so they may globally.

Who decides what?

Let us now turn to Simpol as range of global policies. What would those policies be, and who would decide them?

In principle, Simpol's policy platform could include any desirable policy that nations cannot implement alone for fear of incurring a first-mover competitive disadvantage. Policies on climate change, corporate taxation, financial-market regulation and so on immediately spring to mind, but many other contentious policies – such as disarmament – could potentially be included.[9] But it would be inappropriate, we feel, to attempt to determine Simpol's precise policy content at this early stage. First, this would hardly be democratic, and, second, policies that seem appropriate today may be outdated and inappropriate by the time sufficient political support is available for implementation to proceed. For these reasons, Simpol proposes a two-stage process for developing its policy content: first national, then global.

At the first, *national* stage, once political support in its country had reached a level to make it worth while, the Simpol organization in that country could inaugurate its own policy process. This would involve Simpol supporters in that country engaging with one another with the aim of producing a list of priority global issues along with the proposed policies to solve them. Here, a crowd-based process such as that advocated by Alan Watkins and Iman Stratenus in their book *Crowdocracy* could potentially be useful.[10] Such a process could, if supporters desire, include the consideration of policies already developed by think-tanks, NGOs or other expert bodies. In non-democratic nations, where individual autonomy remains restricted, the government concerned would more likely carry out policy development. In either case, the all-important subsidiarity criterion explained in the previous chapter would be applied, so screening out any unilateral policies. At the same time this stage would ensure that each nation's individual priorities and perspective were taken properly into account.

The second, *global* stage would commence much later, if and when support around the world became sufficiently widespread for the prospect of Simpol's practical implementation to occur. In this second stage, representatives from each nation would be invited to participate in international negotiations with a view to harmonizing their national lists and agreeing a final set of global measures to be implemented simultaneously by all nations.

In this way, while Simpol's ultimate policy content would, of course, require international consensus, the policies to be negotiated, as well as any verification and enforcement measures, would be strongly influenced by citizens in democratic countries whose consent would in any case be required before implementation could proceed. While the agreement of democratic countries would be strongly incentivized by the voting power of Simpol supporters, the agreement of governments in non-democratic nations would, of course, also be needed.

Weeding out global conflicts

In the previous chapter we identified the knotty problem of how appropriate global policies could ever be arrived at when different national societies reside at very different levels of consciousness and would therefore likely propose conflicting and often inappropriate global policies. Here, the elegant way the subsidiarity criterion differentiates policies into *unilateral* and *simultaneous* categories has an important side-effect that automatically excludes a vast swathe of inappropriate or harmful policies that might be proposed by national cultures that are still operating at pre-Worldcentric levels.

This weeding out occurs because most culturally divisive policies tend to have no significant bearing on national economic competitiveness. The unilateral implementation of capital punishment, for example, or abortion, would not cause the nation implementing it to suffer an economic competitive disadvantage. Policies of that kind thus fall into the unilateral-policy category and so would not qualify for inclusion.

By applying the subsidiarity criterion then, a whole host of inappropriate policies emanating from any of the pre-worldcentric levels of development would automatically be screened out before any international negotiation took place, so leaving only those policies in the process that genuinely required simultaneous implementation. This already provides a large part of the solution to the problem of diverse values. Any harmful policies that may still slip through this net, as we'll see next, can be excluded in another way.

To understand how this would work, we need to bear in mind that each national population will hold a different opinion about which global policies each sees as being most desirable and necessary. People in Germany, for example, may regard carbon-emissions reductions as a priority, whereas people in Kenya may see poverty reduction as the main priority. It is therefore vital for each nation's perspective to be appropriately taken into account. The surprise, as we'll now see, is that it is precisely by doing so that any remaining harmful policies can be screened out.

Let's remember, first, that it's only those policies that end up meeting with the agreement of all (or nearly all) nations that can proceed to implementation. If a policy failed to achieve that level of agreement, it would simply fall out of the process. With that in mind, we can recall that there is an inherent conflict between each of the first six (First-Tier) value levels: Modern values conflict with Traditional values and vice versa; Postmodern values conflict with both Modern and Traditional values, and vice versa. This conflict, as we'll now see, can cleverly be taken advantage of.

This is because potentially inappropriate policies that reflect any one of the First-Tier levels, if not already excluded by the subsidiarity criterion, would almost certainly fail to appeal to societies at the *other* First-Tier levels. A policy that reflects a Traditional perspective, for example, would almost certainly be rejected by national societies broadly at Modern or higher. Likewise, policies reflecting a Postmodern perspective would likely fail to meet with the approval either of Traditional societies or of Modern societies and so on. In other words, policies that reflect any level lower than Early or Late Worldcentric are highly likely to fall out of the process for lack of sufficient global agreement.

Meanwhile, the only policies likely to be palatable to *all* levels stem, almost by definition, from the Early or Late Worldcentric levels because these are the only ones in the spiral that *integrate* and take into account all preceding levels. Policies reflecting a worldcentric perspective, in other words, are the only ones likely to be both appropriate and beneficial for global implementation *and* capable of appealing to national societies at all the prior value-levels, albeit that each may have its own particular reason for supporting them.

Given the two-stage policy development process described earlier, it would be during the second *global* stage that the above-mentioned conflict would occur; a conflict likely to result in all policies emanating from the First-Tier levels failing to gather sufficient global support and so falling out of the process. For the few policies emanating from the Worldcentric levels that remained, these, as we suggested before, would be negotiated so that compensations and trade-offs would allow nations that may lose on one policy to win on another. They would also involve sorting policies into groups of two or three complementary policies and prioritizing those groups.

The aim, then, would be to establish an initial set of two or three world-centric policies, which become acceptable to all nations because they include the necessary compensations, exemptions and trade-offs as well as appropriate verification and enforcement measures. Subject to such agreement, then, this first group of policies – the first Simultaneous Policy – could be implemented globally and simultaneously on a mutually agreed date, while the less important groups could be scheduled for later implementation.

Binding global governance of the kind Simpol offers not only serves our civilization's survival but is in the self-interest of all humanity regardless of worldview. For societies at pre-Traditional levels, including so-called 'failed states', the more settled atmosphere that Simpol could bring to international relations through cooperative global governance, aided by a debt-free global redistribution of wealth, would allow citizens in these countries to stabilize, prosper and build viable national economies. No longer would they feel such pressure to emigrate or suffer their present brain drain. Increased international security would be a worldwide pay-off.

By the same token, the lessening of mass migration and the consequent safeguarding of secure national identities should reassure those holding a Traditional worldview in more developed countries who presently feel under threat. Conversely, for those at a Modern level who want the global economy to thrive, the level regulatory playing field that Simpol could provide would allow the global economy to survive and become truly sustainable. Likewise, Simpol is in the self-interest of enterprises that want to stay in business for the long term and not just for the next few years.

For those at a Postmodern level, the ideal of a just and sustainable world, including more localized economies, depends, as we have seen, on cooperation formalized in binding global governance. The laudable aims of multiculturalism can be realized but only if the legitimate needs of national identity required for a healthy Traditional level are respected by adopting the more global and encompassing simulcultural approach we have outlined.

Embryonic global cooperation

Clearly, there remain very many important details to be worked out and questions to answer. But it would be wrong, we feel, to try to predetermine everything at such an early stage. Instead, a more organic and participatory approach is called for: we all need to *participate* in developing the process and in answering any remaining questions along the way.

The kind of international agreement that Simpol could help forge therefore falls far short of being a fully fledged institution of binding global governance. Rather, it might better be thought of as an embryonic praxis. Just as the EU only emerged organically from the embryonic praxis of an agreement between its mining and steel industries, so democratic global governance, too, is most likely to emerge if it starts in a similar way.

Simpol, then, could be described as an embryonic praxis by which a sufficient number of governments could be driven by citizens to legislate on a few very specific policies that would be implemented globally and simultaneously. Such a process, if successful, could then be repeated whenever global problems arise. Whether it later evolves into something resembling a more permanent institution is another matter entirely, and it would be one for citizens to decide.

Nevertheless, we can already visualize the Simpol process to an important degree. The diagram on page 164 provides a useful overview.[11]

Recalling the ten boxes that a worldcentric political campaign would have to tick, you can judge for yourself whether Simpol does so:

1. Is Simpol based on the condition of global and simultaneous implementation?

2. Does Simpol give citizens sufficient power to drive their governments towards global cooperation while also giving them the power to determine the policies to be implemented?

3. Does Simpol incorporate multiple issues, so potentially making cooperation in all nations' *immediate* interests? As a result, is it likely to include measures for ongoing enforcement?

4. Can Simpol's policy-development process avoid the dangers of one-size-fits-all governance?

Simpol
Using Our Votes to Take Back the World

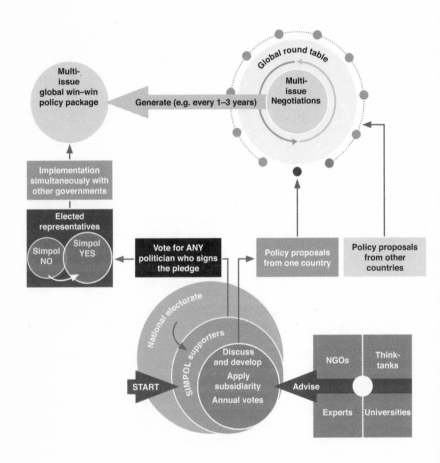

5. Would Simpol be legally binding and enforceable?

6. Would Simpol take non-democratic nations into account while ensuring accountability to citizens in democratic nations?

7. Does Simpol possess a robust subsidiarity criterion that ensures that the principle of national sovereignty is properly upheld?

8. Does Simpol resolve the conundrum that it can be neither an NGO nor a political party?

9. Can Simpol's policy content be arrived at with the whole world's participation while avoiding the inclusion of potentially inappropriate policies?

10. Does Simpol offer a tag or brand that enables citizens, politicians and governments to build trust?

Despite the obvious challenge that binding global governance represents, we hope that by now you'll see it as more achievable than you might at first have imagined.

Talking and walking together

A critical factor in making it a reality is that the possibility of simultaneous action and a viable route to achieving it be actively articulated. People need to start suggesting it. We all need to start talking about it. As more and more people do, a new cooperative future context starts to take shape in people's minds – in the collective psyche. A mental model starts to be built in which fruitful cooperation starts to be understood by the whole society as both desirable and realistic. As the historian Arnold Toynbee put it:

> Apathy can only be overcome by enthusiasm, and enthusiasm can only be aroused by two things: first, an ideal which takes the imagination by storm, and, second, a definite, intelligible plan for carrying that ideal into practice.[12]

If, on the other hand, enough people do not articulate the possibility of simultaneous international action and how it may be achieved, the risk is that global society will be left without even the *idea* of a realistic future context of cooperation let alone any feasible means to achieve it. All players – whether governments, corporations or we ourselves – would then be left locked in the present competitive context, locked, that is, in DGC's vicious circle, a circle that has only chaos and collapse as its end-point. It is the articulation of a future cooperative context and a viable means of achieving it that give birth to the pull or drive towards ever higher and larger levels of governance. It is exactly this drive that has taken human social units from families to tribes to medieval small states to nation states, and it is this evolutionary drive that calls us again now to establish cooperatively a form of binding, people-centred global governance.

The paradox of this and all previous major evolutionary transitions is that, if left to reach a critical stage, competition ultimately ceases to be a strategy for individual survival but instead becomes a strategy for collective suicide. At that point – a point we're fast approaching – cooperation becomes in everyone's self-interest.

In fact, cooperation and not just competition has been the deeper story of evolution all along, as we'll see in the final chapter.

9. An Evolutionary Perspective

By the time the nineteenth century was well under way, two remarkable developments occurred in the United Kingdom, the small island nation that was at the time the world's leading nation in trade, industrial development and military might. The first was a revolution in organization: the banning of slavery. The second was a revolution in consciousness: the theory of evolution through natural selection. Darwin's supplanting of Genesis was to have profoundly contentious ramifications, which continue to this day. Whether innate selfishness is ascribed to genetic hardwiring, whether the survival of the fittest seems to justify predatory capitalism or whether it is denied altogether by religious fundamentalism, we are still trying to make sense of the process of evolution.

Human societies have been subject to evolution just as other life forms, and throughout this book we've been hinting at the evolutionary nature of the predicament in which we find ourselves under globalization. In this final chapter, we argue that, seen from an evolutionary perspective, globalization is part of our natural evolution. It was only to be expected. Equally, however, we will argue that global cooperation and governance are natural, too. They are part of evolution's tendency towards ever-greater scales of cooperation. Perhaps surprisingly, we'll mostly attempt this with reference to today's understanding of the original science of evolution: biology.

New foe or old friend?

As we look back into history, we notice successive waves of expanding trade and new technology confronting human societies with new contexts for governance. In response, ever-larger scales of cooperation and governance evolved to cope:

> Cooperation amongst humans has expanded considerably in scale over the past 100,000 years. Initially cooperation existed only within small family groups. Since then, cooperative organisation has progressively expanded in scale to produce multi-family bands, tribes, agricultural communities, cities, empires, nation states, and now some forms of economic and social organisation that span the globe.[1]

This perspective comes not from a historian but from cutting-edge evolutionary biologist John Stewart. The trajectory of human evolution, although never predetermined, has tended towards ever-larger scales of cooperation and governance, and this will continue, Stewart suggests.

> Modern human societies are obviously not at an end-point of evolution . . . they will go on to form cooperative organisations of larger and larger scale and of greater and greater evolvability.[2]

Given that the scale of human cooperation has continuously expanded, we may wonder why this expansion occurs.

Sometimes cooperation develops easily because two societies may combine since they share an immediate interest, perhaps mutual trade or defence against a mutual external threat. In other cases, as a result of one violently conquering and subsuming the other, two societies merge and become a kind of larger cooperative venture. The important point to note, however, is that wherever two or more societies come into contact, competition between them is inevitable. Unless they see an immediate benefit from cooperating, competition will ensue. In that sense competition, or the potential for it, can be said to be evolution's 'default mode'.

Initially competition between two or more societies may be tolerable, even beneficial, and progress may be stimulated. But sooner or later the space for fruitful competitive expansion runs out and the competition then becomes destructive, and at that critical point, as we explained earlier, competition ultimately ceases to be a strategy for individual survival but instead becomes a strategy for collective suicide.

At such a point it produces the evolutionary pressure for cooperation at a new, higher level and on a larger scale to emerge. Competition becomes so destructive that cooperation becomes the only solution. What the best-selling philosopher of the twentieth century Robert Pirsig calls 'Dynamic Quality, the continually changing flux of immediate reality' begins to get too much for what he calls the patterns of 'static value', and an upset in the systemic field occurs.[3] This dynamism overturns the balance of the hitherto accepted reality – sometimes violently – in order to cause a transformation. In terms of a competitive environment, the field cannot stand any more competition, so cooperation quickly begins to catch on because now it becomes in everyone's interests or they won't survive. So, paradoxically, destructive competition acts as a *driver* of cooperation.

But, although cooperation may be in everyone's interests, it is never assured: it doesn't occur automatically. This is because, as we've seen throughout this book, destructive competition operates as a vicious circle that is very hard to escape. In game theory this predicament is called 'the prisoner's dilemma' because it locks all players into a downward spiral that will ultimately cause their collapse and yet there seems to be no way out.[4] So here is the paradox: destructive competition supplies the drive for cooperation on a larger scale but is also a formidable *barrier* to it. Underlining the crucial importance of overcoming this barrier, Stewart argues that destructive competition applies not only to the evolution of human cooperation but to all living processes:

> The circumstances that cause it are universal. Individuals who use resources to help others without benefit to themselves will be outcompeted. They will be disadvantaged compared to those who use the resources for their own benefit. And the barrier applies no matter what the evolutionary mechanisms are that adapt and evolve individuals. The barrier has applied whether the evolutionary mechanisms are those that adapt corporations, individual humans, other multi-cellular organisms, single cells or autocatalytic sets.'[5]

Destructive competition is therefore a very old foe, one that is universal and, if not overcome by a higher and larger level of cooperation, drives instead towards collapse. Our identification of Destructive Global Competition as today's central barrier to solving global problems is therefore nothing new. It is simply the reidentification of an age-old phenomenon.

One important reason why the destructive side of competition frequently seems to evade identification is our human propensity to see things out of context or in micro-contexts.[6] In particular, this can allow us to develop a misleading focus on differences in absolute rather than relative terms. Taking wealth inequality as one example, leading academic economist Robert H. Frank suggests that while standard economic theory focuses on people's *absolute* wealth it is *relative* wealth that has the greatest influence on how people feel and the decisions they take.[7] Frank demonstrates that ignoring relative economic or financial positions creates drastic economic consequences such as the tragedy of the commons as well as winner-takes-all markets. This occurs because – much as neoliberals may protest – neither individual people nor individual nations can ever be considered in isolation.

Competition, then, is as old as the hills. But so is cooperation. In fact, the only way that evolution overcomes destructive competition is by establishing cooperation (i.e. governance) at a higher level. This is why evolution has produced increasing scales of cooperation and complexity. While competition, most of the time, is evolution's default mode, cooperation is its 'discrete mode', which comes to the fore at critical junctures when competition becomes destructive and threatens wipe-out.

The divergence between individual and group interests is something Darwin understood well. Frank calls this effect 'Darwin's wedge', and it is a good starting point for considering the most cutting-edge reading of the interplay between self-interest and common good that is now emerging. The divergence between individual and group interests is the basis for what leading evolutionary biologists refer to as 'multilevel selection theory', which is concerned with discovering whether or not there is any innate drive for altruism. It also helps explain why the scale of human social groups has tended to expand. Multilevel selection theory states that although selfishness and competition will tend to destroy cooperation *within* a group, competition *between* groups will tend to favour groups that are internally cooperative and altruistic. As evolutionary theorists E.O. Wilson and David Sloan Wilson succinctly put it, 'Selfishness beats altruism within groups. Altruistic groups beat selfish groups. Everything else is just commentary.'[8] Since highly cooperative groups out-compete less cooperative groups and then incorporate them, it is not surprising that the scale of human social groups has increased.

These ideas are not mere theorizing – hence the confidence expressed in their joint statement. Multilevel selection has been shown to affect both the tiniest of biological units such as individual genes and human groups. Based on the work of the economist and Nobel Prize winner Elinor Ostrom, D.S. Wilson has conducted several long-term quantitative research initiatives on 'groups that work'. The outcome of these studies demonstrates that cooperation among human groups and the fostering of altruism is both innate and effective.[9] This cutting-edge analysis now puts to bed the Richard Dawkins mindset that came to be accepted by scientists and politicians alike. 'Let us try to teach generosity and altruism, because we are born selfish.'[10]

The work of D.S. Wilson, Elinor Ostrom and others is finally helping cooperation to claim its rightful place as competition's equal. Important misunderstandings persist, however, especially concerning the appropriate *scale* of cooperation. Even some of cooperation's most vocal advocates, such as Margaret Heffernan, presume that cooperation is best suited to smaller-scale approaches. The solution to the vast ecological and environmental problems we face are more likely to be solved, argues Heffernan, by thousands of individual efforts at city, regional, national and international levels rather than through overarching agreements.[11]

This assumption seems to be based on the fact that Ostrom's research looked only at small-scale examples, such as the governance of local fisheries. But Ostrom herself, in the last of her famous 'eight design principles for common-pool resources', clearly recommends that there must be appropriate coordination among all relevant groups in cases of larger common-pool resources. D.S. Wilson concisely describes the principle emerging:

> Every sphere of activity has an *optimal* scale [authors' italics]. Large-scale governance requires finding the optimal scale for each sphere of activity and appropriately coordinating the activities, a concept called 'polycentric governance'.[12]

This is precisely in line with the vision of this book and with Simpol practice, where, increasingly, many issues we face today are now inescapably global and require governance and coordination on a global scale. And part of this big-picture practice is also to make sure that as many issues as possible continue to be dealt with at lower levels – national or local. It is therefore misleading and may be dangerous to imply that global agreements aren't necessary, even if this misreading of the crucial aspect of scale is unfortunately widespread. E.F. Schumacher, for example, is widely thought by environmentalists to have championed everything small, whereas, in fact, he was absolutely clear that large-scale cooperation was an essential component of structural change. Here he is, from his world-famous *Small Is Beautiful*:

> We need the freedom of lots and lots of small, autonomous units, and, at the same time, the orderliness of large-scale, possibly global, unity and co-ordination.[13]

Global-scale action, like action at all other scales, has its place and, as we hope to have made clear, has today become an absolute and urgent necessity.

A further important point is the way that cooperation occurs. In the micro world of biology as in the macro world of economics, overcoming destructive competition has always consisted, as Stewart explains, in 'Building cooperative organizations out of self-interested components'.[14]

Stewart's point about self-interest is especially important in our own context because for global cooperation to actually occur it has to be in each nation's *immediate* self-interest. It is no use appealing to moral arguments about saving the planet or pointing out that cooperation would be in our *ultimate* best interests. Instead, cooperation has to be designed in such a way that we want it *now*, that it will *benefit* us now. For that to happen, and as this book has tried to show, cooperation has to be properly and intentionally designed. This is a point with which evolutionist D.S. Wilson concurs:

> Now we are at a point in history when the great problem of human life is to accomplish functional organization at a larger scale than ever. The selection of best practices must be intentional, because we cannot wait for natural selection and there is no process of between-planet selection to select for functional organization at a planetary scale.[15]

Since the big bang evolution has devised myriad ways to evolve cooperation in order to overcome destructive competition. To this point, it has done so, as Wilson pointed out, largely through processes of trial and error: natural selection. In human affairs, large-scale cooperation is most easily seen in the way individuals voluntarily submit to appropriate governance. This is a point made by Jared Diamond in his book *Collapse: How Societies Choose to Fail or Survive*. Analysing the reasons why some human societies collapsed whereas others survived, Diamond argues that throughout human history, whenever people have encountered others lacking ties of family or clan relationship, governance eventually had to be established for the necessary enforcement of moral principles.[16]

Governance, then, is crucial. But, as Wilson suggests, if it is to proceed to the global level it must be designed and implemented consciously and intentionally. We will have more to say on conscious evolution shortly.

Evolution's dance

According to this view, competition and cooperation can be considered not so much as opposites – as friends or foes – but more like dance partners. Each takes its turn, at the appropriate point, in leading the evolutionary dance. In this way competition can be said to drive cooperation to ever-higher levels and on ever-larger scales. Competition leads the dance of life for most of the time, but, as the dance reaches its dizzying climax, competition starts wildly gyrating, stepping on toes, bumping into others and falling over itself, at which point cooperation has to take over for the dance to continue at a higher level.

In *Nonzero*, a study of the evolution of human cooperation, Robert Wright uses game theory to chart the interplay between competition and cooperation in human social evolution. Wright draws a distinction between zero-sum games in which one faction's gain is the other's loss and non-zero-sum games, in which each faction's interests overlap or are the same. These games, he argues, have characterized the drivers of human cultural evolution since time immemorial:

> The crevices of social organization – the zones of zero-sum contention [i.e. of destructive competition] between families or villages or chiefdoms or states – keep getting filled in by the cement of non-zero-sumness [by cooperation]; and the zero-sumness [competition] thus displaced keeps retreating to higher levels of organization.[17]

What this broader view suggests is that the deep drivers of all evolution appear to be competition and cooperation *in combination*. If cooperation succeeds in overcoming destructive competition by establishing governance at a new higher level, competition is then released to operate at that new level. For example, when destructive competition at the level of a group of small states was overcome by their incorporation within a single nation state, competition between that group of small states was substantially eliminated. But competition then reappeared at the next level between different nation states. As biologist and palaeontologist Geerat J. Vermeij suggests, 'Cooperation merely shifts competition to a higher level in the organizational hierarchy of life, but hardly diminishes it.'[18] So, while competition drives cooperation to a higher level, cooperation then releases competition again on that new level. This suggests that if global cooperation of the kind we are proposing were ever achieved, we could expect that destructive competition between nations would be substantially eliminated.

One reason that it has taken us so long to recognize the dance between competition and cooperation is that it is very difficult to detect within the timeframe normally used for historical analysis. It only becomes apparent if we zoom out to take a much broader evolutionary perspective. The dance itself and the different roles that competition and cooperation play are recognized by another evolutionary biologist, Elisabet Sahtouris:

> Young species tend to grab territory and resources, maximizing the numbers of their offspring to spread themselves where they can. As species encounter each other, conflict develops in the competition for space and resources. Eventually negotiations leading to cooperation prove useful to the competing species and they reach the higher level of unity.[19]

For humanity, however, the crucial problem is not that we are encountering other species but that through our own expansionary economy our species is outcompeting and eliminating them. In reaching the limits of earth's ability to sustain our own civilization, it might be truer to say that we are encountering ourselves. Or as the cartoonist Walt Kelly puts it, 'We have met the enemy and he is us.'[20]

Looking through this broader evolutionary lens, the dance between competition and cooperation also reveals that, at each level, it is composed of distinct moves or stages. Sahtouris again:

> All evolution – of the great cosmos and of our own planet within it – is an endless dance of wholes that separate themselves into parts and parts that join into mutually consistent new wholes. We can see it as a repeating, sequentially spiralling pattern: unity ➡ individuation ➡ competition ➡ conflict ➡ negotiation ➡ resolution ➡ cooperation ➡ new levels of unity, and so on. Competition and cooperation can both be seen within and among species as they improvise and evolve, unbalance and rebalance the dance.[21]

How fragile we are

Where should we as a species locate ourselves in the dance that Sahtouris describes, immersed as we are in globalization with all its benefits as well as its prodigious competition-driven threats? If the moves in the dance are unity → individuation → competition → conflict → negotiation → resolution → cooperation→ new level of unity, what move of that dance are we engaged in at present? And which move comes next?

The nation state, the highest level of governance that exists throughout the world, is no exception to this dance. It, too, can be said to be following the same cycle. In the diagram below we attempt to trace the nation state's life progress through this cycle or dance. This diagram shows the main dance moves arranged in the form of an S-curve, which, following Dr Sally Goerner, offers a useful visual representation of this naturally occurring cycle.[22]

The Life Cycle of the Nation State

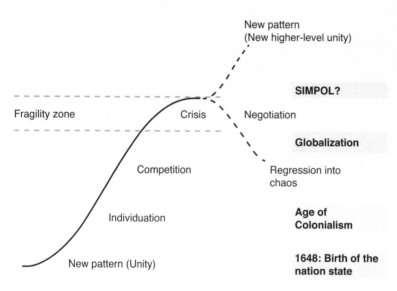

The cycle starts at the bottom of the S with the birth of the modern nation-state system, which was framed as a conceptual reality in 1648 by the Peace of Westphalia. Its significance was that it released nations from the all-powerful influence that religion, especially Roman Catholicism, exercised over their populations. The emergence of the modern nation-state system thus represented the stage Sahtouris calls the 'new pattern' or 'unity'.

No longer in danger of being undermined by religious authorities,

European nations began to sense their newfound secular identity and independence: they had reached the stage of 'individuation'. Feeling themselves to be autonomous independent entities, they then flexed their muscles accordingly, and over the following centuries inevitably came into conflict with each other. These power struggles were characterized by the Age of Colonialism, in which Europe's nations vigorously competed for trading opportunities and overseas settlements: Sahtouris's stage of 'conflict' or competition had begun. Burgeoning national populations, meanwhile, increasingly identified with belonging to their nation. This, as we have suggested, is how the idea of the sovereign nation, from which we now need to release ourselves, became so deeply ingrained.

Colonialism was soon reinforced by the emerging industrial revolution, and, equipped with ever-evolving technologies, this laid the foundations for the era of globalization that was to follow. Now, with the help of information technology and neoliberal deregulation, the overt international competition that characterized the Age of Colonialism has morphed into a more subtle and insidious version, Destructive Global Competition. This brings us to where we are today, located in the 'fragility zone', where competition has become so intense and destructive that the system becomes critical and prone to recurrent crises and collapse. The harsh winds of crisis potentially spell regression into chaos and dissolution. This is where we see humanity currently located. Yet, were we to organize ourselves appropriately, these same winds could fill the sails of our vessel and carry us to the fresh shores of a new pattern, the new, higher-level unity that global governance and global cooperation offer.

Evolutionary transformation is usually thought of as a slow and gradual process, and most of the time it is. However, when a system has entered the fragility zone things can change rapidly. This is what evolutionists often refer to as 'punctuated equilibrium', a rapid shift from one system-level to the next.[23] Considering the many problems humanity now faces, the pressure for such a shift is already mounting, and we must move swiftly if we are to survive. Global warming, the melting of polar ice-caps, the depletion of fossil fuels, terrorism, wealth inequality, mass migration, ballooning national and personal debt, financial crises, nuclear proliferation and the rise of the far right are all signs to warn us we have entered the fragility zone.

We should be prepared either for meltdown – or to commit to shifting to a new level of global cooperation as soon as possible.

Bargaining with evolution

Such a broad evolutionary perspective on our present predicament brings into sharp relief the role of DGC. As we have seen, throughout evolution destructive competition has always represented the key barrier to achieving higher levels of cooperation. This makes it all the more vital that we take it seriously. If we fail to overcome DGC by means of global cooperation we may not survive.

This elucidates just how futile are the bargaining strategies that we described in earlier chapters. As we can now see, to bargain with a new context for governance is to place ourselves on the wrong side of evolution's trajectory. It's as if we are attempting to bargain with evolution itself – which is not a winnable bargain!

It is precisely the inadequacy of such strategies that should signal the establishment of a new system of global governance as the only viable option. That signal, if we interpret it correctly, could be seen as evolution's way of calling to us, and answering her call means acting swiftly to transcend the existing destructively competitive nation-state paradigm and to include it within a new, more appropriate and encompassing, globally cooperative one.

The importance of taking a worldcentric evolutionary perspective is that it enables us for the first time to recognize and understand this. The sociopolitical implications of this realization are not that the global justice movement should abandon its bargaining strategies, rather that it could include them while transcending them by continuing to pursue them alongside a broader, more powerful global political strategy, such as the Simultaneous Policy. The GJM's important campaigns could thus continue as before, while at the same time support and encouragement for Simpol could be developed among its many supporters. In this way the GJM could achieve the critical move from nationcentric either/or thinking to world-centric both/and thinking.

In practical terms each NGO or activist group could accomplish this by carefully reviewing each of its policy demands and subjecting them to the 'subsidiarity criterion' mentioned earlier. Each demand should be soberly assessed and sorted into either the unilateral or simultaneous policy category. If NGOs and activist groups carried out such an assessment they might be surprised to find just how many of their policy demands fall into the simultaneous category.

Adding the Simultaneous Policy ('Simpol?') to the diagram on page

175 represents its potential to fulfil both Sahtouris's stages of 'negotiation' and 'new higher-level unity'. This is because Simpol encompasses two dimensions: it is a *policy* to be developed through which humanity might negotiate a solution to many urgent global problems, while its campaign offers a transformative *process* through which humanity could potentially drive its leaders to implement and thereby realize the needed new pattern – the new higher-level unity.

Simultaneity in evolution

Simultaneous action is not, in fact, some newfangled idea. On closer inspection it turns out to have been cooperation's key mode of implementation in many varying circumstances since the dawn of time. Take the human body, for example, or the body of an animal or of any multicellular organism. Evolutionary biology has made enormous strides in understanding how such organisms came to evolve. John Stewart again:

> If cells could reproduce independently they would compete destructively with each other, making a multi-cellular organism impossible. What was needed was the emergence of constraints that prevented competition between cells. The constraints that evolved were arrangements that ensured that each cell in a multi-cellular organism had the same DNA – i.e. the same governance.
>
> If these constraints fail to continue to act *globally and simultaneously* [authors' italics] across the organism, individual cells will again begin to compete by reproducing as fast as they can. Cancer is an example of this breakdown of constraints in multi-cellular organisms.[24]

Author and journalist Arthur Koestler was another advanced mind who recognized the fundamental importance of global simultaneous implementation in biology. In his study of evolution *Janus: A Summing Up* he tells the story of the evolution of the reptilian egg from its amphibian predecessors. We shall quote him at length, because of the precision of his elegant argument:

> The vertebrates' conquest of dry land started with the evolution of reptiles from some primitive amphibian form. The amphibians reproduced in the water, and their young were aquatic. The decisive novelty of the reptiles was that, unlike amphibians, they laid their eggs

on dry land; they no longer depended on the water and were free to roam over the continents. But the unborn reptile inside the egg still needed an aquatic environment: it had to have water or else it would dry up at an early stage. It also needed a lot of food: amphibians hatch as larvae who fend for themselves, whereas reptiles hatch fully developed. So the reptilian egg had to be provided with a large mass of yolk for food, and also with albumen – the white of the egg – to provide the water. Neither the yolk by itself, nor the egg-white itself, would have had any selective value. Moreover, the egg-white needed a vessel to contain it, otherwise its moisture would have evaporated. So there had to be a shell made of a leathery or limey material, as part of the evolutionary package-deal. But that is not the end of the story. The reptilian embryo, because of this shell, could not get rid of its waste products. The soft-shelled amphibian embryo had the whole pond as a lavatory; the reptilian embryo had to be provided with a kind of bladder. It is called the allantois, and is in some respects the forerunner of the mammalian placenta. But this problem having been solved, the embryo would still remain trapped inside its tough shell; it needed a tool to get out. The embryos of some fishes and amphibians, whose eggs are surrounded by a gelatinous membrane, have glands on their snouts: when the time is ripe, they secrete a chemical which dissolves the membrane. But embryos surrounded by a hard shell need a mechanical tool: thus snakes and lizards have a tooth transformed into a kind of tin-opener, while birds have a caruncle – a hard outgrowth near the tip of their beaks which serves the same purpose and is later shed by the adult animal.[25]

As it turns out, this evolutionary step was going to be crucial to the spread of life from sea to land. And in this step, as Koestler goes on to explain, global simultaneous implementation played the key role:

Now according to the Darwinian schema, all these changes must have been gradual, each small step caused by a chance mutation. But it is obvious that each step, however small, required *simultaneous* [authors' italics], interdependent changes affecting all the factors involved in the story. Thus the liquid store in the albumen could not be kept in the egg without the hard shell. But the shell would be useless, in fact murderous, without the allantois and without the tin-opener.

> Each of these changes, if they had occurred alone, would have been harmful, and the organisms thus affected would have been weeded out by natural selection . . . They are all interdependent within the organism – which is a functional whole and not a mosaic.[26]

Koestler clearly understands the fundamental importance of the role played by global simultaneous implementation in facilitating transformative evolutionary change. Later he unequivocally concludes that 'evolutionary progress . . . requires simultaneous, coordinated changes of all the relevant components in the structure and function of the organic holarchy'.[27]

Alternatively, stepping outside the field of biology for a moment, let us consider the same processes in the field of human language, in particular written communication. If we look at a sentence composed of words, the context of meaning provided by the ordering of words within the sentence applies *globally* (i.e. to all of the words concerned) and *simultaneously* (i.e. to each word, at the same time). What do we have to do to make sense of the following group of words to shape them into a meaningful sentence?

AM AN I? IDIOT NOT

Unless an ordering of the words – that is to say, governance – is effected globally and simultaneously by the higher organizational level that the sentence represents, their meaning is unavailable. The words are just a heap and not a whole. In the example above one can almost feel the words competing with each other for meaning, a kind of 'cancer of the sentence'.

Whether it is global cooperation now or whether it was the big bang fourteen billion years ago, all such transitions appear to be characterized by global and simultaneous implementation. Global simultaneous implementation, like Destructive Global Competition, is nothing new; both are as old as evolution itself.

We've been here before

With the benefit of an evolutionary perspective, we may now allow ourselves to wonder about some previously unimaginable questions:

- Is it reasonable to imagine that a crisis similar to that now confronting humanity might have occurred at some point in our distant past?

- Is it possible that something akin to globalization occurred on some different and smaller scale before?

- And if such a crisis was eventually overcome, as it clearly was, could its solution hold clues to what might be an appropriate solution now?

One of our clues here may be the existence of *fractals*, which are patterns that repeat at different scales and indicate repetition in evolution. These are found throughout nature and are discernible in mathematical processes. Dr Sally J. Goerner says fractals arise from processes we assume could create only disorder, but they are beautiful, useful and orderly.[28]

A remarkable story from the beginnings of life is the development of the nucleated cell. This is particularly relevant to us because it indicates that something akin to globalization has occurred before. Elisabet Sahtouris again:

> Like ourselves, the ancient bacteria got themselves deeper and deeper into crisis by pursuing win/lose economics based on the reckless exploitation of nature and each other. The amazing and inspirational part of the story is that entirely without the benefit of brains, these nigh invisible inventive little creatures reorganized their destructively competitive lifestyle into one of creative cooperation.[29]

The crisis occurred when local food supplies were exhausted. At that point, what Sahtouris describes as 'relatively hi-tech respiring bacteria' called 'breathers' invaded larger, more passive bacteria called 'bubblers', whose function was fermentation, and completely devoured them. She calls this process 'bacterial colonialism or imperialism'. The invaders now multiplied within the conquered colonies until their food supply was exhausted and everyone died. This must have happened countless times before at some point they learned a new strategy – to cooperate:

> Somewhere along the line, the bloated bags of bacteria also included photosynthesizers, 'bluegreens', which could replenish food supplies if the motoring breathers would push the enterprise up toward a lighter part of the primeval sea. Perhaps it was this lifesaving use of solar energy that initiated the shift to cooperation.[30]

Thus a major crisis that threatened bacterial wipe-out within the developing cell eventually triggered a switch to cooperation. The interesting part of the story is *how* this occurred, as Sahtouris goes on to recount:

In any case, bubblers, bluegreens, and breathers eventually contributed their unique capabilities to the common task of building a workable society. In time, each donated some of their 'personal' DNA to the central resource library and information hub that became the nucleus of their collective enterprise: the huge (by bacterial standards) nucleated cells of which our own bodies and those of all Earth beings other than bacteria are composed.'[31]

Cooperation within the cell, it seems, was orchestrated by an emergent central entity: what became the cell's *nucleus*. The emergent nucleus, as Sahtouris describes, proceeded to invite all the competing entities within the dangerously unstable cell to contribute some of their DNA to what she calls the nucleus's 'central resource library and information hub'. The competing entities accepted the process that the nucleus had set in train, and they contributed their DNA. It was as if they chose to share their ideas or policies as to how the cell could be reorganized on a cooperative basis for the future.

After some time and at some point, life within the globalizing cell itself became transformed from a mode of destructive competition to one of fruitful cooperation. Since all the competing bacteria in the cell were affected, we can say with reasonable certainty that the transformation occurred *globally*, but we can only wonder if it might also, perhaps, have occurred *simultaneously*. Be that as it may, Sahtouris continues:

This process of uniting disparate and competitive entities into a cooperative whole – a multi-creatured cell, so to speak – was repeated when nucleated cells aggregated into a multi-celled creatures, and it is happening now for a third time as we multi-celled humans are being driven by evolution to form a cooperative global cell in harmony with each other and with other species. This new enterprise must be a unified global democracy of diverse membership.[32]

'A unified global democracy of diverse membership', as Sahtouris describes it, is very similar to the global-governance framework that Simpol proposes. After many repeated failures, it seems that our bacterial forebears eventually managed to achieve cooperation in the form of the nucleated cell, the cell of which we ourselves are composed, and they did so even without the benefit of brains.

Is it too much to hope that we, with the big triune brains we humans have at our disposal, might be able to achieve cooperation in the form of a nucleated, people-centred global governance? And could we achieve it on our first attempt? Sahtouris concludes:

> Perhaps, in a parallel fractal way, globalization struggles to happen on countless planets in our universe that have evolved civilizations, but we humans cannot afford to be one of the failures, as we have only one chance – the common cell wall that binds us together is the boundary of our planet itself.[33]

Maturity and self-regulation

Instead of thinking about how competing nations struggle to cooperate, let us try for a moment to consider humanity as whole, within a 'common cell wall that binds us together', as if humanity were on its own evolutionary journey. From such a perspective, we might see our species floundering in a crisis of maturation: do we mature and cooperate, or do we carry on competing and perish?

If we likened humanity's evolution to an individual's development, we could imagine it to be a phase of adolescence, on the way to becoming properly autonomous. But being autonomous is not an end in itself; it means being responsible and thereby accountable. In this case we could say humanity seems to be stuck in an adolescent crisis, wanting it all without wanting accountability. Processes of maturation – with their ensuing crises – seem to apply to all species, and Sahtouris also finds the metaphor of adolescence helpful:

> The adolescent who strikes out with a false sense of maturity, believing he or she knows it all, can be expected to get into some kind of trouble before maturing into an adult. And the adolescence of civilized humanity is running true to form . . . Like any adolescent who is suddenly aware of having created a very real-life crisis, our species faces a choice – the choice between pursuing our dangerous course to disaster or stopping and trying to find mature solutions to our crisis.[34]

In terms of evolution, we could be standing on the brink of species collapse or, potentially, a shift to a new and higher level of self-awareness and to a deeper fulfilment of who we are. A 'mature solution' seems the only choice with a future.

One of the concepts that frequently defines maturity in organisms, and is regularly the sticking point for an adolescent, is the *ability to self-regulate*. A prime example is the human body. Our body is a marvel of interlocking systems with discrete individual functions that relate with each other. The basic drivers of the body are self-preservation and reproduction, but the operating mode of the systemic whole is self-regulation. In this purpose, each cell and each organ cooperates and self-regulates. The heart, aided by the lungs, has a central self-regulating function especially in how it influences behaviour through its control of the autonomic nervous system.

While the overall self-regulation functioning of the body is *autonomic* – that is to say does not require conscious effort – we can apply intentional self-regulation to our bodies. We can influence our heart rate and thereby our central nervous system and overall well-being by what we think, the way we behave and even how we breathe. Conscious self-regulation is increasingly becoming the most important new idea in healthcare, chiefly because it works, and it puts patients back in charge of their own lives. Self-regulation is also increasingly the goal in mental health and is being implemented through methods such as mindfulness, mentalization and cognitive behaviour therapy (CBT) being integrated into mainstream approaches. Self-regulation turns out to be the key to self-driven behaviour change and becoming properly autonomous and accountable.

This brings us back to adolescence. Adolescents have a particularly hard time with self-regulation. Children initially need regulation from the outside, from their parents, and when they enter adolescence their task is to integrate this parental regulation so they gradually learn to self-regulate alongside the external regulation. Eventually, as young adults, maturity is deemed to be reached when they are able to look after and take responsibility for themselves; self-regulation is a precursor to becoming autonomous and accountable. But, in the meantime, adolescents need sufficient boundaries, rules, role models and guidance so they learn eventually how to self-regulate without being burned up in the fires of instant gratification. Even if they reject it initially, adolescents need governance as a counterbalance to their increasing autonomy. It is not until they leave home and begin paying their own bills and taking full responsibility for their livelihoods – as all parents have to learn – that adolescents understand how to self-regulate responsibly and take their place as citizens. As for adolescents, so for humanity as a whole: we have to learn to be accountable for our desires, our habits, our livelihoods, our impulses and our needs. And this means learning to self-regulate. The only difference is the scale. We have to self-regulate – not just on an individual or local scale – but globally.

We urgently need to complement the competition of our global market with self-regulating governance and cooperation on the same scale, and, surprisingly, the same arguments easily fit into the frame of economics. Until now we have seen ideas about regulation and models of governance (big or small government) come in and out of fashion. Both models are polarized, and both have failed; both are founded on a conception of regulation based in either *control* or *no control,* which is mirrored respectively in the two modes of trade, protectionism or free trade. As the world becomes increasingly globalized, it becomes increasingly hard to deny that in many fields regulation is essential. But the model has to change. We have to choose it and allow ourselves to be voluntarily bound by it, which is where self-regulation comes in. Self-regulation is of a completely different order to the control/no control polarity and is inherent in the biological systems from which we are drawing our evolutionary paradigm. This concurs with what is emerging in all other fields, while currently economics and politics lag a long way behind.

We need to learn to self-regulate by regulating our activity – our economies, our banks, our militaries, our profligate habits and so on – and this can now only be done together through simultaneous global cooperation. Then, perhaps, we may consider ourselves grown-up enough to leave home and ask ourselves the question: what will we become? To reach our species' maturity, the paradox is that 'leaving home' means we must come home to all of who we really are – not just the world's greatest competitors but also its supreme cooperators – and this means learning conscious self-regulation on a scale the matches the scale of human activity.

Conscious evolution

When thinking about evolution, we have a tendency to suppose that it happens all by itself, that it's a purely random process of natural selection in which we can play no purposeful part. Stewart, by contrast, is one of a bevy of new scientific thinkers who propose that evolution itself is evolving by devising new ways to evolve more quickly and effectively. This, as D.S. Wilson also suggested, is because the methods evolution has used so far – blind trial-and-error and change-and-test processes – are no longer adequate. Under today's globalized pace of change, global cooperation is highly unlikely to be achieved by the process of blind trial and error: it is unlikely to happen all by itself. Instead, as Stewart suggests, 'The evolutionary process itself is evolving . . . transitioning from a process that stumbles forward blindly, to one that advances consciously and intentionally.'[35]

In considering the factor of conscious intention, futurist and systems theorist Ervin Laszlo concurs with Stewart and D.S. Wilson that consciousness – our thinking – has the unique capacity to mitigate the vicissitudes of change. Grasping the nature of the evolutionary processes that unfold around them, conscious members of a social system can purposefully and effectively intervene.[36]

This factor of conscious *intentionality* is sometimes referred to as 'conscious evolution', and this is a point where scientists and mystics are increasingly finding common ground. In the prestigious journal *Astronomy*, the particle physicist and cosmologist Professor Edward Kolb proposes nature's most miraculous transformation to be that the universe evolved the capacity to contemplate and understand itself.[37]

If global cooperation and governance of the kind we have described is highly unlikely to emerge by chance, humanity needs to take responsibility for consciously establishing it, and to do that we need to devise and then to coalesce around a viable, practical and appropriate strategy. It is our hope that this book may offer an answer to what such a strategy might look like and how it might work.

As we've argued throughout *The Simpol Solution*, to intervene appropriately and to establish a form of global governance we need a worldcentric level of consciousness to proliferate among a relatively small, yet critical, mass of people. Armed with worldcentric thinking, new values and new modes of action such as Simpol arise. We can then consciously participate in our own evolution. We can assist it and help ourselves to consciously establish global cooperation and governance. It is to that task that evolution now calls us.

But nothing will happen without *you*. You – we – as many of us as possible need to act together, consciously and intentionally, to make it happen.

Afterword: Coming Home

The time seems to have come for humanity to cooperate and realize our species' maturity. It is time for us to grow up, time for us to come home. We have only one chance, and we have been away too long.

In the most objectively accurate, as well as in the most profound, sense possible, we are all in the same boat. In terms of game theory, humanity is now playing a non-zero-sum game: a game where it's in all our interests to cooperate. As Robert Wright suggests, there's no better metaphor for a non-zero-sum relationship than 'being in the same boat'.[1]

Global cooperation, as we have argued, will not happen if we simply sit back and take no action because we are now in the age of conscious evolution. It requires our active, conscious participation. As we start to take proper responsibility for actively navigating the vital transition from destructive global competition to fruitful global cooperation, we may ask ourselves what better concept we could have to guide us than the idea of *simultaneity* itself.

Simultaneous action and the new context of cooperation that it both enables and invites us towards could be described as 'the great reconciler' because it successfully reconciles two timeless, universal and yet seemingly irreconcilable opposites, those of unity and diversity. Even if we act simultaneously alongside others we still retain our own individuality, our diversity or our unique national sovereignty. We don't stop being who we are; we don't have to surrender our *identity*, we just enlarge it. And yet by acting together simultaneously we also achieve unity. We maintain our unique individuality and yet stand together, stronger in our unity. We make ourselves greater than the sum of our parts. We retain our national or tribal civic identity, but we add a global one to it.

In our increasingly interdependent globalized world, then, simultaneity has the capacity to reconcile our diverse self-interests with our united common interest. Using a process such as Simpol, unity and diversity can be reconciled, *self*-interest and *common* interest become one. And there, we suggest, resides our underlying spiritual purpose, the underlying lesson globalization is trying to teach us: *that we are not separate from one another*. We are not two but one. We are not just great competitors but great cooperators, for how else could we – how else *should* we – cross this crucial and historic evolutionary threshold, if not hand in hand, if not as one humanity, if not simultaneously, if not *together*?

Inherent to the idea of simultaneity – of global reconciliation and oneness – are the act of forgiveness and the mutuality principle known as the Golden Rule: to do globally as we would be done by. To support Simpol is to understand fully the vicious circle of Destructive Global Competition and how it effectively forces political leaders, business people, indeed everyone to engage in and condone behaviours we know to be harmful. To support Simpol is to forgive those in charge and ourselves. It is to understand that although no one is really to blame for our predicament we are all jointly responsible for overcoming it – and that we can do it if we choose to.

Simpol may not have all the answers. Simpol is not designed to address every problem but is tailored towards solving *global* problems. This means that all the various solutions presently being pursued by NGOs, governments and others still remain important at regional, national and local levels. For the global level, Simpol seems to answer more key questions and meets more key criteria than any other proposal we have seen so far. If this is correct, and with the world deteriorating as we write, perhaps the important question now is not so much whether Simpol can work but whether a better idea is immediately available? If not, we invite you to help get the ball rolling by using your vote in the powerful way Simpol offers. You can sign on to the campaign for free at simpol.org.

Remember, it cannot happen without *you*, without each of us actually *taking* that action. We may individually have little to lose by taking such a step, but possibly there is a whole world to gain. At the very least we will have reclaimed our sovereignty and dignity as individual citizens along with our right to decide on our common global future – and potentially we will have the chance to establish a form of people-centred global governance that expresses our common humanity, that acknowledges that we are not just great competitors but supreme co-operators and that releases us to fulfil the mature destiny of our species.

Notes

Introduction

1. http://www.telegraph.co.uk/news/politics/georgeosborne/8804027/Conservative-Party-Conference-2011-George-Osborne-speech-in-full.html.

Chapter 1

1. Fortune Magazine: http://fortune.com/2012/10/15/theres-no-quit-in-michael-porter/; 15 October 2012.

2. M.E. Porter, *On Competition*, Harvard Business School, Boston, Massachusetts, 1998, p. 16.

3. D. Harvey, *A Brief History of Neoliberalism*, Oxford University Press, Oxford, 2005.

4. P. Vaillancourt Rosenau, *The Competition Paradigm*, Rowman and Littlefield, Lanham, Maryland, 2003, p. 11.

5. D. Harvey, 2005.

6. World Economic Forum website: http://reports.weforum.org/global-competitiveness-report-2014-2015.

7. Article by Brian Francis, lecturer in economics at the University of the West Indies, writing in *Nationnews:* http://www.nationnews.com/nationnews/news/68686/-tourism-caribbean-economies.

8. W. Davies, *The Limits of Neoliberalism: Authority, Sovereignty and the Logic of Competition*, Sage Publications, London, 2014, p. 190.

9. Party Political Broadcast by the UK Conservative Party, *Britain in the Global Race*, March 2013.

10. http://www.theguardian.com/commentisfree/2014/oct/19/unending-economic-crisis-powerless-paranoia.

11. *Ibid.*

12. J. Luyendijk, *Hello Everybody! One Journalist's Search for Truth in the Middle East*, Profile Books, London, 2010.

13. J. Luyendijk, *Dit kan niet waar zijn* (That Can't Be True), Atlas Contact, Amsterdam, 2015. Published in English as *Swimming with Sharks*, Faber and Faber, London, 2015.

14. Joris's talk in Holland was on 13 May 2015 and was organized by the paper *De Correspondent* at the State Theatre in Amsterdam.

15. Retrieved from https://en.wikipedia.org/wiki/Michael_Porter, 15 July 2015.

16. http://www.theguardian.com/education/2015/jun/23/school-sport-crossroads-london-2012-legacy.

17. P. Vaillancourt Rosenau, 2003, p. 10.

18. *Ibid.*

19. *Ibid.*

20. 'Lose–Lose: The Penalties of Acting Alone Stall Collective Effort on Climate Change', by Fiona Harvey, Comment and Analysis, *Financial Times*, 6 December 2006.

21. For a fuller explanation of 'regulatory chill', see D. Blair, 'Race to the Bottom Denial: Reassessing the Globalization–Environmental Regulation Relationship', paper presented at the Midwest Political Science Association 66th Annual National Conference, Chicago, 3 April 2008, by David J. Blair, Department of Political Science, Huron University College, London, Ontario; http://www.allacademic.com/pages/p268485-1. php.

22. *Act Two: How Google Is Muscling Its Way into the Advertising Mainstream*, by Richard Waters, Comment and Analysis, *Financial Times*, 19 January 2007.

23. See http://www.channelnewsasia.com/news/asiapacific/indonesia-president-mulls/ 3030298.html?utm_source=newsletter&utm_medium=email&utm_campaign=the_ tjn_weekly_friday_12_august_2016.

24. See http://www.oecd.org/tax/beps-about.htm and http://ec.europa.eu/taxation_customs/ taxation/company_tax/common_tax_base/index_en.htm for more details.

25. Simon Bowers, *Guardian*, 18 June 2015; http://www.theguardian.com/world/2015/ jun/18/uk-reject-eu-plans-combat-multinational-tax-avoidance.

26. See *Financial Times*, 3 December 2012; http://www.ft.com/cms/s/0/cac9ebe8-3d5c-11e2-b8b2-00144feabdc0.html#axzz3hGWUXve1.

27. See, for example, Oxfam's report, *Wealth: Having It All and Wanting More*; http://policy-practice.oxfam.org.uk/publications/wealth-having-it-all-and-wanting-more-338125.

28. 'S. Africa Relaxes Empowerment Rules', by Caroline Southey, International Economy, *Financial Times*, 15 December 2006.

29. *The London Paper*, 22 January 2007.

30. D. Harvey, 2011, *op cit*.

31. Retrieved from http://uk.reuters.com/article/uk-financial-soros-idUKTRE51K0AV20090221, 21 November 2016.

32. *The Scotsman*, 29 November 2009.

33. M.E. Porter, *On Competition*, Harvard Business School, Boston, Massachusetts, 1998, p. 155.

34. W. Davies, 2014, p. 193.

Chapter 2

1. Based on consciousness theorist Ken Wilber's explanation in 'Excerpt A: An Integral Age at the Leading Edge, Part III: The Nature of Revolutionary Social Transformation' (p. 1); retrieved in October 2004 from http://wilber.shambhala.com/html/books/ kosmos/excerptA/part3-1.cfm.

2. See G. Braden, *Deep Truth: Igniting the Memory of Our Origin, History, Destiny, and Fate*, Hay House, Carlsbad, California, 2012.

3. J. Diamond, *The World Until Yesterday*, Allen Lane, London, 2012.

4. See B. Tuchman, *A Distant Mirror: The Calamitous Fourteenth Century*, Ballantine, New York, 1978, p. 14.

5. Retrieved from http://www.ted.com/talks/george_papandreou_imagine_a_european_ democracy_without_borders.

6. As reported in the *Guardian*, 5 December 2012; https://www.theguardian.com/uk/2012/ dec/05/corporation-tax-rate-cut-autumn-statement.

7. http://www.bbc.co.uk/news/business-36768140.

8. What we, the authors, call the Myth of the Sovereign Nation is akin to what the world-renowned sociologist Ulrich Beck referred to as 'methodological nationalism'. An account of John Bunzl's meeting with Professor Beck can be found at https:// johnbunzl.wordpress.com/2015/02/24/my-first-and-last-meeting-with-ulrich-beck/.

9. WEF Global Competitiveness Report 2014–15; http://www3.weforum.org/docs/WEF_ GlobalCompetitivenessReport_2014-15.pdf, p. 60.

10. 'Mass Migration into Europe Is Unstoppable', by Gideon Rachman, Comment, 12 January 2016, *Financial Times*; http://www.ft.com/cms/s/0/64d058c4-b84f-11e5-b151- 8e15c9a029fb.html#axzz410QeZO2F.

11. 'Comment Is Free' in the *Guardian*, 29 June 2016; https://www.theguardian.com/ commentisfree/2016/jun/29/key-lesson-of-brexit-globalisation-must-work-for-all-of- britain.

12. See, for example, http://www.waronwant.org/what-ttip.

13. See, for example, https://www.cnet.com/uk/news/robots-could-make-half-the-world- unemployed-in-30-years-says-prof/.

14. J. Lyndley-French, 'Why the UN and the EU Are Stalling', in J. Möhring, and G. Prins (eds), *Sail On O Ship of State*, Notting Hill Editions, London, 2013, p. 195.

15. 'A Ritual to Read to Each Other', by William Stafford, in R. Bly, J. Hillman and M. Meade (eds), *The Rag and Bone Shop of the Heart*, Harper Perennial, New York, 1993.

16. D. Blair, 2008.

17. The Brothers Grimm in the original 1812 edition of *Children's and Household Tales*.

Chapter 3

1. On the difficult necessity of combining a new politics with a psychological understanding, see N. Duffell, *Odd Bedfellows: Psychotherapy, History and Politics in Britain* (Self and Society Series), Taylor and Francis, London and New York, 2015.

2. J. Hillman and M. Ventura, *We've Had a Hundred Years of Psychotherapy – And the World's Getting Worse*, HarperCollins, New York, 1993.

3. 'Regulate Us, Please', *Economist*, 8 October 2005, p. 38.

4. D. Korten, *When Corporations Rule the World*, Kumarian Press, West Hartford, Connecticut, and Berrett Kohler Publishers, Oakland, California, 1995, p. 212.

5. G. Soros, *The Crisis of Global Capitalism: Open Society Endangered*, Little, Brown and Co., London and New York, 1998, p. 196.

6. See K. Higgs, *Collision Course: Endless Growth on a Finite Planet*, MIT Press Cambridge, Massachusetts, 2014.

7. http://www.channel4.com/news/google-boris-should-get-his-facts-right-on-tax.

8. N. Duffell, *Wounded Leaders: British Elitism and the Entitlement Illusion: A Psychohistory*, Lone Arrow Press, London, 2014.

9. S. Grosz, *The Examined Life*, Chatto and Windus, London, 2013.

10. D. Siegel, transcript of 'The Neurobiology of Trauma Treatment: How Brain Science Can Lead to More Targeted Interventions for Patients Healing from Trauma', webinar session broadcast 14 November 2014, with Daniel Siegel, interviewed by Ruth Buczynski, National Institute for the Clinical Application of Behavioral Medicine, p. 16.

11. E.O. Wilson, *The Social Conquest of Earth*, Norton, New York, 2012, p. 1.

12. D. Barrett, *Supernormal Stimuli: How Primal Urges Overran Their Evolutionary Purpose*, Norton, New York, 2010.

13. D. Siegel, 2014.

14. K. Marx, *A Contribution to the Critique of Political Economy*, with some notes by R. Rojas (1977 edn), Progress Publishers, Moscow, 1859.

15. G.B. Shaw, *Man and Superman: A Comedy and a Philosophy*, 'Maxims for Revolutionists', Constable, London, 1903, p. 229.

Chapter 4

1. S.R. Covey, *The Seven Habits of Highly Effective People: Powerful Lessons in Personal Change*, Simon and Schuster, New York, 2013.

2. As he explained when interviewed by Jeremy Paxman; see http://www.bbc.co.uk/news/uk-24648651.

3. Prime Minister Winston Churchill addressing the House of Commons in November 1947, Official Report, House of Commons, 11 November 1947; 5th series, cols 206–7.

4. The publication *Voter Turnout Since 1945: A Global Report, 2002*, available from the Institute for Democracy and Electoral Assistance (www.idea.int), shows that for many years voter turnouts were on the increase but from the 1980s onwards they went into decline. It is perhaps no coincidence that it was around this time that the Reagan–Thatcher 'big bang' deregulation of financial markets took place.

5. *Guardian*, https://www.theguardian.com/theguardian/1999/oct/14/features11.g23.

6. *The Times*, 15 January 2014.

7. Nicholas Teo of KGI Securities, as quoted in a BBC report by Karishma Vaswani; http://www.bbc.co.uk/news/business-37933376.

8. See *Voter Turnout Since 1945: A Global Report*, 2002.

9. J. Habermas, *Legitimation Crisis*, Polity Press, London, 1973.

10. Retrieved from http://www.bbc.co.uk/news/uk-politics-26843996.

11. https://www.theguardian.com/commentisfree/2016/jun/28/brexit-great-news-eu-britain-sovereignty?CMP=share_btn_link.

12. See article by Nicholas Snow at https://fee.org/resources/if-goods-dont-cross-borders.

13. In respect of this and other references to Conscious Capitalism, Conscious Capitalism is a registered trademark of Conscious Capitalism, Inc.

14. http://www.independent.co.uk/news/world/asia/bangladesh-clothing-workers-still-exploited-five-months-after-factory-fire-panorama-investigation-finds-8833102.html.

15. http://www.bangladeshaccord.org.

16. M. Strong, *Be the Solution: How Entrepreneurs and Conscious Capitalists Can Solve All the World's Problems*, John Wiley and Sons, Hoboken, New Jersey, 2009.

17. M.E. Porter, 1998, p. 45.

18. M. Porter and C. Van der Linde, 'Green and Competitive: Ending the Stalemate', *Harvard Business Review*, Boston, Massachusetts, 1995; http://www.uvm.edu/~gflomenh/ENRG-POL-PA395/readings/Porter_Linde.pdf.

19. *Ibid.*

20. G. Monbiot, *The Age of Consent: A Manifesto for a New World Order*, Flamingo, London, 2003, pp. 56–7.

21. Global Justice Now was formerly the World Development Movement.

22. From http://www.wdm.org.uk/climate-change/report-back-world-social-forum-2013-tunis (with some corrections and some passages removed).

23. *Ibid.*

24. *Guardian*, 9 June 2014.

25. *Ibid.*

26. M. White, *The End of Protest: A New Playbook for Revolution*, Alfred A. Knopf (Penguin Random House), Toronto, 2016.

27. *Guardian*, 3 November 2005.

28. To understand how fracking is strongly driven by competitiveness concerns, see *Fracking: Are Environmentalists Missing the Point?* http://www.huffingtonpost.co.uk/john-bunzl/fracking-are-environmenta_b_4659564.html.

Chapter 5

1. A. Hussey, *The French Intifada: The Long War Between France and Its Arabs*, Granta, London, 2014.

2. Importantly, both are embedded in a rationalist 'either/or' mode of thought, what writer and philosopher Robert Pirsig calls a 'Subject–Object Metaphysics'; see R. Pirsig, *Lila: An Enquiry into Morals*, Bantam, London, 1991.

3. A.S. Gupta, article entitled 'The World Social Forum Sprouts Wings', 2005, retrieved from http://www.forumsocialmundial.org.br.

4. See 'Listening to Shahram Nazeri', in R. Bly, *Stealing Sugar from the Castle: Selected and New Poems*, 1950–2013, W.W. Norton and Co., New York, 2013.

5. Melanie Klein's prose is somewhat challenging in the original, so readers are recommended an excellent summary of her work by her namesake J. Klein in *Our Need for Others and Its Roots in Infancy*, Tavistock Publications, London, 1987.

6. Retrieved from http://www.melanie-klein-trust.org.uk/depressive-position.

7. N. Duffell and H. Løvendal, *Sex, Love and the Dangers of Intimacy: A Guide to Passionate Relationships When the 'Honeymoon' Is Over*, Thorsons, London, 2002.

8. K. Wilber, *Sex, Ecology, Spirituality: The Spirit of Evolution*, Shambhala, Boston, 1995.

9. A. Einstein, 'Self-Portrait' (essay dated 1936), *Out of My Later Years*, Citadel Press, New York, 1995.

10. M.K. Gandhi, *An Autobiography*, Navajivan Publishing House, Ahmedabad, 1927.

Chapter 6

1. Why this is so is explained in J. Bunzl, *Global Domestic Politics: A Citizen's Guide to Running a Diverse Planet*, International Simultaneous Policy Organisation, London, 2013.

2. B. Adams, *The Law of Civilization and Decay: An Essay on History*, Macmillan, New York and London, 1895.

3. I. McGilchrist, *The Master and His Emissary: The Divided Brain and the Making of the Western World*, Yale University Press, New Haven and London, 2010.

4. J. Piaget, *The Equilibration of Cognitive Structures: The Central Problem of Intellectual Development*, University of Chicago Press, Chicago, 1985.

5. Retrieved from https://en.wikipedia.org/wiki/Clare_W._Graves, 12 July 2016.

6. D.E. Beck and C. Cowan, *Spiral Dynamics: Mastering Values, Leadership, and Change*, Blackwell Publishing, Oxford, 1996, p. 28.

7. *Ibid.*

8. This is fully explained in K. Wilber, *Integral Psychology: Consciousness, Spirit, Psychology, Therapy*, Shambhala Publications, Inc., Boston, 2000. For the differences between AQAL and Graves's, Beck's and Cowan's Spiral Dynamics models, see pp. 229–32.

9. For a full and helpful exposition of the various values levels, the reader is referred to Don Beck's and Chris Cowan's very useful and informative *Spiral Dynamics*, 1996, information from which we gratefully acknowledge.

10. *Ibid.*, p. 66.

11. Joseph Campbell's seminal work on comparative religion and archetypes, *The Hero with a Thousand Faces*, was first published in 1949 and is available in various editions.

12. J. Mackey and R. Sisodia, *Conscious Capitalism: Liberating the Heroic Spirit of Business*, Harvard Business Review Press, Watertown, Massachusetts, 2014.

13. P.H. Ray and S.R. Anderson, *The Cultural Creatives: How 50 Million People Are Changing the World*, Three Rivers Press, New York, 2001.

14. E. Beck and G. Linscott, *The Crucible: Forging South Africa's Future*, self-published, 2001.

15. For an in-depth discussion of the differences between Early and Late Worldcentric political thinking, see John Bunzl, 'Discovering an Integral Civic Consciousness in a Global Age', in *Journal of Integral Theory and Practice*, 2012, Vol. 7, No. 1, pp. 105–23.

16. As explained in 'The Handout' by Ken Wilber contained in *Integral Politics: A Summary of Its Essential Ingredients*; retrieved 7 July 2009 from http://www.kenwilber.com.

17. Our claim that Simpol represents a Late Worldcentric form of politics has been independently corroborated by the publication of three articles in the peer-reviewed *Journal of Integral Theory and Practice*, 2009, Vol. 4, No. 4, pp. 121–40; 2012, Vol. 7, No. 1, pp. 105–23; 2012, Vol. 7, No. 3, pp. 25–42.

18. K. Wilber, 1995, pp. 59–61.

19. R.M. Pirsig, 1991.

20. J. Diamond, *Guns Germs, and Steel*, Vintage, New York, 1998.

21. Indra Adnan, futurist and founder of the Soft Power Network, proposed this view at the June 2016 Alter Ego conference, http://www.alterego.site, a gathering of eighty leaders in the field of integrating spiritual and psychological tools into policy-making that Nick Duffell attended.

22. R. Rohr, *Falling Upward: A Spirituality for the Two Halves of Life*, SPCK, London, 2012, p. 9.

Chapter 7

1. Pippa Norris, 'Global Governance and Cosmopolitan Citizens', Chapter 8 in J. Donahue and J. Nye, *Globalization and Governance*, Brookings Institution Press, Washington, DC, 2000; http://unpan1.un.org/intradoc/groups/public/documents/APCITY/UNPAN 002060.pdf.

2. A proposal for fundamentally reforming the monetary system can be found in J. Bunzl and J. Robertson, *Monetary Reform: Making It Happen!*, International Simultaneous Policy Organisation, London, 2003.

3. Such redistributions would have to be carefully managed and controlled by independent agencies to avoid corruption. These safeguards could form an integral part of the global agreement discussed later in the book.

4. Commission on Global Governance, *Our Global Neighbourhood*, Oxford University Press, New York, 1995, pp. 236–9.

5. For details of voting power by country for the International Monetary Fund, see http://www.imf.org/external/np/sec/memdir/eds.aspx For the World Bank, see http://web.worldbank.org/WBSITE/EXTERNAL/EXTABOUTUS/ORGANIZATION/

6. For more information, see https://en.wikipedia.org/wiki/Currency_transaction_tax.

7. For further details, see http://en.wikipedia.org/wiki/New_World_Order_%28 conspiracy_theory%29.

8. Although we have referred to policies having an adverse effect on a nation's *economic* competitiveness, policies adversely affecting a nation's competitiveness in the military or other spheres could also be included.

9. Included in this category, of course, would not only be policies having no adverse impact on competitiveness but also those likely to have a *positive* impact; that is, those giving individual nations a competitive advantage.

10. See, for example, K. Sehm-Patomäki and M. Ulvila (eds), *Global Political Parties*, Zed Books, London, 2007.

11. This is what the German Green Party found to its cost when it was in a coalition government in the 1990s.

12. P. Mason, *PostCapitalism: A Guide to Our Future*, Allen Lane, London, 2015, pp. 277–84.

13. T. Piketty, *Capital in the Twenty-First Century*, Belknap Press of Harvard University Press, Cambridge, Massachusetts, and London, 2014, pp. 515–39.

14. P. Turchin, *Ultrasociety: How 10,000 Years of War Made Humans the Greatest Cooperators on Earth*, Beresta Books, Chaplin, Connecticut, 2016, p. 223.

15. https://en.wikiquote.org/wiki/Margaret_Mead suggests it to be a 'disputed' quotation.

16. K. Wilber, Excerpt A: *An Integral Age at the Leading Edge. Part III: The Nature of Revolutionary Social Transformation* (p. 2). Retrieved 11 October 2004 from http://wilber.shambhala.com/html/books/kosmos/excerptA/part3-2.cfm.

17. Wilber makes this suggestion in an audio interview at http://worldwidetippingpoint.com/2011/11/ken-wilber-on-humanitys-sixth-known-shift.

Chapter 8

1. You can see the list of current UK MPs who have signed the Simpol Pledge at http://uk.simpol.org/index.php?id=508 .

2. The Simpol Pledge that politicians are invited to sign can be viewed at http://www.simpol.org/fileadmin/user_upload/Articles/ISPO_Forms/MP_PPC_Pledge_Form_-_New.pdf.

3. Canada Elections Act (SC 2000, c. 9); http://laws-lois.justice.gc.ca/eng/acts/e-2.01/page-89.html#h-228.

4. Simpol's Founding Declaration can be viewed at http://www.simpol.org/fileadmin/user_upload/Articles/Founding_Docs/ISPO_Draft_Founding_Declaration_-_Simpol_version.pdf.

5. *Financial Times*, 10 October 2008.

6. According to BrainyQuote: http://www.brainyquote.com/quotes/quotes/m/michaelenz501997.html.

7. Robust measures and controls to ensure that funds did not fall prey to corruption or diversion could, of course, form an integral part of any agreement.

8. I. Goldin, *Divided Nations: Why Global Governance Is Failing, and What We Can Do About It*, Oxford University Press, Oxford, 2013.

9. For a list of potential policy areas that might be included, see http://www.simpol.org/index.php?id=14.

10. A. Watkins and I. Stratenus, *Crowdocracy: The End of Politics*, Urbane Publications, Chatham, 2016.

11. With special thanks to Dirk Weller, National Coordinator of Simpol-Germany, who devised the original diagram from which this was drawn.

12. Arnold J. Toynbee Quotes (n.d.); Quotes.net, retrieved 22 February 2016 from http://www.quotes.net/quote/4644.

Chapter 9

1. J. Stewart, *Evolution's Arrow: The Direction of Evolution and the Future of Humanity*, Chapman Press, Canberra, 2000, p. 57.

2. *Ibid.*

3. Letter from Robert M. Pirsig to Anthony McWatt of Liverpool University, 2 January 1998.

4. See https://en.wikipedia.org/wiki/Prisoner%27s_dilemma for a fuller explanation.

5. J. Stewart, 2000, p. 57.

6. This problem is beginning to be recognized by neuroscience as a major factor that occurs as humans transfer perceptions into concepts owing to the difference in brain hemisphere perspectives. The conceptual reality favoured by left-hemisphere brain perspective is a narrowing in on detail. Thus it creates micro-contexts at the expense of the larger perspective of the right hemisphere, which takes in the big picture and the web of relationships. This has been clearly described by Iain McGilchrist in his groundbreaking analysis contained in *The Master and His Emissary: The Divided Brain and the Making of the Western World*, Yale University Press, New Haven, Connecticut, and London, 2010. Through a neuro-psychological lens (as explained in Duffell, 2014) conservatism can paradoxically be seen as risky, because of left-brain blindness to larger contexts, such as global belonging issues, relying on the most primitive defences of splitting and projecting. The right hemisphere, by contrast, tends to favour what neuroscientists call a 'global' perspective.

7. R.H. Frank, *The Darwin Economy: Liberty, Competition, and the Common Good*, Princeton University Press, Princeton, New Jersey, 2011.

8. E.O. Wilson and D.S. Wilson, *Rethinking the Theoretical Foundation of Sociobiology*, Departments of Biology and Anthropology, Binghamton University, Binghamton, New York, and the Museum of Comparative Zoology, Harvard University, Cambridge, Massachusetts, 2007, p. 348.

9. D.S. Wilson, *Does Altruism Exist? Culture, Genes, and the Welfare of Others*, Yale University Press, New Haven, Connecticut, 2015.

10. R. Dawkins, *The Selfish Gene*, Oxford University Press, Oxford, 1976.

11. M. Heffernan, *A Bigger Prize: Why Competition Isn't Everything and How We Do Better*, Simon and Schuster, London, 2014, p. 366.

12. D.S. Wilson, 2015, pp. 12–13.

13. E.F. Schumacher, *Small Is Beautiful: A Study of Economics As If People Mattered*, Abacus, London, 1974, pp. 53–4.

14. From a personal email to John Bunzl dated 11 June 2002.

15. D.S. Wilson, 2015, p. 147.

16. J. Diamond, *Collapse: How Societies Choose to Fail or Survive*, Penguin Books, New York, 2006.

17. R. Wright, *Nonzero: History, Evolution and Human Cooperation*, Abacus, London, 2001, p. 63.

18. G.J. Vermeij; from a personal email to John Bunzl, 18 January 2006, for which we are very grateful.

19. E. Sahtouris, *EarthDance: Living Systems in Evolution*, iUniverse, Lincoln, Nebraska, 2000, p. 107.

20. http://www.thisdayinquotes.com/2011/04/we-have-met-enemy-and-he-is-us.html.

21. E. Sahtouris, E., 2000, p. 24.

22. S.J. Goerner, *After the Clockwork Universe*, Floris Books, Edinburgh, 1999, p. 143.

23. For an explanation of punctuated equilibrium see https://en.wikipedia.org/wiki/Punctuated_equilibrium.

24. John Stewart; from a personal email to John Bunzl dated 11 June 2002 for which we are very grateful.

25. Excerpts from A. Koestler, *Janus: A Summing Up*, Random House, New York, 1978, pp. 175-6.

26. *Ibid.*

27. *Ibid.*, p. 184.

28. S.J. Goerner, 1999, pp. 122–3.

29. *The Biology of Globalization*; article by Elisabet Sahtouris, www.ratical.org/LifeWeb/Articles/globalize.html.

30. *Ibid.*

31. *Ibid.*

32. *Ibid.*

33. E. Sahtouris, 2000, p. 272.

34. *Ibid.*, p. 287.

35. *The Evolutionary Manifesto*, John Stewart, http://www.evolutionarymanifesto.com/man.html

36. E. Laszlo, *Chaos Point: The World at the Crossroads*, Hampton Roads Publishing Company, Newburyport, Massachusetts, 2006, p. 108.

37. *Astronomy*, February 1998, p. 37. Edward Kolb has worked on many aspects of the big bang cosmology, including baryogenesis, nucleosynthesis and dark matter. He is author, with Michael Turner, of the popular textbook *The Early Universe*, Westview Press, Boulder, Colorado, 1990, and was awarded the 2010 Dannie Heineman Prize for Astrophysics.

Afterword

1. R. Wright, 2001, p. 30.

Further Reading

Adams, B. (1895), *The Law of Civilization and Decay: An Essay on History*, Macmillan and Co., New York and London

Beck, D.E. and C. Cowan (1996), *Spiral Dynamics: Mastering Values, Leadership and Change*, Blackwell Publishing, Oxford

Bunzl, J. (2013), *Global Domestic Politics: A Citizen's Guide to Running a Diverse Planet*, London: International Simultaneous Policy Organisation, London

Bunzl, J. (2012), 'Discovering an Integral Civic Consciousness in a Global Age', in *Journal of Integral Theory and Practice*, 2012; Vol. 7, No. 1, pp. 105–23, Integral Institute, Boulder, Colorado

Bunzl, J. (2006), *People-Centred Global Governance: Making It Happen!*, International Simultaneous Policy Organisation, London

Davies, W. (2014), *The Limits of Neoliberalism: Authority, Sovereignty and the Logic of Competition*, Sage Publications, London

Diamond, J. (2006), *Collapse: How Societies Choose to Fail or Survive*, Penguin Books, New York

Diamond, J. (2012), *The World Until Yesterday*, Allen Lane, London

Diamond, J. (1998), *Guns, Germs, and Steel*, Vintage, New York

Duffell, N. (2015), *Odd Bedfellows: Psychotherapy, History and Politics in Britain* (Self and Society Series), Taylor and Francis, London and New York

Duffell, N. (2014), *Wounded Leaders: British Elitism and the Entitlement Illusion – A Psychohistory*, Lone Arrow Press, London

Duffell, N. and H. Løvendal (2002), *Sex, Love and the Dangers of Intimacy: A Guide to Passionate Relationships When the 'Honeymoon' Is Over*, Thorsons, London

Frank, R.H. (2011), *The Darwin Economy: Liberty, Competition and the Common Good*, Princeton University Press, Princeton, New Jersey

Gandhi, M.K. (1927), *An Autobiography*, Navajivan Publishing House, Ahmedabad

Goldin, I. (2013), *Divided Nations: Why Global Governance Is Failing, and What We Can Do About It*, Oxford University Press, Oxford

Goerner, S.J. (1999), *After the Clockwork Universe*, Floris Books, Edinburgh

Grosz, S. (2013), *The Examined Life*, Chatto and Windus, London

Habermas, J. (1973), *Legitimation Crisis*, Polity Press, London

Harrington, B. (2016), *Capital Without Borders: Wealth Managers and the One Percent*, Harvard University Press, Cambridge, Massachusetts

Harvey, D. (2005), *A Brief History of Neoliberalism*, Oxford University Press, Oxford

Higgs, K. (2014), *Collision Course: Endless Growth on a Finite Planet*, MIT Press, Cambridge, Massachusetts

Klein, J. (1987), *Our Need for Others and Its Roots in Infancy*, Tavistock Publications, London

Koestler, A. (1978), *Janus: A Summing Up*, Random House, New York

Korten, D. (1995), *When Corporations Rule the World*, Kumarian Press, West Hartford, Connecticut, and Berrett-Koehler Publishers, San Francisco, California

Laszlo, E. (2006), *Chaos Point: The World at the Crossroads*, Hampton Roads Publishing Company, Newburyport, Massachusetts

Luyendijk, J. (2010), *Hello Everybody! One Journalist's Search for Truth in the Middle East*, Profile Books, London

Mason, P. (2015), *PostCapitalism: A Guide to Our Future*, Allen Lane, London

McGilchrist, I. (2010), *The Master and His Emissary: The Divided Brain and the Making of the Western World*, Yale University Press, New Haven, Connecticut, and London

Milanovic, B. (2016), *Global Inequality: A New Approach for the Age of Globalization*, Belknap Press of Harvard University Press, Cambridge, Massachusetts

Monbiot, G. (2003), *The Age of Consent: A Manifesto for a New World Order*, Flamingo, London

Novak, M. and R. Highfield (2012), *Super Cooperators: Beyond Survival of the Fittest. Why Cooperation, Not Competition, Is the Key to Life*, Canongate Books, Edinburgh

Piaget, J. (1985), *The Equilibration of Cognitive Structures: The Central Problem of Intellectual Development*, University of Chicago Press, Chicago

Piketty, T. (2014), *Capital in the Twenty-First Century*, Belknap Press of Harvard University Press, Cambridge, Massachusetts

Pirsig, R. (1991), *Lila: An Enquiry into Morals*, Bantam, London

Robertson, J. and J. Bunzl (2003), *Monetary Reform: Making It Happen!*, International Simultaneous Policy Organisation, London

Sehm-Patomäki, K. and M. Ulvila (eds) (2007), *Global Political Parties*, Zed Books, London

Sahtouris, E. (2000), *EarthDance: Living Systems in Evolution*, iUniverse, Lincoln, Nebraska

Samuels, A. (2015), *A New Therapy for Politics?*, Karnac, London

Samuels, A. (2001), *Politics on the Couch: Citizenship and the Internal Life*, Other Press, New York

Schumacher, E.F. (1974), *Small Is Beautiful: A Study of Economics as If People Mattered*, Abacus, London

Soros, G. (1998), *The Crisis of Global Capitalism: Open Society Endangered*, Little, Brown and Co., London

Turchin, P. (2016), *Ultrasociety: How 10,000 Years of War Made Humans the Greatest Cooperators on Earth*, Beresta Books, Chaplin, Connecticut

Vaillancourt Rosenau, P. (2003), *The Competition Paradigm*, Rowman and Littlefield, Lanham, Maryland

Watkins, A. and I. Stratenus (2016), *Crowdocracy: The End of Politics*, Urbane Publications, Chatham, Kent

White, M. (2016), *The End of Protest: A New Playbook for Revolution*, Alfred A. Knopf (Penguin Random House), Toronto

Wilber, K. (1995), *Sex, Ecology, Spirituality: The Spirit of Evolution*, Shambhala, Boston, Massachusetts

Wilber, K. (2006), *Integral Spirituality: A Startling New Role for Religion in the Modern and Postmodern World*, Integral Books (Shambhala Publications, Inc.), Boston, Massachusetts

Wilson, D. S. (2015), *Does Altruism Exist? Culture, Genes, and the Welfare of Others*, Yale University Press, New Haven, Connecticut

Wilson, E.O. (2012), *The Social Conquest of Earth*, Norton, New York

Wright, R. (2001), *Nonzero: History, Evolution and Human Cooperation*, Abacus Random House, New York

Index

SOME AUTHORS WE HAVE PUBLISHED

James Agee • Bella Akhmadulina • Tariq Ali • Kenneth Allsop • Alfred Andersch
Guillaume Apollinaire • Machado de Assis • Miguel Angel Asturias • Duke of Bedford
Oliver Bernard • Thomas Blackburn • Jane Bowles • Paul Bowles • Richard Bradford
Ilse, Countess von Bredow • Lenny Bruce • Finn Carling • Blaise Cendrars • Marc Chagall
Giorgio de Chirico • Uno Chiyo • Hugo Claus • Jean Cocteau • Albert Cohen
Colette • Ithell Colquhoun • Richard Corson • Benedetto Croce • Margaret Crosland
e.e. cummings • Stig Dalager • Salvador Dalí • Osamu Dazai • Anita Desai
Charles Dickens • Bernard Diederich • Fabián Dobles • William Donaldson
Autran Dourado • Yuri Druzhnikov • Lawrence Durrell • Isabelle Eberhardt
Sergei Eisenstein • Shusaku Endo • Erté • Knut Faldbakken • Ida Fink
Wolfgang George Fischer • Nicholas Freeling • Philip Freund • Carlo Emilio Gadda
Rhea Galanaki • Salvador Garmendia • Michel Gauquelin • André Gide
Natalia Ginzburg • Jean Giono • Geoffrey Gorer • William Goyen • Julien Gracq
Sue Grafton • Robert Graves • Angela Green • Julien Green • George Grosz
Barbara Hardy • H.D. • Rayner Heppenstall • David Herbert • Gustaw Herling
Hermann Hesse • Shere Hite • Stewart Home • Abdullah Hussein • King Hussein of Jordan
Ruth Inglis • Grace Ingoldby • Yasushi Inoue • Hans Henny Jahnn • Karl Jaspers
Takeshi Kaiko • Jaan Kaplinski • Anna Kavan • Yasunuri Kawabata • Nikos Kazantzakis
Orhan Kemal • Christer Kihlman • James Kirkup • Paul Klee • James Laughlin
Patricia Laurent • Violette Leduc • Lee Seung-U • Vernon Lee • József Lengyel
Robert Liddell • Francisco García Lorca • Moura Lympany • Thomas Mann
Dacia Maraini • Marcel Marceau • André Maurois • Henri Michaux • Henry Miller
Miranda Miller • Marga Minco • Yukio Mishima • Quim Monzó • Margaret Morris
Angus Wolfe Murray • Atle Næss • Gérard de Nerval • Anaïs Nin • Yoko Ono
Uri Orlev • Wendy Owen • Arto Paasilinna • Marco Pallis • Oscar Parland
Boris Pasternak • Cesare Pavese • Milorad Pavic • Octavio Paz • Mervyn Peake
Carlos Pedretti • Dame Margery Perham • Graciliano Ramos • Jeremy Reed
Rodrigo Rey Rosa • Joseph Roth • Ken Russell • Marquis de Sade • Cora Sandel
Iván Sándor • George Santayana • May Sarton • Jean-Paul Sartre
Ferdinand de Saussure • Gerald Scarfe • Albert Schweitzer
George Bernard Shaw • Isaac Bashevis Singer • Patwant Singh • Edith Sitwell
Suzanne St Albans • Stevie Smith • C.P. Snow • Bengt Söderbergh
Vladimir Soloukhin • Natsume Soseki • Muriel Spark • Gertrude Stein • Bram Stoker
August Strindberg • Rabindranath Tagore • Tambimuttu • Elisabeth Russell Taylor
Emma Tennant • Anne Tibble • Roland Topor • Miloš Urban • Anne Valery
Peter Vansittart • José J. Veiga • Tarjei Vesaas • Noel Virtue • Max Weber
Edith Wharton • William Carlos Williams • Phyllis Willmott
G. Peter Winnington • Monique Wittig • A.B. Yehoshua • Marguerite Young
Fakhar Zaman • Alexander Zinoviev • Emile Zola

Peter Owen Publishers, 81 Ridge Road, London N8 9NP, UK
T + 44 (0)20 8350 1775 / E info@peterowen.com
www.peterowen.com / @PeterOwenPubs